"Building on the success of the first volume, Kiasunomics©2 has returned to explain, in clear and simple prose, how economic principles shape our everyday lives, and influence the decisions we make. Kiasunomics©2 explores many topics near and dear to many Singaporeans — public housing, education, and even shopping! The book also wonderfully illustrates how exciting and original research can help us better understand our ever-changing environment, and guide us to make better and more informed choices."

Professor Tan Eng Chye
President, National University of Singapore

"The authors have mastered the knack of explaining complex behavioural economics concepts in language that is easy for a layman to understand. They contextualise these insights to Singapore, which make them even more relevant. Their research is first-rate, and the insights interesting. A great follow-up to Kiasunomics©!"

Mr Piyush Gupta
Chief Executive Officer and Director, DBS Group

"Economics comes alive in our daily behaviour and decisions. Using the life journey of the protagonist Teng from his birth to adulthood, the authors adopted an easy conversational style to describe common decisions we all made to minimise living costs, optimise opportunities and maximise investment potential. It is a light-hearted yet so-real rendition of how we effectively manage our 'kiasuism' and fear of missing out on anything."

Ms Claire Chiang
Co-Founder, Banyan Tree Holdings

Kiasunomics© 2

Economic Insights for Everyday Life

Kiasunomics©2

Economic Insights for Everyday Life

Sumit Agarwal

Ang Swee Hoon

Sing Tien Foo

National University of Singapore, Singapore

World Scientific

NEW JERSEY · LONDON · SINGAPORE · BEIJING · SHANGHAI · HONG KONG · TAIPEI · CHENNAI · TOKYO

Published by

World Scientific Publishing Co. Pte. Ltd.

5 Toh Tuck Link, Singapore 596224

USA office: 27 Warren Street, Suite 401-402, Hackensack, NJ 07601

UK office: 57 Shelton Street, Covent Garden, London WC2H 9HE

National Library Board, Singapore Cataloguing in Publication Data
Name: Agarwal, Sumit. | Ang, Swee Hoon. | Sing, Tien Foo.
Title: Kiasunomics© 2 : economic insights for everyday life / Sumit Agarwal,
    Ang Swee Hoon, Sing Tien Foo.
Description: Singapore : World Scientific, [2020]
Identifier(s): OCN 1135957625 | ISBN 978-981-12-1839-2 (paperback) |
    ISBN 978-981-12-1709-8 (hardcover)
Subject(s): LCSH: Economics--Singapore--Psychological aspects. |
    Consumer behavior--Singapore.
Classification: DDC 330.019--dc23

British Library Cataloguing-in-Publication Data
A catalogue record for this book is available from the British Library.

For any available supplementary material, please visit
https://www.worldscientific.com/worldscibooks/10.1142/11741#t=suppl

Desk Editor: Jiang Yulin
Design and layout: Loo Chuan Ming

Printed in Singapore

Contents

Foreword

I first read *Kiasunomics*© back in 2017, when Sumit, Swee Hoon, and Tien Foo sent me a copy. It was interesting and easy to read.

I have some background in economics — I completed a BSc (Econ) degree back in 1991 — and I have to admit that economics concepts are not easily explained to the layman. I enjoyed how the authors contextualised the topics to Singapore, and made the issues easy to understand.

In January 2020, Swee Hoon passed me the draft for *Kiasunomics*© 2, and I had the privilege of a preview before the book was published.

I believe most of us will find the authors' insights on topics such as app-hailing, mobile payments, mobile wallets particularly interesting, with these technologies being recent innovations that have very quickly become part and parcel of consumer behaviour in Singapore. 'Like Father, Like Son?' will resonate with many parents. Inter-generational housing wealth is a topic that many in my generation are probably thinking about.

More importantly, many academics know that I am a champion of research into Singapore issues. We are a crucible of policy experimentation. Many countries are curious about how Singapore manages issues like ageing, education for a new era, housing for masses, inequality, and environmental protection. Even in managing the coronavirus disease, or COVID-19, other countries are interested in what we do.

I do not think that doing research on Singapore topics, versus gaining an international audience and publishing in top-tier journals, are mutually exclusive. Local research in fact distinguishes Singapore universities from other universities around the world.

I would therefore like to thank Sumit, Swee Hoon, and Tien Foo for their enthusiasm in local research. I am glad that they are donating the royalty proceeds from *Kiasunomics*© to bursaries and scholarships, and have pledged to do the same for *Kiasunomics*© *2*.

Ong Ye Kung
Minister for Education
(2015 – 2020)

Acknowledgements

Our thanks to our research collaborators as well as our National University of Singapore colleagues whose interesting and meaningful research help to make this book possible:

BASU Debarati

CHAROENWONG Ben

CHENG Shih Fen

CHEONG Alan

CHIA Liu Ee

CHOI Hyun-Soo

CHOMSISENGPHET Souphala

CHONG Juin Kuan

CHU Junhong

DIAO Mi

FAN Yi

GHOSH Pulak

GOETTE Lorenz

HE Jia

HO Teck Hua

KEPPO Jussi

KOO Kang Mo

LI Jing

LI Keyang

LIM Cheryl

LIM Yong Long

LIU Haoming

MAHANAAZ Sultana

MEIER Stephen

PAN Jessica

PAREEK Bhuvanesh

PNG Ivan P.L.

QIAN Wenlan

QIN Yu

REEB David M.

RENGARAJAN Satyanarain

RUAN Tianyue

SERU Amit

SONG Changcheng

TAN Poh Lin

TEO Ernie

TIEFENBECK Verena

VOLLMER Derek

WANG Davin Hong Yip

WANG Zhiwen

WONG Wei-Kang   ZHANG Jian

WU Jing   ZHANG Xiaoyu

YAN Jubo   ZHU Hongjia

YANG Nan   ZOU Xin

YANG Yang

YEUNG Bernard

Our heartfelt appreciation also extends to the organisations who generously shared their data with us so that research can be conducted to benefit the society.

The talented staff at World Scientific – Chua Hong Koon, Jiang Yulin and Jimmy Low – deserve praise for their role in shaping this book.

We also thank Professor Andy Rose, Ms Chua Nan Sze and Ms Dawn Chin at National University of Singapore Business School; Professor Lam Khee Poh and Associate Professor Yu Shi Ming at School of Design and Environment, and Dr Seek Ngee Huat and Board Members of the Institute of Real Estate and Urban Studies (IREUS) for their encouragement and support.

Finally, our overriding debt continues to be our families who provided the time, support and inspiration to our research and preparation of this book.

Note from the Authors

- The Singlish term *kiasu* means "scared to lose".

- Some of the research findings presented in the book are from SSRN (Social Science Research Network) working papers. Readers without full access to the SSRN working papers can email to any of the authors for a copy of the working paper.

- Unless otherwise stated, values prefixed with simple dollar '$' are in Singapore dollar.

List of Acronyms

ABFER   Asian Bureau of Finance and Economic Research

AQI   Air Quality Index

ARF   Additional Registration Fee

ATM   Automated Teller Machine

AYE   Ayer Rajah Expressway

BTO   Build-To-Order

CBD   Central Business District

CEA   Council for Estate Agencies

CHAS   Community Health Assist Scheme

CO   Carbon Monoxide

COE   Certificate of Entitlement

COV   Cash-over-Valuation

CPF   Central Provident Fund

CSC   Collective Sale Committee

ECP   East Coast Parkway

EIP   Ethnic Integration Policy

ERP   Electronic Road Pricing

EU   European Union

FFS   FE Lakeside, FCL Topaz and Sekisui House

GDP   Gross Domestic Product

GFA   Gross Floor Area

GPS	Global Positioning System
GST	Goods and Services Tax
HDB	Housing and Development Board
HIP	Home Improvement Programme
HOS	Home Office Scheme
IMF	International Monetary Fund
IRAS	Inland Revenue Authority of Singapore
IREUS	Institute of Real Estate and Urban Studies
IU	In-Vehicle Unit
JTC	Jurong Town Corporation
K2	*Kiasunomics©2*
KTM	Keretapi Tanah Melayu
LED	Light Emitting Diode
LTA	Land Transport Authority
MAS	Monetary Authority of Singapore
MEP	Ministry of Environmental Protection
MOE	Ministry of Education
MRT	Mass Rapid Transit
NEA	National Environment Agency
NETS	Network for Electronic Transfers
NO_2	Nitrogen Dioxide
NTU	Nanyang Technological University
NTUC	National Trades Union Congress

NUS   National University of Singapore

OCD   Obsessive Compulsive Disorder

PhD   Doctor of Philosophy

PIE   Pan Island Expressway

PSI   Pollutant Standards Index

PSLE   Primary School Leaving Examination

QR   Quick Response

REITs   Real Estate Investment Trust

SARS   Severe Acute Respiratory Syndrome

SERS   Selective En bloc Redevelopment Scheme

SIBOR   Singapore Interbank Offered Rate

SO_2 Sulphur Dioxide

SSRN   Social Science Research Network

SSS   Silver Support Scheme

TV   Television

URA   Urban Redevelopment Authority

US   United States

UVD   United Venture Development

WHO   World Health Organization

Introduction

After the launch of *Kiasunomics*© in 2017, we received very encouraging feedback. We had wanted Singaporeans to know our research and draw learnings for their daily living. We wanted our research to benefit beyond the academic circle. And we have achieved that.

Not just Singaporeans but people outside Singapore were equally intrigued by our research and the book. Singaporeans began to take a hard look at their behaviour such as energy usage, spending, house purchases, and golf playing; while non-Singaporeans were fascinated by cultural nuances that influence our behaviour.

We gave talks at book festivals, libraries, conferences, and companies; and were featured in newspapers, magazines, and radio. We are very encouraged and deeply thankful to those who supported us.

And so, following the tradition of blockbuster movies and doing what comes naturally to Singaporeans, we decided to do the *kiasu* thing – write a sequel!

Kiasunomics©*2* or *K2* for short, brings together the same characters from the original book with new neighbours added in. The journey of Teng, the protagonist, continues as he seeks to optimise his taxi driving income so that his two young sons have a head start in life.

K2 covers our research on contemporary topics such as app-hailing and mobile payments to understand the impact of surge pricing on how much extra we pay for rides, and the benefits of mobile wallets to businesses. These are found in Chapters 1 and 6. The effects of the Home Office Scheme in encouraging entrepreneurship are discussed in Chapter 12.

Singaporeans' perennial favourite topics on property prices and retirement are further researched into and discussed in *K2*. While the first *Kiasunomics*© book talked about the effect of residential addresses ending with '8' on prices, *K2* covers how property developers bid to protect the prices of their existing land parcels. This is discussed in Chapter 15.

En bloc sales is another hot topic. If you have a property that you think might have an en bloc potential, check out Chapter 13. It highlights the effects of property characteristics on en bloc potential. And if you are wondering whether your old HDB still has some value, look no further than Chapter 3 on the decaying value of HDB flats and private condominiums.

As parents, we want our children to do better than us. So, has Singapore progressed such that with each generation, we are doing better than the generation before? Chapter 9 titled 'Like Father, Like Son?' relates this very concern that Teng has and furnishes insights from our study on inter-generational housing wealth.

Fascinating also is how effective word-of-mouth is in influencing behaviours. In Chapter 8, the story unfolds of how a neighbour's bankruptcy can influence spending patterns among selected individuals in the neighbourhood. We also shouldn't think that to be effective, mass communication must have all the bells and whistles. Chapter 14 shows that simple no-frills messages can effectively change Singaporeans' habit of saving energy.

Besides these Singaporean issues, *K2* also discusses our research outside Singapore from which we can glean some insights. Such issues as pollution and corruption (Chapters 10 and 11) instruct us on how companies engage in such behaviours and the repercussions on the society. Chapter 4 on sunny day effect reminds us to be more mindful in curbing our spending when we are in a good mood.

We hope this sequel brings more learnings to Singaporeans as we become smarter consumers.

As with *Kiasunomics©*, all the royalty proceeds from *Kiasunomics©2* will go towards bursaries and scholarships.

Fickle Fingers

Teng, a taxi driver in Singapore, and his wife Siew Ling have two sons – six-year-old Ethan and two-year-old Ervin. Together with his parents, affectionately called Ah Kong and Ah Mah by the grandsons, they live in a modest government-subsidised HDB (Housing and Development Board) flat in Serangoon.

His earnings as a taxi driver had become increasingly difficult to maintain due to rising competition from ride-hailing app services such as Grab and previously Uber.

Uber, the larger of the two app services and the first entrant into the Singapore market, was sent packing after five years by Grab in August 2018. Grab, a Malaysian start-up, kept their finger on the customer pulse – listening and adapting to local needs and cultures of markets that it had entered. It saw an opportunity in Southeast Asia's massive traffic jams and provided GrabBike – motorcycle taxis that could weave in and out of traffic in such markets as Indonesia, Thailand and

Vietnam. With a keen ear on what different markets wanted, Grab began chiselling away Uber's market share. The eventual exit of Uber from Singapore fortified Grab's position with offerings beyond car sharing, including food delivery, offers on limited edition merchandise such as special-flavoured KitKat and even mobile wallet. By late 2018, another ride-hailing app, Indonesian Gojek, entered the fray.

On top of competition is the next generation of road pricing to be introduced in Singapore. To curb vehicles on the road, the current ERP (Electronic Road Pricing) that charges by entry into busy roads during peak hours will be eventually replaced by charges based on road usage. The more distance covered, the higher the toll. As a taxi driver, Teng wondered whether it would still be worth the while to cruise for passengers.

All these spell a headache for taxi drivers who have seen their earnings dwindle. More taxi drivers have been throwing in the towel and exiting the taxi trade, some even preferring to become full-time Grab drivers.

Ah Kong and Ah Mah had been concerned with Teng's unstable earnings but he had assured them then that he knew where and when he could pick up passengers easily. And he remembered the budgeting and financial planning advice he had received from a well-meaning finance professor from NUS (National University of Singapore) whom he had given a ride to some years back. The professor had enlightened him of his research that showed some taxi drivers do not know how to target their earnings effectively.[1] And thankfully, he had signed up

---

[1] For more on this research on how taxi drivers set targets, see Sumit Agarwal, Ang Swee Hoon and Sing Tien Foo (2018), *Kiasunomics: Stories of Singaporean Economic Behaviours*, Chapter 2 "Taxi Driver, Where Are You?" (Singapore: World Scientific Publishers). To read the academic article, see Sumit Agarwal, Diao Mi, Jessica Pan and Sing Tien Foo (2015), "Are Singaporeans Cab Drivers Target Earners?" Working Paper, National University of Singapore, https://papers.ssrn.com/sol3/papers.cfm?abstract_id=2338476. This research has also been published as a commentary; see Sumit Agarwal and Diao Mi, "Why it's so difficult to get a cab," *Today*, (6 October 2016), https://www.todayonline.com/commentary/why-its-so-difficult-get-cab

to be a Grab driver too as almost everyone he knows has a Grab app on their mobile phone.

But with two growing young kids and ageing parents to look after, household expenses were mounting. Teng was finding it more challenging to make ends meet. Siew Ling's salary as a sales assistant at a nearby shoe store could barely cover the enrichment classes that she and Teng wanted the boys to attend.

"Should I become a full-time Grab driver?" Teng thought.

Ever since his parents raised their concerns about his taxi-driving vocation, the thought of making a career switch nagged at him now and then. Sometimes on a slow day while driving along the highway, Teng wondered whether it was still worth the while to stay on as a taxi and Grab driver. Or should he switch to be a full-time Grab driver? He had heard from his cabby friends who had decided to stop driving taxis altogether and become full-time Grab drivers that the expenses were less. It seemed that the rental of the car is lower too.

But with his easy-going personality, Teng tended to let matters slide. "Never mind. Don't think too much. Just do good and be kind to others," as he muttered his mantra while rubbing the small Goddess of Mercy statuette that his wife had carefully placed on his taxi dashboard on his first day of taxi driving, to ward off evil spirits.

Weather Changes

In 2019, Singapore experienced unusual weather for several months. From January to August, the island state had sweltering heat with temperatures rising to 39°C with not much rain. The same scorching weather was also experienced in Europe, India and several other parts of the world.

"This must be due to global warming," mentioned Siew Ling. "Thankfully we have changed our lights to LED to save on electricity. That helps in gas emissions."

"And remember the news report you told me about saving on air-con bills? I want to conserve but how can I do that since the weather is so hot? I need to use the air-con more often," Ah Mah chimed in.

Ah Mah was referring to the time when she was shutting the windows and turning on the air-conditioning unit when there was heavy construction next to their flat. While their electricity bill was higher whenever there was such construction, their bills remained high even after the construction ended.[2]

Teng and Siew Ling learned from the news that Singaporeans tend to continue using air-conditioning because it has become a convenient habit even though there is no more noise or air pollution from nearby construction. Ever since then, the family has become more mindful of air-con usage.

Eventually there was some respite from the hot weather. Rain had been torrential. The weather extremes saw an increase in visits to the doctor. Many were falling sick.

The rainy weather had also made it difficult to commute. That was good news for Teng. His services were in demand whether through taxi or Grab. Once, when there was a sudden downpour, Teng received a flurry of bookings both through the taxi as well as Grab. With so many requests and having to constantly keep an eye on the road, he wasn't sure which booking he should respond to.

---

[2] For more on this research on the effects of nearby construction on utilities bills, see Sumit Agarwal, Ang Swee Hoon and Sing Tien Foo (2018), *Kiasunomics: Stories of Singaporean Economic Behaviours*, Chapter 14 "Mama, Don't Forget to Switch on the Air-Con," (Singapore: World Scientific Publishers). To read the academic article, see Sumit Agarwal, Satyanarain Rengarajan, Sing Tien Foo and Derek Volmer (2015), "Effects of Construction Activities on Residential Electricity Consumption: Evidence from Singapore's Public Housing Estates," Working Paper, National University of Singapore, https://papers.ssrn.com/sol3/papers.cfm?abstract_id=2371314

On the one hand, the NTUC Comfort taxi that he had been driving for so many years had fixed rates. On the other hand, Grab had a surge pricing mechanism which allowed fares to escalate when there was unusually high demand.

Surge Pricing

Surge or dynamic pricing is a system used by car-sharing apps that adjusts fares according to passenger demand in a particular area at a particular time. Some ride-hailing apps claim that they use surge pricing to encourage more drivers to get out on the road when demand is high such as on rainy days.

Grab introduced surge pricing with its JustGrab services in 2017. JustGrab allows commuters to book a ride from the closest private car or taxi at a similar price. It pools together taxis from participating fleets as well as private cars that have independent drivers not affiliated with a taxi company. Prices are based on a dynamic surge factor mechanism where taxi trips booked via the JustGrab service are priced dynamically within the Grab service platform using Grab's surge pricing scheme.

Teng, as a driver for NTUC Comfort as well as for Grab, was in two minds as his fares vary. Taxis hired through either street pick-up or the taxi company's own booking app have fixed meter prices based on location and time that do not vary according to real-time market conditions. However, taxis hired through Grab's app are priced dynamically according to the surge price mechanism.

Teng recalled how his parents were once left stranded because of a heavy downpour and they couldn't get a cab. And the surge prices were, to him, quite astronomical at times compared to fixed meter prices. While on the one hand it's a pure money-making transaction to use the surge price, he felt badly as he remembered all too well how some people especially the elderly could not afford the high fares when they needed the ride most.

Teng had not quite got a handle on how surge pricing works and how the supply of taxis is affected when such pricing takes place. He had talked to several of his taxi driver friends who claimed they know much about surge pricing but didn't seem to know what they were saying when probed further.

"More like bravado talk than anything else," thought Teng.

The Young Man

Then one day, while on a break at the crowded Pek Kio market, it so happened that Teng was sitting next to a Grab driver eating kaya toast with half-boiled egg over a cup of coffee. He was curious why such a young man would be driving Grab. Doesn't he have any other job?

It turned out that the young driver had been a research assistant at NUS Business School working on a research project involving taxis. The project had just been completed and his contract ended. So while in between jobs, the man decided to be a Grab driver to earn some money in the meantime.

"How come Grab can charge fares that are sometimes cheaper than taxi fares?" asked Teng, in his Singapore English. He was curious how Grab does it. He understood that in the early days, discounts were given when Grab was competing with Uber for market share. But with Uber out of the picture, discounts are still sometimes given for rides in conjunction with food purchases on GrabFood.

"Well, Grab has so many investors interested in injecting capital into this start-up," said the young man.

"Have you heard of SoftBank? This Japanese company injected lots of money into Grab. So with the capital raised, Grab can subsidise the fares and incentivise their drivers."

"Oh . . . So they have lots of money," said Teng as he tried to figure out the business model.

"Let me tell you about my previous job. I was at NUS working for my professor after I graduated. He had this very interesting study on how surge pricing affects the supply of taxis on the road," said the young man, happy to share what he knew with Teng.

Teng was keen to listen. After all, this was an issue that he had been grappling with for a while and none of his taxi driver friends seemed interested or to know enough about it.

"Compared to taxi prices, the fares of ride-hailing services such as Grab are set dynamically by the ride-hailing app's algorithm that takes into account the demand and supply of rides," said the young man.

"Oh wait . . . Go slow please. You're talking to an 'uncle' who has only 'O' level, OK? I've no research experience at all," laughed Teng while acknowledging his limited formal education.

"Sorry, Uncle. Let me explain slowly. Grab's prices are determined by supply and demand. It is not fixed by the meter. In other words, it's dynamic or flexible, depending on the situation. When demand is very high, the fare can go up a lot, much higher than the metered taxi fare.

"Let's call this the surge factor. I know it's a big word. But bear with me. The surge factor represents the relative price difference between the fares charged using a ride-hailing app and a standard taxi," explained the young man slowly.

The surge factor represents the relative price difference between the fares charged using a ride-hailing app and a standard taxi.

"For instance, if the Grab fare is $10 and the taxi fare is $9.50, then the surge factor is low because the price difference is small. But if the Grab fare is $15 and the taxi fare is $9.50, then the surge factor is high because the price differential is large.

"So, why would Grab fare be so high, you might ask. That happens when there is more demand than supply for Grab. This would be the case when it is raining heavily and many people need a ride than there is supply of Grab cars or taxis."

"Or when the MRT breaks down," interjected Teng as he recalled the numerous MRT (Mass Rapid Transit) breakdowns that Singaporeans have experienced.

"But for taxis," the young man continued, "the fare is based on distance travelled as measured by the meter rather than on demand. This results in Grab prices possibly becoming higher than taxi prices. When Grab prices are higher than taxi prices, the surge factor is more than one.

"Is this OK so far?"

"Eh . . . Yes. I think I understand," replied Teng tentatively.

"Now, here's the reverse. When there is more supply of Grab cars than there is demand, that is, there are more non-hired Grab cars on the road than there are people wanting a ride, it is likely that the Grab fare will be cheaper than the metered taxi fare. If that is the case, the surge factor is equal to or less than one."

"OK. I think I follow so far. Surge factor is greater than one when Grab fare is more than taxi fare. Surge factor is one or less when Grab fare is less than taxi fare," clarified Teng just so that he got it correct.

The young man nodded.

"But please, don't get more technical. Otherwise, I think I'll be lost," pleaded Teng.

"Don't worry, Uncle. You are doing fine. We'll take it slowly," smiled the young man encouragingly.

"My professor used two sets of data. The first dataset is on taxi mobility. This contains the number of taxi trips across all operators and the trip types at every 30-minute interval. This means we know where each trip started and where it ended. We also know whether the ride was initiated through a booking, a street pick-up, a limo service or whatever.

"Because my professor wanted to find out the effect of surge pricing on taxi supply, he focused on taxi bookings of the two taxi operators who at that time forbade their drivers from participating in the Grab service. By doing that, he can tell the effect of surge pricing on the availability of taxis from these two operators in a particular area.

"His data were collected every 30 minutes. Do you know why? Because that would allow us to see whether there are differences during peak hours and end-of-school hours versus non-peak hours. Is this good?"

"Yup, I got it so far. How about the second dataset?" enquired Teng.

"The second dataset contains a panel of all taxis in Singapore. We also collected the data at every 30-minute interval. Here, we know for each taxi whether the taxi is available or hired, and its location. This allows us to understand the supply of taxis. 'Available' taxis means they are available for hire, which means there is excess supply since they are not used; while 'Hired' taxis means they have been booked already by demand. And we do this for each operator in each area every 30 minutes. Understand?"

"Got it!" said an excited Teng.

The young man continued. "So we know the supply of taxis. How about Grab's supply of cars? Grab offers a range of ride services – GrabHitch, JustGrab and so on. We studied JustGrab. JustGrab allows commuters to book a ride from the closest private car and participating taxi at the same price. So there's private cars with independent drivers not affiliated with a taxi company as well as taxis from participating fleets which included about half of taxis in Singapore at that time.

"Now, remember that at the time of the study, not all taxi companies allowed their taxis to use Grab services. So the supply of taxis in our study is based on operators that forbid their taxis from participating in the JustGrab service.

"Unfortunately, Grab doesn't want to share with us their data. We understand. It's proprietary. So what my professor did was to use a proxy for JustGrab supply."

"What is a 'proxy'?" asked Teng, scratching his head.

"Ahh . . . A 'proxy' means a 'substitute'. In our study, because we could not get data from Grab, we used taxis from taxi operators that permit their taxis to participate as JustGrab cars as a measure of the supply of Grab cars."

"Is that accurate?" asked Teng. "JustGrab has other drivers too."

"You are right. Our proxy for Grab supply is not perfect because private drivers are not included. Also, taxi drivers from participating Grab operators can choose whether to drive as a Grab driver or not. However, since at the time of the study, participating operators do not have other ways of booking rides through a smartphone app, the affiliated taxi drivers are most likely to choose to drive as a Grab driver," explained the young man.

"So even though we do not have data from Grab on direct rides, we can study the relationship between Grab and taxi bookings due to the overlap of Grab cars and certain taxi operators in Singapore.

"Moreover, since the taxis that operate using the Grab platform are able to observe the surge factor, their driving behaviour should be similar with those of private car drivers. But then like you said, we do not have all the data. Not having the private car data from Grab means that our Grab supply is likely to be underestimated. It's not perfect.

Ideally of course my professor would love to have Grab data. We wish Grab would share with us some of their data. As academics, my professor will rigorously analyse the data and help Grab and the society with the findings.

"Anyway, I won't go into the technical mumbo jumbo. The bottomline is that statistically, we can control for this bias in our analyses."

Teng wasn't so sure that he could intelligently follow how the data were analysed. But he was eager to learn the findings. After all, he didn't really care about technical details. He'd leave that to the experts. All he wanted was to know the results and how they affected him as a taxi driver, and his family and friends as commuters.

"OK, are you ready?" asked the young man as he wanted so much to share the findings. "We found that Singaporeans are not very sensitive to the higher price of ride-hailing services when there is surge pricing. It's like the 'got no choice' mentality. When the surge factor is high and there is a lack of available taxis as substitutes, people will just pay the higher fare."

"Yah. I agree. They have no choice. What else can they do?" agreed Teng.

The young man continued, "But that's not the interesting part. The interesting part is – we found that the number of taxis available do not match with the surge factor within an area during the time when there is surge pricing. Let me explain.

> **[T]he number of taxis available do not match with the surge factor within an area during the time when there is surge pricing.**

"When we book a taxi, the supply of taxis comes from the same pool of taxis as those available for street pick-ups. So when people are booking a ride either through Grab or calling for a taxi, of course the taxi driver will prefer to take up the booking because he earns the additional booking fee of $3 to $5. Street pick-ups, on the other hand, becomes less attractive. And so the number of street pick-ups goes down because taxis are diverted to pick up passengers from such bookings."

"That makes sense," thought Teng as he obviously would rather have more booking rides than street pick-ups because of the booking fee earned.

The young man continued. "So, during the time of a taxi booking, the total number of taxis available in that area does not change. This means that the available taxis on the road in that vicinity can absorb these bookings, at least for a short period of time."

"But what about when it is raining?" asked Teng.

"Good question. Rain is relevant because obviously rain affects demand. More people need a ride when it is raining, especially when it is raining heavily.

"The problem with rain is that not all taxi drivers are able to observe the surge factor due to rain. Only drivers near the area where it is pouring can observe the rain and know whether a high demand for taxis is likely to occur. So whether it is raining or not is common information only to drivers in the rainy area.

"Now, rain may increase taxi supply because drivers are anticipating more demand. But rain can also raise concerns about road conditions, safety and congestion. There are some drivers who avoid driving on rainy days."

Teng nodded as he knew of some taxi drivers who do not like driving when there's a heavy downpour.

"We found that in general, during rainy periods, taxi supply increases by 0.37 percent. But when it rains and the surge factor goes up by 10 percentage points, guess what happens? The total taxi supply goes down by 2.3 percent. Down, OK? Not up.

"And as to be expected, we found that when the surge factor is high and people are booking either through Grab or directly from the taxi company, there are more booked taxis and fewer 'Available' taxis. Taxis on the street are diverted to absorb the demand from such bookings and there are less for street pick-ups."

"Yah, that makes sense," nodded Teng.

"But let me ask you this. If you were a smart passenger and there is surge pricing, how should you book your ride?"

The young man paused for effect.

"Let me tell you how much a passenger can save if he books a taxi directly instead of using Grab when there is surge pricing," said the young man as he lowered his voice as if to share a secret.

"Shh . . . It's quite a lot, OK? We did a rough calculation based on the average distance of travel. We found that when the surge factor is higher than one, if a person switches from using ride-hailing to booking a taxi through the taxi operator, he saves about . . . You guess?" teased the young man as he felt Teng's anticipation.

"10 percent?" Teng hazarded a guess.

"18 percent!" said the young man excitedly and yet trying hard not to raise his voice. "That's a lot! If your ride cost $10, you'll be saving $1.80!"

Teng wasn't quite sure whether to feel good or bad because obviously he's a beneficiary of increased taxi bookings but he would also have made more driving on the Grab service.

"The good news for passengers though is that only the surge factor during the last half hour or so affects current taxi bookings. So the effect of surge factor

> [T]he effect of surge factor is temporary. The impact becomes zero after an hour.

is temporary. The impact becomes zero after an hour. This means Singaporeans, especially those not in a hurry, can self-select whether to take Grab or book a taxi if they don't want to pay unnecessarily more for the ride.

"Or they can wait out till the surge pricing is over. Or use another mode of transportation. After all, Singapore is small and we can go from one place to another using alternative transportation such as the bus or MRT."

"Wow! So my parents can save 18 percent if they use taxi booking instead of Grab when there is surge pricing. And if they can outwait the rain, the surge pricing will go away after half hour to one hour," said Teng as he digested the information. "I should tell Pa and Ma this, and even to Siew Ling as I can't be driving them around all the time."

Better Prediction

For Teng as a taxi driver, this meant it pays for him to look at the weather forecast so that he can anticipate areas where there'll be rain and hence increased taxi demand. He's a bit of a *kiasu*. So knowing such information before other drivers would give him an advantage. He wished Singapore's weatherman would provide more granular information on location and time of rain. Then he would be around that vicinity when it starts raining to maximise bookings.

Such information would be beneficial not only to him, but also to the taxi company. If the taxi company could make better predictions of taxi booking demand, then congestion could be alleviated and there would be fewer idle taxis in no-rain areas.

The young man had told him that if a taxi operator could predict demand more accurately by 15 percent, this would lead to an almost 10 percent of additional reduction in vacant roaming time for drivers.

When taxis are better utilised on the roads by carrying passengers instead of vacant roaming, it makes for a greener environment.

The young man had also told Teng that there is a prototype already developed outside Singapore with 500 taxi drivers where recommendations are given by the taxi company on where to drive to for more pick-ups. These drivers experienced almost 30 percent reduction in their vacant roaming time.

"Wouldn't that be fantastic if my taxi company could give recommendations on where these 'hot spots' are? Provided of course they are accurate," thought Teng.

The Future of Taxis

"What about this new ERP that I hear about?" asked Teng to the young man, who seemed to keep up-to-date on transport matters.

"Oh, that one. Some call it ERP 2.0," replied the young man. "The toll you pay is based on distance. And I think it uses some GPS system."

"Doesn't that mean that when I drive around looking for passengers, it will cost me more if I can't find one?" asked Teng as he mentally calculated the average distance he drives without a passenger on board.

"That's right. The new distance-travel toll would put a damper on taxi cruising. If you drive Grab, you know where your next passenger is from bookings, at least for most of the time. Then you'll be cruising less and save on costs," rationalised the young man.

"But what about the older people who don't use Grab? I don't think they know how to use these ride-hailing apps," said a concerned Teng thinking of his parents.

"That's true," answered the young man. "Young people just use the app instead of flagging down a taxi along the road, even though at

> **It's usually the old folks who still flag down taxis. I see the demand for flagged-down taxis declining.**

times it might just be cheaper to flag down a taxi. It's usually the old folks who still flag down taxis. I see the demand for flagged-down taxis declining. And with the new distance toll, I think that may further discourage taxis from cruising for passengers, thus making it harder to flag down an empty taxi."

"Do you think taxis will become obsolete?" asked Teng.

Seeing the disheartened look on Teng's face, the young man offered some comfort.

"Uncle, look at it positively. Times have changed. I see the new distance-travel toll discouraging cruising. Which means as a taxi driver, you'll have to be smarter. You have to know where to find passengers easily to reduce the distance travelled. You'll also need to depend more on bookings for the 'confirmed' passenger. If you do this, your earnings will be higher as you drive less looking for passengers. Moreover, you won't be so tired and you'll be safer on the road. And think about this – there'll be less pollution on the road when fewer empty taxis are cruising about."

Teng had much to consider. His prospects as a taxi driver did not look too promising. He might have to consider taking up a sideline job or maybe even setting up his own business.

WANT TO KNOW MORE?

This chapter is based on Sumit Agarwal, Ben Charoenwong, Cheng Shih-Fen and Jussi Keppo (2019), "Fickle Fingers: Ride-Hail Surge Factors and Taxi Bookings," Working Paper, National University of Singapore, https://papers.ssrn.com/sol3/papers.cfm?abstract_id=3157378

Productivity

"So hot, so hot," grumbled Ah Mah at Singapore's sweltering heat.

"I never remember Singapore to be so hot. Last time when I was young, I could wear long-sleeve blouse when going out. Now I cannot *tahan* (tolerate) the weather. I perspire so much even when I'm wearing my short-sleeve cotton blouse. Singapore is getting too warm for me."

"It's because you are older now. And fatter too. More fat means more insulation. So you feel warmer," joked Ah Kong. He thought his wife had been pampered by the air-conditioned comfort since shutting their windows to block out the noise from nearby construction.

Truth be told, he also shared the same sentiment as his wife. Singapore is getting hotter.

And he knows this from the walks he makes bringing his grandson to school. Every morning, Ah Kong and Ah Mah will bring Ethan to his kindergarten. The morning walk is quite pleasant. They call it 'exercise' and it gives them time alone with Ethan, talking to him about school and his friends. But it's the walk back in the afternoon when they bring Ethan home that is unbearable under Singapore's enervating heat. Ah Kong and Ah Mah would feel quite spent.

Wiping beads of perspiration off their forehead, they would then head to the cool air-conditioned comfort afforded by the nearby community centre. This saves them from incurring air-conditioning expenses at home.

"I've got to make more cooling tea for the family. *Liang teh* is good, especially for Teng since he's driving around so much. The cool tea will balance the heatiness from this kind of weather. Remember to remind me to buy ingredients from the Chinese medicine shop on our way home," Ah Mah told Ah Kong.

Air Pollution and Productivity

That evening, as Ah Mah served the family the *liang teh* she had carefully prepared, the family chatted about the weather.

"Crazy weather, isn't it? So hot for so long, and then suddenly rain so much on another day. I'm sure quite a number of people will fall sick," complained Siew Ling.

"Do you think the hot weather makes the air more dusty?" asked Ah Mah.

"I know it's not like the haze we experienced in 2013 and 2015. I remember people were using more water and air-con then, and falling sick.[1] But with hot weather for weeks or months, with little rain, don't you think the air pollution has gotten worse?"

---

[1] For more on this research on the effects of haze on Singaporeans' utilities consumption, see Sumit Agarwal, Ang Swee Hoon and Sing Tien Foo (2018), *Kiasunomics: Stories of Singaporean Economic Behaviours*, Chapter 16 "Smoke Gets in Your Eyes," (Singapore: World Scientific Publishers). To read the academic article, see Sumit Agarwal, Sing Tien Foo and Yang Yang (2017), "Risk Avoidance and Environmental Hazard: Effects of the Transboundary Haze Pollution in Singapore," https://papers.ssrn.com/sol3/papers.cfm?abstract_id=2942096

"Can you imagine the haze in Sydney from the forest fire last December?" commented Siew Ling.

"I think you'd better drink more water. And better still, don't stay outside so long. Maybe the outside air is not as good as before. I still remember the haze then. Some people stopped working completely," coaxed Ah Mah.

"Wow! Ma, you are quite a *kiasu*," remarked Teng at the lengths his mother would go to ensure he stayed well.

The reality is that Ah Mah dotes on her son. Teng has been filial to invite her and Ah Kong to live with them. In return, as a parent, she should be looking out for his and his family's health.

"It is true, Ma. I remember when there was the haze, some of my taxi driver friends stopped driving. Just a slight change in the air quality was enough to influence their decision on whether to drive," Teng contributed.

"You mean they were so affected by the haze?" enquired Siew Ling with only a remote memory of the haze.

"Yah. My company was concerned because a drop in taxis meant fewer taxis on the road, which therefore meant less income," added Teng.

"They did a study and found that taxi drivers drove less when the PSI (Pollutant Standards Index) increased. PSI has five categories: Good (0 to 50), moderate (51 to 100), unhealthy (101 to 200), very unhealthy (201 to 300), and hazardous (above 300).

"They found that taxi drivers drove less by 14 minutes each day when the PSI moved from good to moderate. Considering that the average driving time when PSI is good is 522 minutes per day, this is equivalent to a 2.7 percent drop from the average time a taxi driver spends on the road."

"Wow! I didn't know taxi drivers are so sensitive to the haze. I can't

> **[E]very increase in the PSI by 50 led to a reduction of 30 minutes of driving.**

recall you stopping to drive so much when there was haze," said Siew Ling.

Teng carried on. "On top of that, my company found that on average, every increase in the PSI by 50 led to a reduction of 30 minutes of driving. Of course, this gets worse at higher PSI levels. So when the air quality worsens, it is likely that there will be fewer taxis on the road."

"Then surge prices can become even higher, right? There may be more demand than supply," exclaimed Ah Mah, who had been caught in a dire situation before – when it was raining heavily, taxis were not easy to get and the prices of Grab cars went extremely high.

"Perhaps you are right, if people still want to go out despite the haze. But I think people would rather stay at home. So both demand and supply drop," replied Teng.

"Maybe these drivers took a longer break in coffeeshops instead of driving around for passengers?" enquired Siew Ling, trying to understand better how taxi drivers behave.

"I don't think so," responded Teng. "My company found that taxi drivers didn't take a longer break from driving. They stopped driving altogether when the pollution condition worsened. In fact, many took shorter breaks to try to earn as much as possible before calling it a day should the air quality worsen."

"Hmm . . . That means poor air quality is not only a health threat, but it can also pose as an economic challenge. Productivity is affected," said Siew Ling who was quite happy that she was drawing such inferences.

"Sadly so. Despite working in the comfort of their cab, taxi drivers are less productive when there is air pollution because inevitably they'll be exposed to pollutants the moment they step outside of their home," agreed Teng.

"I remember my company saying something else . . . something like in the United States, there was a study done and they found a 5.5 percent drop in productivity when there is an increase in ozone exposure, or something like that."

"Wow! If this happens all the time, then we won't be very productive," added Ah Kong. Ah Kong has retired but he always has a strong ethic of working hard no matter what.

"I wonder whether other people, not just taxi drivers, will also drive less? Especially since cars in Singapore are so expensive," wondered Siew Ling.

"Maybe if they drive less, there'll be less traffic, and that will help reduce air pollution," Ah Mah joined in.

Sunk Cost Fallacy

Just then, their doorbell rang. Their neighbour, Professor Sing from NUS, dropped by to give them some snacks he had brought from Japan. He had attended a conference there and as usual, brought food souvenirs home for the family and friends.

"Here's some Kit Kat from Japan. They come in exotic flavours – red bean, crème brulee and even cheesecake. Quite interesting eh?" smiled Professor Sing.

"Thank you. You're so kind," said Teng. "Sing, may I ask you this . . . We were just talking about taxi drivers driving less when there is haze or possibly very bad air pollution. Then my wife asked whether other Singaporeans would drive less or not. What do you think?"

"I don't know about the effects of air pollution. But I know given our high car prices, Singaporeans do not drive less. Do you have time? I can share with you about a study done by two NUS Business School professors and an NTU professor," replied Professor Sing.

"Oh! You mean NUS and NTU profs do research together?" asked a curious Teng.

"I know, I know. We're competitors, right? But we're also collaborative. So these two NUS professors, Ivan Png and Ho Teck Hua, and Sadat Reza from NTU, used data from over 8,000 cars of one particular brand. For the life of me, I can't remember which one. Anyway, when each car was sent for servicing, they tracked the kilometres driven and analysed the usage against the overall cost of ownership and congestion on Singapore's roads.

"Interestingly, they found that people drove more when they had bought a car at a higher price. The higher price could be because of higher COE (Certificate of Entitlement) or Additional Registration Fee (ARF).

"And the more driving associated with high car ownership costs was not confined just to young drivers who might be buying the car for the first time. Even experienced and wealthy car owners drove more when the car ownership became more expensive."

"Huh? How can that be? Ironic, isn't it? Isn't COE supposed to curb traffic jam? Now a high COE is encouraging more driving!" quizzed Teng.

"Yup, you're right. It is indeed ironic. Tackling traffic congestion is a major challenge. The Singapore Government has made car ownership costly and kept public transport alternatives like buses and MRT affordable and efficient to keep cars off the roads.

"My friends from other countries are often shocked at how much we have to pay to own a car. Before buying a car, we have to bid for the right to own a car via COE through a monthly auction where prices fluctuate depending on demand and supply."

"Eh, Sing. I think these people are so *kiasu* that they want to maximise every dollar they spent on the car. They want to make every dollar worth the while," said Teng.

> [I]ncreasing car prices had the unintended consequences of stimulating driving among people who had bought the cars.

"You are absolutely right. As a taxi driver, you would probably realise this already. Let me explain my colleagues' research," as Professor Sing continued.

"We would have thought that to tackle traffic congestion, we should make car ownership costly. But my colleagues found that increasing car prices had the unintended consequences of stimulating driving among people who had bought the cars. In other words, as Teng said, car buyers reasoned that as they had already paid so much for a car, they should get maximum use out of it!

"So let's say it's you, Teng. You bought a car and it costs about $100,000 all in, including COE. You have already invested a lot into the car. And on top of that, the investment cannot be easily reversed. It's not like stocks where you can sell the investment quite easily. So what would you do?"

"Drive more?" replied Teng with some hesitance.

"Exactly. You'd drive more. You would mentally justify the high cost by using the car more. Instead of easing congestion, a high COE adds to the congestion by having the unintended effect of encouraging people to drive more."

"I think I understand why people think that way. I'd probably feel the same way too," agreed Teng. "It's being *kiasu*."

"While that might be the case, my colleagues also found that this kind of thinking is not permanent. It changes over time. What this means is that people do not always think they should use their car so much. For the first 48 months of car ownership, usage is high to compensate for the initial high purchase price. Then as the car ages, usage gradually decreases. But the higher the initial cost, the longer this will take," Professor Sing elaborated further.

Everyone nodded.

"My colleagues even worked out how many extra kilometres this phenomenon added to Singapore's roads," said Professor Sing, while trying to recall the numbers.

"During the time when they studied COEs, the number of COEs had been reduced from something like 10,000 to 6,500. This reduction resulted in more than a doubling of COE prices from $11,000 to over $24,000. So let me ask you. On average, for each month, how many more kilometres do you think people will drive their cars given the increase in COEs?"

Ah Kong who was listening attentively was the first to respond.

"300 kilometres! 10 kilometres more each day."

"You crazy ah! Singapore is only 50 kilometres wide from East to West, and 27 kilometres from North to South. Do you know how much is 300 kilometres?" Ah Mah scolded her husband. She sometimes thinks that Ah Kong doesn't think through before he talks.

Only Ah Mah can speak like that to Ah Kong. Everyone else in the family knows too well they should be polite to the patriach.

"How long is our coastline? Teng, quickly Google for the information," urged Ah Mah.

"193 kilometres" was Teng's response after a quick search on his smartphone. He was surprised that his mother even knew about Google. He wondered whether she had learnt it from her grandsons.

"Uncle, 300 kilometres is indeed too high," replied a very amiable Professor Sing, trying to diffuse the momentarily tense moment.

"Eh . . . Maybe 100 kilometres more?" said Siew Ling.

"Almost," said Professor Sing. "My colleagues found car owners would drive their cars 86 kilometres more per month than they would have otherwise. That's 5.6 percent more than their average driving distance."

"Hmm . . . I get it. They want to max out given the high price they have paid for their car since they've already paid for it and are stuck with it," nodded Siew Ling.

> [I]n business, sunk costs are not considered in future business decisions because the cost will be the same regardless of the outcome of a decision.

"That's right. It's a sunk cost," explained Professor Sing.

Seeing the confused look on everyone's face when he mentioned sunk cost, he continued. "A sunk cost is a cost that has already been incurred and cannot be recovered. So in business, sunk costs are not considered in future business decisions because the cost will be the same regardless of the outcome of a decision."

"I wonder whether the same thing would be true too for the casino levy. You know, the government increased the levy for Singaporeans from $100 to $150. Do you think once someone pays the levy and enters the casino, he will spend as long as he can there?" asked Teng.

"That's an interesting question," smiled Professor Sing. "According to the reasoning given by my colleagues, the answer would be a 'Yes'. If you've already paid a levy to play in a casino and you start losing, you are more likely to stick with it as you've already invested in the levy and believe it will be a waste to walk away, even though staying may mean spending more."

"So fascinating. Is there a special name to call this phenomenon?" asked Teng.

"Ah yes. It's called the 'Concorde Fallacy'. Do you remember the supersonic aircraft called Concorde that flew between London and New York? It's named after that plane," answered Professor Sing.

"Concorde was a very expensive plane. Well, even after it became clear that there was no economic justification to run Concorde, the British and French governments continued to fund the joint development. Maybe it's the emotional attachment to what they've already invested in – time, money and reputation, or whatever.

"Hey sorry. I would like to stay on but I can't. I'm tired but I need to prepare for tomorrow's lecture."

"Thanks so much for the Kit Kat, Sing. Thanks for the explanation too," said Teng as he closed the door.

"It's quite interesting isn't it to know that people's behaviour changes because of the amount spent on buying a car?" remarked Siew Ling.

As the family sat down together again at the dining table, the conversation on car usage continued.

"I know Singapore wants to avoid massive traffic jams by limiting the number of cars on the road. And to do that, the government has kept car ownership cost prohibitively high. But those who can afford a car will not want to leave their car at home. Otherwise, it will seem to be a waste of the huge money spent on buying the car. Maybe the government should think of other ways to curb congestion," said Siew Ling.

At this point, Teng paused for a moment. He recalled something that his taxi friends had said.

"I remember my friends saying that the government realised it too – that relying on high car ownership costs to manage congestion may not be effective. So there's some talk about shifting the tax from car ownership to usage rate instead."

"When will this start?" Siew Ling asked.

"Some say 2021, but who knows. It seems that a new sophisticated road-pricing system will be implemented. They refer to it as ERP 2.0 or Electronic Road Pricing 2.0. I spoke to this young man the other day. He's a research assistant at NUS and he gave me some updates. It will use GPS to determine the amount drivers pay based on distance, time, location and vehicle type. Drivers will receive real-time information about the cost and which roads are experiencing higher congestion."

"Will this affect your taxi? You drive a lot and throughout the day," added Siew Ling, the wife who is concerned with expenses.

Before Teng could reply, Ah Mah said, "I think more people will take public transportation that is not only cheap but also convenient. Your father and I were at the community centre this morning and they encouraged working people to take the MRT early to reduce crowding."

Incentives to Ease Congestion

Earlier that day, Ah Kong and Ah Mah were at the community centre attending a talk organised to encourage people to take public transportation during off-peak periods for their morning commute.

"But if everyone were to take the MRT, then each train carriage will be super crowded. I'll be squeezed like sardines in a tin can. Why would I want to do that?" quizzed Ah Mah.

"And if you were working, you'd have no choice but to do this twice every day during peak periods – when going to work and when coming home. Urgh . . . Having to stand so close to each other and bear with the armpit smell. How horrible," Ah Mah shuddered.

"Let's just go and listen. We are not affected since we don't need to travel during peak periods. Let's hear what the LTA (Land Transport

Authority) has to say. Maybe they have brilliant ideas," said Ah Kong, somewhat sarcastically as he was still sore with the numerous MRT breakdowns he had experienced.

"Thank you everyone for coming to this talk. Please grab a seat quickly as we will begin soon," announced an administrator from the community centre. As usual, she tapped on the microphone to make sure that was working.

"I'm sure all of you have encountered instances when the MRT is so crowded that you either have to stand very closely to one another or worse, miss the train and be late for work or an appointment. Today, we have Mr Yang from the LTA to share with us steps that the LTA is doing to alleviate overcrowding in trains. Mr Yang, please."

It turned out that Mr Yang was in charge of special projects at the LTA which included studies on incentivising Singaporeans to take the MRT during off-peak hours.

"I wonder whether our neighbour, Josie, knows Mr Yang," whispered Ah Mah to Ah Kong. Josie used to work at the LTA, although now she has moved on to the NEA (National Environment Agency).

"Shh . . . He's going to speak," whispered Ah Kong to remain polite and attentive.

Here's what Mr Yang had to say:

"Overcrowding is a serious issue. In New York, 40 percent of its subway train delay incidences are caused by overcrowding. We want to avoid such a situation.

"We recognise that riding in a crammed MRT can be a miserable commute for people especially if this occurs twice a day, five days a week, when going to work and back home.

"Whilst spending on more personnel, trains and infrastructure may help to alleviate overcrowding, the reality is that there are diminishing returns on such investments when the demand for these extra resources is concentrated only at certain times. First, there are physical limits to adding more trains. Worse, these expensive additional trains would be left idle during off-peak hours.

"So we started thinking of other strategies that we can do to alleviate overcrowding. One solution is to persuade commuters to stagger or spread out their journeys. Why should everyone travel at the same time? Instead, we want to encourage people who can shift their travel time, to take the MRT at less busy times.

"The question then is how to make this shift not only successful but also lasting."

Mr Yang waited for a while to let the information sink in, and then continued.

"In some countries, the authorities impose surcharges during peak hours to discourage such travel. But studies have shown that such surcharges have little impact on travel patterns. I'm sure you don't like to see fare hikes, right? Well, studies also show that surcharges only add to commuter resentment to having pay more. Moreover, imposing surcharges is politically unpopular.

"So what can the LTA do to encourage Singaporeans to stagger their commute time so that people can have a more comfortable MRT journey especially during peak hours?

"We partnered with NUS Business School to examine which type of incentive scheme would be effective. Today, I'll be sharing with you one of several studies that we've conducted."

Mr Yang looked around the audience, made up of mainly retirees, to see that they registered what he had said so far.

He thought to himself. "Sigh . . . It's unfortunate that the audience doesn't have many working adults. This is not exactly the target audience we want. Hopefully they'll convey today's message to their children. Perhaps we'll have to conduct more of such talks at workplace areas during lunch time."

Aloud, Mr Yang addressed the crowd. "In this study, we recruited 350 regular morning commuters as participants. We monitored their MRT commute for 20 weeks first to see the average time they exit the station.

"Then we asked ourselves, 'If we were to give them some incentives, would they use the MRT earlier and hence, exit the station earlier?' In other words, we want to encourage them to use the MRT before their usual time so that ridership can be spread out across times to minimise overcrowding during peak periods.

"So we divided these 350 commuters into three groups. One group did not receive any reward. They are what we call the Control group. They travelled as usual and paid the normal fare. The other two groups received an incentive. One group was rewarded a full rebate of their fare if they exited the station before 7:45 AM. In other words, they travel for free. We call this group 'Early Treatment'. The other group received a full rebate if they exited by 8:00 AM, and we call this group 'Late Treatment'.

"Now, you can well imagine that if you were one of the participants and you just missed the free travel cut-off time, you might be upset that you had just missed getting free travel, right? So to avoid such disappointment, those who narrowly missed the cut-off time were given a 50-cent discount during a 15-minute grace period from 7:45 to 8:00 AM (for the 'Early Treatment') and 8:00 to 8:15 AM (for the 'Late Treatment').

"Let me show you the various groups and incentives:

Group	Behaviour	Reward
Control	Travel as normal	No incentives given
Early Treatment	Exit MRT station before 7:45 AM	Full rebate of fare
Late Treatment	Exit MRT station before 8:00 AM	Full rebate of fare

"We then monitored their travel patterns during the 10 weeks when the incentives were given. After the incentive programmes were over, we continued to monitor their commute for another 30 weeks to see whether the incentive programmes were persistent in changing commute behaviour. So altogether, we monitored their travel patterns for 60 weeks – 20 weeks before the rewards were given, and 40 weeks after they were given, of which 10 weeks were the reward period."

"Is this all good? You follow me?" asked Mr Yang.

The audience nodded. Satisfied, Mr Yang carried on, speaking slowly and clearly.

"Here are the findings:

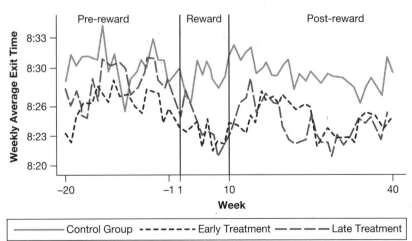

33

"On the left margin is the exit times in the morning when commuters go to work. Remember that we want to encourage them to exit earlier than usual to relieve congestion during the peak period.

"The solid line is the Control group that did not receive any reward. They travel on full fare. The short dashed line is the Early Treatment group where commuters receive a full fare rebate if they exited the station before 7:45 AM. The long dashed line is the Late Treatment group where commuters receive the same rebate if they exited before 8:00 AM.

"There are three time periods that we want to study. The two vertical lines demarcate the 10-week reward period, separating it from before the programme started and after the programme ended.

"If you look at the graph, not everyone succeeded in exiting before the cut-off exit time, but you can see that they tried. Looking at the 10-week reward period, you can see the exit times for the Early and Late Treatment groups went down immediately in response to the reward. When the 10-week reward programme was over, we see the exit time went up for both groups. That's to be expected because there was no more reward.

"But what is interesting is that the difference in exit times between those who received the rewards and the Control group that didn't receive any rebate persists. Look at the lines to the right of the graph during the Post-reward period. The short and long dashed lines continued to be way below that of the solid line. Remember that the solid line denotes commuters who didn't receive any reward, and the short dashed and long dashed lines are those who received rewards for being early.

"What this means is that having received the reward in the weeks prior, these commuters continued to exit the station earlier than those who did not receive any rewards, although not as early as they did when they were incentivised. So, incentivising them did work."

Mr Yang looked around the audience to make sure they understood.

"Here's another finding that shows the percentage of commuters who exited by 8:00 AM.

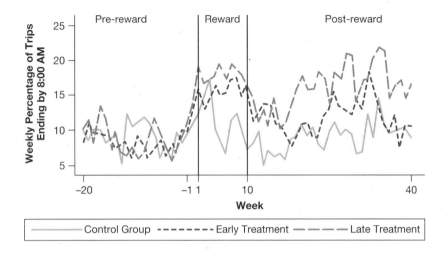

"After receiving the reward, the percentage of passengers who completed their trip by 8:00 AM went up compared to those who didn't receive any reward. And this behaviour continued even after the reward was discontinued.

"All in, during the 10-week reward period, we were able to shift 271 trips out of the peak period of 8:15 to 9:00 AM. After the reward period, we continued to shift 553 trips out of peak period. So congestion was largely alleviated.

"So, you might ask – Why did commuters in the reward groups persist in using the MRT earlier? After all, there were no more financial rewards to be gained.

"Now, we must bear in mind that the reward, a full rebate of fare, is really not a huge reward. On average, the fare is $1.30 and that is miniscule considering our average income. Public transportation in Singapore is relatively cheap compared to other developed countries.

"So, here's what we think. We think it's because of this phenomenon called habit formation. During the reward period, not only did commuters receive financial rewards, as small as that might be for being an early bird, but they also learned through the experience the non-monetary benefits associated with early travel such as less crowded trains and less stress from being late for work. They began to enjoy these non-monetary perks and stayed on with this travel pattern even when there were no more financial rewards. A habit has been formed. And a good one at that!

> **[O]ffering a temporary incentive or 'nudge' could induce lasting change in behaviour even well after the financial rewards are withdrawn.**

"In summary, our findings showed that offering a temporary incentive or 'nudge' could induce lasting change in behaviour even well after the financial rewards are withdrawn.

"I see that many of you here are retirees. But still young at heart! Please encourage the working adults in your family to go to work earlier to beat the crowd so that more people, including themselves, can enjoy a more hassle-free journey. Thank you."

The discussion was then open to the floor.

Someone behind Ah Kong and Ah Mah asked, "You carried your study only among 350 people and gave incentives for only 10 weeks. If the LTA were to give these rewards nation-wide to encourage non-peak period travel, it can be very expensive. You also mentioned that infrastructural improvements would require higher capital and the returns were not sustainable. How does giving rewards compare to the cost of adding a new train?"

It seemed Mr Yang was well prepared for this question as he replied without hesitation.

"Thank you for the question. We've asked this too among ourselves. Allow me to give you an example. A train, and let me be as specific as possible – the Kawasaki Heavy Industries C151 – with a capacity to hold 2,000 passengers costs about $13 million. The parallel scenario would be how much would it cost to shift 2,000 passengers to travel and exit earlier using such a reward programme? Does that seem to be a fair comparison?"

Some in the audience nodded in agreement.

"I had said earlier that the average train ride is about $1.30. Over the 10-week period, we paid $1,346 in rebates – $417 to Early Treatment commuters and $929 to Late Treatment commuters – to effectively shift them to use the train earlier and exit before the peak period to relieve congestion.

"If we were to extend this to shifting 2,000 passengers daily, which is what adding a train would do, we would hit the $13 million cost of adding that train in slightly less than 3.5 years. Now, that's not very cost effective, is it?"

Mr Yang raised his eyebrow as he asked the last question. The audience, though mainly retirees, was fairly sharp when it comes to money matters and nodded.

"But, think about it," Mr Yang nudged. "We really do not need to reward people every time they travel earlier. We just need to reward them for only a limited period of time; in our study, it was 10 weeks. People's commuting behaviour can change and we've shown that to be the case. They travel earlier. And importantly, the change persists for a while. Then when the early-travel behaviour dissipates, we can re-introduce the reward programme.

"So, let's say we conduct the reward programme for 10 weeks and discontinue it and re-introduce it some four to five months later. Then we can have a seven-month cycle including the 10 weeks of reward, right?

"If that is the case, we find that under this scenario, we can enjoy similar benefits of adding a train for some 20 years before the cumulative costs of the reward is as much as the cost of buying a new train.

"And mind you, this does not even take into account the operational costs of maintaining the train. Moreover, the reward programme is flexible and can be tweaked should travel behaviour change, while investing in a train is a sunk cost."

Another question was raised.

"What plans does the LTA have then to encourage commuters to change their travel pattern?"

Mr Yang paused for a while, debating in his mind how much he should reveal.

"The LTA will certainly be collecting more data to ensure that whatever schemes we introduce will work and are cost effective. One possibility is the use of travel smartcards that have data on how a commuter travels. This will allow us to tailor individualised incentive schemes based on each commuter's travel patterns instead of a generic reward system."

When the talk was over, Ah Mah told Ah Kong, "I think we should tell Siew Ling this just in case she has to take the MRT to work in the future."

Ah Kong turned to her, knowing how much she spoils the grandsons. "It seems that while being rewarded financially changes behaviour, people can learn and appreciate the non-monetary rewards also. And will continue their changed behaviour when there are no more financial rewards given. I think we can learn from this with regards to rewarding our grandsons. We cannot always reward them for good behaviour. They have to learn that there are other benefits to good behaviour."

Ah Mah nodded in agreement.

WANT TO KNOW MORE?

This chapter is based on the following research: Sumit Agarwal, Cheng Shih-Fen, Jussi Keppo and Yang Yang (2017), "The Impact of Air Pollution on Labour Productivity," Working Paper, National University of Singapore; Sumit Agarwal, Koo Kang Mo and Sing Tien Foo (2017), "Haze and Productivity," Working Paper, National University of Singapore; Sumit Agarwal, Koo Kang Mo and Sing Tien Foo, "Air quality affects productivity: Study," *The New Paper*, (14 May 2019), https://www.tnp.sg/news/views/air-quality-affects-productivity-study; Ho Teck Hua, Ivan P.L. Png and Sadat Reza (2018), "Sunk Cost Fallacy in Driving the World's Costliest Cars," *Management Science*, Vol. 64 (4), pp. 1761-1778, https://mpra.ub.uni-muenchen.de/82139/1/MPRA_paper_82139.pdf; Yang Nan and Lim Yong Long (2018), "Temporary Incentives Change Daily Routines: Evidence from a Field Experiment on Singapore's Subways," *Management Science*, Vol. 64 (7), pp. 3365-3379, https://pubsonline.informs.org/doi/abs/10.1287/mnsc.2017.2731

CHAPTER

How Much is My HDB Flat?

Singapore's property market has been in the doldrums since the cooling effects were implemented by the government. Peter, a real estate agent, is one of Teng's close friends since they were primary schoolmates.

He was the one who advised Teng and Siew Ling on which flat to buy when they shifted out of their Woodlands flat, having made quite a sizeable profit after the nearby railway tracks to Malaysia were removed. The absence of the tracks meant no noise from the trains. The more agreeable surroundings elevated property prices in the vicinity.[1]

They have much to thank Peter for. He had shared with them information

---

[1] For more on this research on the effect of the removal of KTM railway tracks on surrounding property prices, see Sumit Agarwal, Ang Swee Hoon and Sing Tien Foo (2018), *Kiasunomics: Stories of Singaporean Economic Behaviours*, Chapter 3 "New Wife, New Life," (Singapore: World Scientific Publishers). To read the academic article, see Diao Mi, Qin Yu and Sing Tien Foo (2016), "Negative Externalities of Rail Noise and Housing Values: Evidence from the Cessation of Railway Operations in Singapore," *Real Estate Economics*, Vol. 44, pp. 878-917.

that his real estate agency had found – information about prices of properties with number '4' and '8'. Addresses with '4' were considered unlucky while those with '8' were considered lucky. It turned out that although properties with '8' in the address commanded a price premium of over 2 percent while those with '4' were sold at more than 1 percent discount, there was more to it than meets the eye.

Lucky addresses commanded a premium only in non-prime areas. In prime areas, there was no price difference in addresses with '4' and '8'. Peter was the one who enlightened them that house addresses were also used as a sign of conspicuous consumption. By virtue of owning a property in a prime area, people already know that such residents are wealthy regardless of whether their address has an '8' or a '4'. Hence, the lucky or unlucky address is not suggestive of wealth. But in non-prime areas, addresses with '8' cost a premium because property owners want to signal to others that they are sufficiently wealthy to pay higher prices for the auspicious number.[2]

Peter also educated them on the value of having a property near an MRT station. They were surprised to learn that having a MRT station nearby could increase property prices by as much as 13 percent.[3]

And so, on Peter's advice, Teng and Siew Ling settled on buying their Serangoon flat as it was near the MRT interchange station with an

---

[2] For more on this research on the effects of lucky and unlucky addresses on property prices, see Sumit Agarwal, Ang Swee Hoon and Sing Tien Foo (2018), *Kiasunomics: Stories of Singaporean Economic Behaviours*, Chapter 8 "Mind Your 4s and 8s," (Singapore: World Scientific Publishers). To read the academic article, see Sumit Agarwal, He Jia, Liu Haoming, Ivan P.L. Png, Sing Tien Foo and Wong Wei-Kang (2016), "Superstition, Conspicuous Spending, and Housing Markets: Evidence from Singapore," Working Paper, National University of Singapore, http://ftp.iza.org/dp9899.pdf. This research was also published as a commentary, see Sumit Agarwal, "The 'lucky 8' premium in housing unit prices," *The Straits Times*, 19 September 2014, https://www.straitstimes.com/opinion/the-lucky-8-premium-in-housing-unit-prices

[3] For more on this research on the effect of MRT stations on property prices, see Sumit Agarwal, Ang Swee Hoon and Sing Tien Foo (2018), *Kiasunomics: Stories of Singaporean Economic Behaviours*, Chapter 9 "Circling Up," (Singapore: World Scientific Publishers). To read the academic article, see Diao Mi, Fan Yi and Sing Tien Foo (2017), "A New Mass Rapid Transit (MRT) Line Construction and Housing Wealth: Evidence from the Circle Line," *Journal of Infrastructure, Policy and Development*, Vol. 1 (1), pp. 64-89.

auspicious number, and near a good neighbourhood school for their two boys.

Complaining Uncles and Aunties

Peter has always been a carefree and jovial character. But the long-drawn quiet real estate market seemed to have subdued him somewhat.

"I can't believe that one day I'll be saying this. But adulthood is tough," sighed Peter one day when he was at Teng's place.

"We are now in our 40s. We are fathers. And I can feel tons of responsibility on me. I wish we were the two small boys again, playing marbles back then. Remember the golden marble that you had? We were so carefree. Enjoyed life. No worries."

"Hey, life's like that. That's part of growing up. Look at me. People used to say driving a taxi makes easy money. But now there's Grab and Gojek. It's technology. Progress. Otherwise, if we remain the same and nothing changes, how then do we progress?" said Teng, trying to placate his best friend.

"I guess you're right. And what is life if there were no challenges?" said Peter, who seemed to have regained that little bit of bounce.

"You know, for the last few weeks, my clients have been grumbling about their old HDB flats. These uncles and aunties bought their flats some 30 or 40 years ago, directly from the government. Some even bought theirs almost 60 years ago. And they've lived in them ever since.

"Of course then when they bought them, the flats were spanking new. Everything worked. Everything's clean and new. They were so happy. Now after 30, 40 years, these uncles and aunties are complaining.

"They say they have retired. Their children have married and moved out. The flat is too big for them. They want to sell to move in with their children or downsize to a smaller flat. But selling their flat is not easy because it is old. This doesn't work, that doesn't work. And they also complain that banks do not give loans to potential buyers because the remaining lease is short. Blah, blah, blah.

"So they say that in the end, the value of their HDB flat is not there. That they should have bought a condo instead. Buy a condo? Are they crazy? They couldn't even afford a condo then!

"Every day, I have to hear these uncles and aunties complain and complain."

"But is it true? Do HDB values go down and go down very fast when the flat reaches a certain age?" enquired Teng, somewhat concerned as he started to count mentally how old his Serangoon flat is.

"Aiyah! These uncles and aunties just like to complain. They must always have something to complain about. If it's not this, it's that. That's being Singaporean, right?

"When they bought the flat so cheaply from the government years ago, they didn't complain. They lived there for so long, with all kinds of subsidies, and they didn't complain. Now, even if they weren't selling, they complain because they say the value has come down since it is old.

"Come on. Think of how much it is worth now compared to the price they paid then and the number of years they've lived in it.

"And of course things do depreciate with age, right? Look at cars. *Lagi* (Even) worse. The price goes down immediately once you buy it."

"Peter, seriously. Tell me, is it true that HDB flats depreciate after a certain age? I need to know for my house," Teng persisted with his questioning.

"Yes and no," yawned Peter, as he stretched across the sofa. The Singapore heat is making him drowsy and talking about old HDB flats isn't something that will particularly perk him up.

Teng waited patiently for Peter's explanation. He knows Peter too well to hurry him. He's a cool cat and enjoys taking his time at almost everything. He'll let it pass. And anyway, it's not that he's selling his flat right away. He can wait till Peter comes around to explain.

Interest Rates

For almost a decade, Singaporeans have been enjoying low bank lending rates of close to 1 percentage point. Such low rates meant that many were able to get a mortgage loan for close to 1.5 percentage points, or were able to finance a car, and possibly even get a small business loan at very low rates at the same time.

But in late 2018 to early 2019, the rates started moving up to almost 3 percentage points. Teng was concerned as his mortgage rate was a floating one. This meant the rate fluctuates depending on economic circumstances.

"How, dear? It looks like interest rates are going to double. This means that our mortgage payments will double too," voiced a concerned Teng to Siew Ling.

Like most Singaporeans, Teng had borrowed to finance his flat. Although both he and his wife work, they also have to look after his parents and their two young sons, putting a strain on liquidity. Servicing the debt will become more difficult if rates increase.

"Currently, we pay $1,500 every month for mortgage and another $1,500 for kids' education, transportation, and groceries. And then another $800 for dining out, seeing the doctor and buying clothes. As they age Pa and Ma have been going to see the doctor more often now than before. All these expenses add up. If interest rates increase, we are pretty much tapped out at the end of the month. It's going to be very tight. We need to tighten our belt," said Teng, shaking his head.

"Oh no! Maybe we should have opted for the fixed-rate mortgage offered by HDB. With flexible rates, we now have this uncertainty hanging over our head. What if interest rates go even higher?" said Siew Ling with a tinge of regret, her eye brows knitted closer together into a slight frown.

> **The fixed-rate option comes with some strict restrictions ... [a]nd the rate is priced higher than bank loan rates.**

"Hey, you shouldn't think like that. The fixed-rate option comes with some strict restrictions that may not work out well for us. And the rate is priced higher than bank loan rates. What if interest rates did not go up? What if rates went down instead? Then you'll be cursing that we signed on to the higher fixed-rate option," explained Teng to quell his wife's regret.

"Sigh . . . How much more do we have to pay if interest rate doubles?" asked a concerned Siew Ling. She had never liked making financial decisions when there is much uncertainty.

"Well, our $1,500 mortgage payment includes paying down the principal loan as well as interest. Not the whole lot is interest. So if rates go up from 1.5 percent to 3 percent, it is likely that the interest portion of our mortgage payment can go up to as high as $1,500," answered Teng.

"We certainly should continue paying our mortgage. No defaulting on that one. We're not in such a dire situation although I can imagine some people having a hard time making ends meet. Remember our friend Muthu who became a bankrupt? I often wondered how his wife and children are coping."

"Teng, maybe we can borrow on our credit cards and take on debt to support our current expenses?" offered Siew Ling, who as quickly as she said it, changed her mind. "But that would be borrowing from the future for today's expenses. I don't feel comfortable with that. And it would not be a good example to set for our children to follow."

"And credit card interest is ridiculously high. Or we can just cut down on our expenses. I think that would be more sensible," suggested Teng as a third option.

"But what can we cut down on?" asked a worried Siew Ling. "As it is, Pa and Ma go to the polyclinic and with their Pioneer discount card and the CHAS (Community Health Assist Scheme) card. We're already paying less for these necessary expenses."

"We should cut down on things that are expensive but not necessary. I think the term is 'durable and discretionary' items," explained Teng.

"What does that mean?" asked Siew Ling.

"These are things like electronics stuff like an iPad and mobile phone, clothes and restaurant meals. Expensive things that we don't really need," explained Teng. "And we should also cut down on eating out. We shouldn't eat out so often. And I think from now on, if we do go out and eat, we should choose places that are cheaper."

"And for the boys, we shouldn't be buying them iPad to play. Ethan can play on my phone instead," added Teng as he recalled how they were contemplating buying an iPad just so the boys can play games on them.

Siew Ling agreed. "And no puppy, either. Ethan has been asking for a pet dog ever since his classmate Jay got one. It's not something we need to have. And we would need to feed the dog and change its litter. Such expenses are not one-off. They are recurring expenses."

"Teng, I must confess this," admitted Siew Ling. She was a bit reluctant to say, feeling somewhat ashamed. But she felt she had to get it out.

"I didn't tell you this before, but previously, I had harboured dreams of having a bigger house. So when we were looking for a house, I was actually thinking of buying an even bigger place than this one, thinking that my income would probably increase and you'd earn more as a taxi and Grab driver. I was thinking of a bigger house in anticipation of our future increased incomes. Luckily, we didn't get one."

"I don't blame you. Everyone dreams of having a big house and they think they'll have higher salaries in the future," reassured Teng.

"In fact, some friends I know bought bigger homes than they needed in anticipation of future housing needs like when they have more children or when parents live with them. But doing so would mean increasing their burden to pay a higher mortgage. And especially when interest rates go up, they could face a more severe financial crunch.

"And many are becoming entrepreneurial and joining start-ups. While that's great for innovation, it's also risky. Their business may go bust and they won't be able to service their loans.

"Luckily, we were prudent to have bought a place within our means and that requires a smaller mortgage payment every month.

"When we see Peter next time, we should ask him about interest rates and mortgage payments."

SIBOR

The following Saturday, there was an open house for an executive flat at Teng's block and Peter was busy showing potential buyers the place. By 7 PM, the open house was closed and Peter headed to Teng's place for dinner.

"How was the open house? Were there many interested buyers?" asked Siew Ling.

"It's not bad but not that great either. I think I have one or two genuine buyers interested in the flat," replied Peter.

"But I don't know for sure. In the end, it all boils down to price. And especially now when there's uncertainty concerning interest rates, the price must be comfortable to the buyers. They must be able to service the housing loan."

"Hey . . . Siew Ling and I want to ask you this. This interest rate thing . . . How ah? You think it will go up and up or what?" asked Teng.

"Aiyah! How can I predict? If I can predict accurately, then I don't need to be a real estate agent anymore," laughed Peter.

"I tell you . . . Every time Trump opens his mouth and threatens a trade war with China, the market goes down. Then we all think we are heading for a recession and interest rates go up. And then later, when Trump says 'No, United States and China are good friends and trade agreement looks good', the market reacts positively. Maybe Trump is manipulating the market!"

Everyone laughed. Peter is a joker.

"But seriously, rising rates affect not only us but our economy too. Not just you and me but businesses as well – we will all be less likely to take out new loans at higher rates. That will hurt economic growth."

Peter continued. "I think perhaps banks need to think about how they plan for the future and consider how the transmission of SIBOR (Singapore Interbank Offered Rate) will affect bank lending behaviours to individuals and businesses.

"For instance, commercial banks can consider how increased SIBOR rates will affect their current portfolio of services. First, they will not get many people buying houses as the higher interest rate will make housing less affordable.

"Second, many people may default on their mortgage payments. This means banks will have credit risk on their portfolio. We are already seeing evidence of this in Singapore with the mortgage slowdown due to rising interest rates and the latest round of property curbs.

"Third, the impact of rising interest rates may also extend to people shying away from credit cards and car loans. Businesses may also be less likely to take out commercial loans because of the high interest rates."

Peter paused for a while to catch his breath.

"My! My primary school classmate who barely passed his exams is speaking like a pro," Teng thought with a mental jaw drop.

"How about interest rates and gold price?" asked Siew Ling, who as a fashionista, is interested in gold jewellery. "I remember years ago, gold shot up to $72."

> **Gold price soars when there is uncertainty. It is seen as a safe haven because currency and stock prices take a tumble when there is economic chaos.**

"Yes, that was in December 2011," answered Peter. "Since then, gold has softened. Gold price soars when there is uncertainty. It is seen as a safe haven because currency and stock prices take a tumble when there is economic chaos. But you must remember, gold does not give you any interest or dividends, unlike fixed deposits or stocks. The returns is only when you sell.

"The popular opinion is that interest rate hikes have a bearish effect on gold prices. This means when interest rates increase, gold price falls. But in reality, studies have not shown conclusively that there is a relationship between interest rates and gold price."

"Peter, how did you get to know all these things? I thought you are just a real estate agent?" asked a curious Teng.

"How do I know? Have you heard of SkillsFuture? I signed up for some courses to improve my knowledge of finance. Since the property market is quite slow, I thought I might as well go for these self-improvement courses.

"I want to eventually take some insurance courses, too. I think I should prepare myself to become an insurance agent. To me, being an insurance agent and a property agent is complementary. When I sell a house, I can also sell fire insurance to the new home owner. Then each property I sell can bring me more commission."

Teng was quite surprised. He didn't realise that his friend had been taking these self-enrichment courses, and thinking so strategically about improving his career too.

"You know what else I think?" Peter asked.

Without waiting for a response, he continued, "I think the U.S. Federal Reserve may keep raising interest rates if it thinks the U.S. economy is overheating. But if the Fed thinks the economy is doing fine, it will keep the rates flat. This will influence SIBOR rates in Singapore. Perhaps to buffer Singaporeans from this, banks may want to think of offering customers fixed-rate mortgages and take the interest-rate risk away from them. This may be an attractive option during times of uncertainty.

"I'm not sure whether our MAS (Monetary Authority of Singapore) has policies governing interest rates in Singapore. If not, maybe it should consider having exchange rate and interest rate policies.

"But no matter what, Singaporeans should be more financially literate to guard themselves against fluctuations in interest rates. Teng, you should consider taking some personal finance courses using your SkillsFuture funds."

Teng and Siew Ling looked at each other. They weren't sure they totally understood what Peter was saying. The gist seems to be that high interest rates may slow down the economy. But whether interest rates will go up or down is anybody's guess.

As it turned out, the later part of 2019 saw interest rates remaining low.

Property Depreciation

"Peter, how about the value of HDB flats as they get older? Remember? We talked about this the last time you were here but you were too tired to explain to me," said Teng as he jogged his friend's memory recalling the balmy weekend afternoon. "Now that Siew Ling is here, maybe you can explain it to both of us?"

"Ah yes . . . The one where the uncles and aunties are complaining about every day," said Peter while shaking his head. He could feel a headache coming as the imagery of the old folks floated through his mind.

"OK, this is what it is. People have been complaining that as their HDB flats get older, their resale value declines because the flats are old and banks don't want to give loans for properties with less than 60 years left in their lease. And the government has also restricted the use of CPF (Central Provident Fund) for the purchase of HDB flats with less than 60 years in the remaining lease.

"Of course we understand their concern. After all, housing is an asset that serves the dual needs of consumption and investment for buyers. Consumption because they live in it, and investment because they want to sell it at a higher price than when they first bought it.

> [H]ousing is an asset that serves the dual needs of consumption and investment for buyers. Consumption because they live in it, and investment because they want to sell it at a higher price than when they first bought it.

"Even though the government has this action plan for successful ageing such as organised exercises and dancing for old folks, these uncles and aunties are unlikely to outlive the 99-year lease period of a HDB flat. Instead, they would want to monetise their flat by selling the balance of its unused lease or bequest it to their children.

Hence, having a high value for their old flat is important to them.

"So, in comes NUS again. Remember how I've previously shared with you some research by NUS professors? Well, here they are again researching on this very topic that not only uncles and aunties, but you and I also want to know – do old HDB flats depreciate faster than private properties?

"What NUS did was they obtained data from the URA (Urban Redevelopment Authority) and the HDB on transaction prices of resale properties from 1997 to 2017. That's a 20-year period covering almost 620,000 resale properties. This comprised almost 480,000 HDB flats, 68,000 99-year leasehold non-landed residential properties and 72,000 freehold non-landed residential properties."

"Ahh . . . So the professors studied these three sets of properties so that the comparison can be fair when they compare HDB with non-landed properties as both sets are not landed. And between HDB and leasehold condos because both are 99 years," interjected Siew Ling, smiling because she understood what the researchers were thinking.

"Yes, you are right," said Peter. "They wanted a fair comparison of the ageing effect across these three groups of properties. Moreover, since the question is about whether property age affects value, then other factors that are non-age related must be controlled for. Things like . . ."

"How big the house is," Teng jumped in. Being a little *kiasu*, he wanted to show he was as smart as if not smarter than his wife.

"Yup, that's right. They controlled for housing size, housing type, number of housing units in the neighbourhood as well as distances to the nearest MRT and to the CBD (Central Business District). After all, these non-age factors could potentially affect property value," elaborated Peter.

"So, do you think the value of HDB flats depreciated faster or slower than private properties?"

"Faster," Teng said so confidently.

"Why?"

"Private properties have their management committee to look after the estate. They have money to do up the place nicely. Moreover, these owners paid a pretty huge sum of money to buy private property. Surely they will look after it very well," Teng replied with gusto.

Peter chuckled.

"If this were an exam, that would have been a trick question! You've gotten tricked. Old HDB flats depreciated less than private housing. Surprising, right?"

Peter took out his iPad to show his friends a chart.

"This is the professors' findings. The solid line is HDB flats, the dashed line is private leasehold non-landed properties, and the dotted line is private freehold non-landed properties.

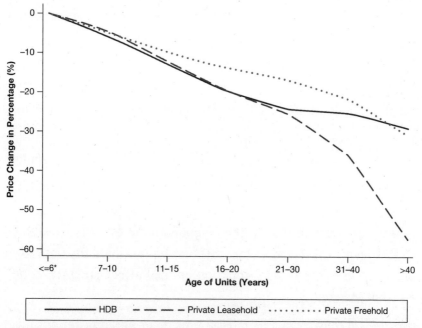

*Note: For HDB, the age group "<=6" includes only properties aged between 5 and 6 years old.

"The horizontal axis shows the age of the property. Since we cannot sell an HDB flat during the first five years, '<=6' means properties aged from five to six years old. The vertical axis is the change in transacted price in percentage terms.

"As you can see, the percentage change in transacted prices fell as the property aged. In the first 10 years, HDB flats depreciated by only 1 percent faster than private properties.

"After 10 years, private freehold properties depreciated at a slower rate compared to private leasehold properties and HDB flats. In fact, the latter two have a similar depreciation rate for up to 20 years.

"After 20 years, you can see the solid line is higher than the long dashed line. This means the rate of depreciation is slower for HDB than leasehold properties.

"In fact, the professors calculated that when non-landed properties are above 20 years old, the depreciation rate for HDB flats is only around 3 percent. Leasehold private properties depreciate by more than 30 percent while freehold private properties depreciate by more than 10 percent.

> [W]hen non-landed properties are above 20 years old, the depreciation rate for HDB flats is only around 3 percent.

"Understand so far?" asked Peter as he tried to read his friends' faces.

Both Teng and Siew Ling nodded, with eyes wide-opened.

Peter continued.

"Now, look at properties 30 years and older. After 30 years, you'll see that the solid line for HDB flats is flatter than the dotted and dashed lines. This means that ageing slows down the resale price decline for HDB flats compared to private residential properties. In contrast, the depreciation lines for the two private properties decline at a steeper rate after 30 years."

Teng sighed with relief. He did a quick mental calculation of their Serangoon flat and he didn't think it was more than 30 years old yet.

"*Heng* ah! Thankfully HDB flats do better. Why's that so?"

"Well, what do you think? For private properties, what has happened? For HDB flats, what has the government been doing?" asked Peter as he pushed Teng to think deeper.

"Maybe I was wrong in thinking that condo owners are rich enough and willing to maintain their properties well," replied Teng.

"Well . . . I wouldn't put it exactly that way," Peter responded. "With increasing ageing effects, old private properties become under-maintained. The building as well as the surroundings such as landscaping need even more maintenance. This means higher costs. Owners have to incur higher maintenance expenses and set aside more in the sinking fund to address building deterioration. This problem is even more serious for leasehold private property owners who face the double whammy of both ageing and lease decaying effects on their property price.

> [H]ome improvement programmes and upgrading schemes by the government help to manage the effects of ageing on resale prices.

"Now, look at HDB flats. What has the government done? The government has various enhancement schemes to improve building conditions and spruce up surrounding amenities. All these home improvement programmes and upgrading schemes by the government help to manage the effects of ageing on resale prices."

"Really?" asked a puzzled Siew Ling. "So these uncles and aunties have been wrong?"

"It's a matter of perception, right?" explained Peter.

"So what happens to private properties then?" asked Teng.

People are complaining that their old HDB flats have lost their value. But an NUS study showed that older HDB flats are able to hold up their value better than private condo.

Old properties tend to depreciate.

It gets increasingly difficult to maintain as a condo estate becomes older.

But for HDB estates, there are enhancement schemes to improve building conditions. These help to slowdown the effects of ageing on resale prices.

When a property is more than 20 years old, the depreciation rate for HDB flats is lower than that for leasehold and freehold private properties. HDB flats deteriorate the slowest because of such enhancement schemes.

Why do properties depreciate after a certain age?

Leases are for 99 years. Banks do not give housing loans for properties that have less than 60 years left in the lease. So, few people want to buy them.

"You've heard of en bloc sale?" winked Peter.

"Well, the ageing effect of these private properties are further hastened by economic obsolescence especially when private housing prices increase significantly. So guess what? There's profit to be made by selling in a rising market and there's an incentive to get rid of older buildings. This results in en bloc sales of older private properties where these old properties get to be redeveloped. Many older but structurally sound residential developments have been sold en bloc to private developers and redeveloped into new and high density residential developments."

"Ahh . . . No wonder there's these en bloc sales," as a light bulb seemed to be turned on in Teng's head.

"And HDB upgrading schemes are always brought up during elections. Being able to retard depreciation of old HDB flats is a sweetener to voters," smiled Siew Ling.

"Do you think the elections are coming?" Peter asked.

"Who knows. But if I were to decide, I would have it before recession sets in," said Siew Ling as the conversation drew to a close.

WANT TO KNOW MORE?

This chapter is based on Sumit Agarwal, "Consumers feel the pinch of rising interest rates," *Channel News Asia*, (22 February 2019), https://www.channelnewsasia.com/news/commentary/higher-interest-rates-mortage-singapore-sibor-best-banks-11261734; "HDB flats above 30 years depreciate less than private non-landed housing: NUS study," *Channel News Asia*, (13 February 2019), https://www.channelnewsasia.com/news/singapore/hdb-flats-depreciate-better-private-non-landed-housing-nus-study-11237604; "According to NUS study, HDB flats older than 30 years depreciate less than private freehold properties," *The Independent*, (14 February 2019), http://theindependent.sg/according-to-nus-study-hdb-flats-older-than-30-years-depreciate-less-than-private-freehold-properties/; Romesh Navaratnarajah, "Older HDB Resale Flats Depreciate Slower than Private Condos: Study," *Property Guru*, (14 February 2019), https://www.propertyguru.com.sg/property-management-news/2019/2/178139/older-hdb-resale-flats-depreciate-slower-than-private-condos-study

Good Sunshine Day, Good Shopping Day?

As a retail sales assistant, Siew Ling gets days off from work on a rotational basis. This week, her day off would fall on Thursday. She was looking forward to it, hoping that Thursday would be sunny as there had been unseasonal torrential downpour for the last few days. A rainy day would ruin a shopping trip.

From young, Siew Ling has always loved shopping. Being in the retail trade, and selling shoes at that, she enjoys it very much. With an eye for what's fashionable, she noticed that some Asian tourists she had served in the shoe store tended to over accessorise. Their sartorial sense seemed to be "more is better."

In contrast, Singaporeans, she felt, generally have a more conservative taste in design except for a few millennial and Gen Y shoppers who have an *avant garde* inclination. And they seemed to spend quite readily, especially with the increasing use of mobile payments. Cash is becoming obsolete.

"These young Singaporeans . . . They seem to think money grows on trees," she had recounted to Teng before. "I'm stunned at how they spend. They don't seem to save. And I wonder whether they keep track of their expenses given that they use their mobile wallet to pay."

"They have too comfortable a life. They have not experienced hardship yet. Wait till they move out of their parents' house and start a family. Then they'll know," Teng added. And he knew this from his personal experience growing up as a spoilt Dragon baby only to realise much later as a father the importance of financial prudence.[1]

Brushing those thoughts aside, Siew Ling was smiling to herself about her forthcoming day off.

"I can bring Ethan along with me shopping. He can walk alone by himself now without tiring too quickly. Also, since Ervin was born, I haven't spent as much time as I used to with Ethan. This would be good mother-son bonding time," thought Siew Ling, feeling a little guilty that she hadn't been spending enough time with her older son since the birth of the young one. But she was mindful not to tell Ethan in advance of this pending trip. She had noticed that on several past occasions, she and Teng had thought it better to inform Ethan ahead of what they were planning to do as a family so that he learns what it means to plan and prepare. But when plans go awry due to unforeseen circumstances, Ethan would throw a tantrum and not be open to reason.

"You promised we will go to the zoo today. Now we're not going!"

---

[1] For more on this research on how belonging to a cohort of Dragon babies affects education and consumption, see Sumit Agarwal, Ang Swee Hoon and Sing Tien Foo (2018), *Kiasunomics: Stories of Singaporean Economic Behaviours*, Chapter 1 "Dragon Babies, There Are So Many of You," (Singapore: World Scientific Publishers). To read the academic article, see Sumit Agarwal, Qian Wenlan, Sing Tien Foo and Tan Poh Lin (2018), "Dragon Babies," Working Paper, National University of Singapore, https://papers.ssrn.com/sol3/papers.cfm?abstract_id=3032575. This research has also been published as a commentary; see Sumit Agarwal and Qian Wenlan, "Dragon babies, muted achievements," *The Straits Times*, (27 January 2017), https://www.straitstimes.com/opinion/dragon-babies-muted-achievements

screamed Ethan, bawling as he sat on the floor, waving his hands angrily in the air.

"Yes, we did say we were going to the zoo. Mummy and Daddy want to go to the zoo. We want to bring you and *di di* (younger brother) to the zoo, too. But now it is going to rain heavily. We can't go," explained Siew Ling.

"But you promised," yelled an uncompromising Ethan.

"Yes, we promised. But the weather is not co-operating. We did not expect it to rain so heavily," said Siew Ling trying to be the voice of reason.

"A promise is a promise. How can you break your promise?" Ethan simply refused to listen to his mother's explanations.

"Yes, promises are to be kept. But this is beyond our control. We cannot tell the sky not to rain. If it were sunny, we would definitely go," reasoned Siew Ling.

"If we go in the rain, you and *di di* may fall sick. And that would be worse. You'll be coughing and sneezing. You cannot play for the next few days. You have to take medicine and stay at home. You cannot go to school. Do you want that?"

Despite explaining patiently in different ways with a multitude of examples, Ethan would not listen and remained petulant and tearful. Siew Ling and Teng had enough of his behaviour. They would just leave Ethan to mope on his own and later when he was calmer, they would make it up to him with some ice cream.

As parents, Siew Ling and Teng learnt their lesson. Until the child is old enough to reason maturely, they should not tell him too much of their plans in case the plans get scuttled. Otherwise, they'd have to put up with unnecessary tantrums and sulky faces, something they did not need nor look forward to.

"Maybe it's just our kids. Perhaps other parents don't have the same issue with theirs," Siew Ling had said to Teng.

Orchard Road

Although the shopping mall Nex is nearby, Siew Ling wanted to go to Orchard Road. She had not gone there for ages and wanted to know how it has changed. Additionally, she needed to buy a power bank for her phone and Teng had reminded her to get batteries for their various electronic devices.

Thursday came. Siew Ling woke up to a sunny day, one that was not too hot. The sky was somewhat cloudy but one could feel the sun soft rays penetrating through to give that bit of oomph into life. The shopping trip was on.

But before that, Siew Ling went for a swim at the Serangoon Swimming Complex while Ethan was still at kindergarten, with the sun beating gently on her shoulders as she swam stroke for stroke in the water. She felt invigorated and good. After all, when she's working, she's cooped up inside the shopping mall shielded from the sun. And the last couple of days had been gloomy with rain.

After Ethan returned from kindergarten and with a quick change of clothes, they took the North-East MRT line from the Serangoon station to Dhoby Ghaut. It was a comfortable ride and she thought how fortunate they were that public transportation in Singapore is so accessible.

The shopping centre closest to the Dhoby Ghaut station is Plaza Singapura. It is one of Singapore's oldest shopping mall with Yaohan, a Japanese department store, being its anchor tenant in the 1970s through to the late 90s. In the early 2000s, it underwent a major revamp that saw the mall being connected directly to the Dhoby Ghaut station. The renovation and direct MRT link gave the mall a shot in the arm. With more renovation work done thereafter, the mall was given a new façade with a long wave frontage. A new wing was added that increased its retail space. It is now again a 'happening' shopping place.

Siew Ling knows that with online shopping becoming more common, many offline stores are experiencing declining sales. Shops have open and closed. She wondered which ones had fallen victim to e-commerce.

Brushing these thoughts aside, the good weather made her feel good. And Ethan seemed to be in a good mood too to spend time with mummy after school.

Shopping

Mother and son headed for lunch first at the food court. Still fresh in her mind was the world economic turbulence and the impact on their job security and mortgage payments, but Siew Ling was generally feeling happy. They were eating at the food court where prices are lower than those in fast-food chains and restaurants. So she decided to splurge on bubble tea for herself and Ethan instead of just drinking from their bottled water.

Next, it's to the electronics store Challenger on the 4th floor. As a member there, she could benefit from membership discounts whenever she needed to buy electronic gadgets.

Ethan had been a good boy. He followed Siew Ling wherever she went, without complaining that he's tired. He even volunteered to carry the shopping bag for her.

"OK. Power bank and batteries," Siew Ling reminded herself of what she needed to buy.

She saw some power banks sitting neatly on two shelves. Some were brands she had heard of and some completely foreign to her. She was overwhelmed by not only the number of brands but also the multitude of varieties. There was a range of Xiaomi models from 5000 mAh to 20000 mAh, with prices from $18 to $50.

"This brand 'Xiao Mi' sounds familiar. Is it the brand that's in the news lately?" thought Siew Ling. She was confusing Xiaomi with Huawei, the brand in the middle of the U.S.-China spat concerning Huawei's spying and 5G capabilities.

"There's this Asus ZenPower. 'Asus' also sounds familiar. But it's quite expensive.

"What is this brand? 'Pineng'. Sounds like 'Penang' the state in Malaysia," as Siew Ling smiled to herself at her own joke. "But it's quite cheap. 10000mAh at $21."

Seeing that she needed some help, a sales assistant came by.

"Hello. May I help-joo?" asked the man in his early 20s, speaking like most Singaporean sales people with the 'j' sound for 'you'.

"Ah yes. I'm looking for a power bank. How come the prices are so different?" asked a somewhat confused Siew Ling.

"The higher the mAh the higher the price," explained the young sales assistant. "And also you must feel the weight. Some are quite heavy. The light ones tend to be more expensive.

"People prefer the light and small ones. So sometimes for the same mAh, two brands can have different prices because of size and weight. It depends on your preference which type you prefer."

"Are they all reliable? I don't want one that spoils quickly," Siew Ling told the sales assistant.

"To me, they are all the same. But if you are afraid, then buy the brand name one," advised the young man.

"I'm not going to compare so many different models. I'll just get the higher-priced one. I think high price must mean good quality," Siew Ling said to herself.

She was in a positive mood. Today had been a glorious day. It was sunny but not too hot, she managed to have a swim, and Ethan had been a good boy.

"Next, batteries. That should be easy."

Besides the regular Eveready and Duracell batteries and a no-name brand, there were rechargeable batteries too. And they were pricey.

The sales assistant explained, "These rechargeable batteries are more expensive. You pay more at the beginning. But you can use and re-use them again and again. So you don't have to buy new batteries each time. They last a long time. So you pay more now but you save later because you don't have to replace them so fast like ordinary batteries."

"But I also don't know which type Teng wants," Siew Ling said to herself. "Never mind. I'm not going to think too much. I'll just get the most expensive rechargeable batteries and let Teng sort out the recharging."

"Mummy, can we have some ice cream? I'm tired," Ethan said softly to his mummy. He loves her. He wished she could spend more time with him. *Di di* isn't quite a good company yet. He can't play hide-and-go-seek. And he always falls when he runs. And Ah Mah and Ah Kong talk way too much about how to be a good boy. That conversation is getting tiresome on Ethan. And on top of that, they smell, especially when the day is hot.

"OK, Ethan. Since you're such a good boy today, you can have double scoops of ice cream and with a topping," said a beaming Siew Ling. "And mummy will also have the same!"

Ethan cheered. "Mummy is really in good mood," he thought.

Good Shopping Day?

When Teng got home after work that day, he was greeted by smiling faces from Ethan and Siew Ling.

"You guys had a great day shopping ah?"

"Daddy, Daddy. I had bubble tea and double scoops of ice cream today!" exclaimed an excited Ethan.

"Wow! That's a lot," said Teng, somewhat surprised that Siew Ling allowed him to have so many treats.

"And Mummy did too!" added Ethan.

"Hmm . . . Why is Siew Ling so generous?" thought Teng.

"And I got the batteries you wanted. There were way too many to choose from so I just got you the most expensive one," Siew Ling said.

"And my power bank. Even worse. So many choices. So I just closed one eye and picked a somewhat higher-end one. I think if I pay a higher price, then it is probably of better quality."

Teng thought this was somewhat unusual of his wife. She seemed quite indifferent to price when she would usually hum and haw when making purchases. And they just had a recent conversation about cutting down on discretionary expenses in anticipation of economic uncertainty. But he didn't want to admonish her. She seemed happier than usual and he didn't want to spoil her day. But he was curious to know what made her shop in such a carefree manner.

Sarah

Teng thought of asking Sarah, their teenage neighbour, who is now studying at a junior college. Josie, her mother, had proudly told them how well Sarah did for her 'O' levels and besides doing her subjects at 'A' levels, she is reading up on her own about psychology as that's what she intends to study when she enters NUS.

"So wonderful that your daughter has grown up and doing so well in her studies," Ah Mah had congratulated Josie. "A big girl now. Soon, you won't have to take care of her anymore. In fact, she'll be taking care of you."

"No lah, Aunty. A mother's job is never done. No matter how old Sarah is, I'll still be worrying for her," said Josie.

So when Teng bumped into Sarah the other day, Teng asked her whether she knew anything about psychology that might make a person spend more than they usually would.

"Uncle Teng, I've not taken any formal psychology courses yet. So I don't know much about psychology, although we get guest speakers every now and then who talk to us on various topics including psychology. Can I go find it out for you? Give me two weeks?" asked Sarah, wanting to help but unsure how much she really can.

Sunshine Effect

Sarah came by some weeks later. "Uncle Teng. I've something here that might just be what you were looking for."

"Huh? What is it? Teng, what were you looking for?" asked a confused Siew Ling.

"Eh . . .," Teng was sheepish. He didn't want to upset Siew Ling that her shopping behaviour the other day was somewhat too spendthrift for his liking. Now, he's been caught finding out more about her aberrant behaviour.

"You come and listen. Maybe both of us can learn from what Sarah has to share with us," Teng said, trying to diffuse Siew Ling's confusion.

"Hi Auntie Siew Ling. Uncle Teng wanted to find out whether there's a psychological explanation for people spending more than they usually would," explained Sarah.

"Oh! That's interesting. We can all learn from that," said Siew Ling, not realising that she was the reason for this discussion. She did think it was somewhat odd that Teng would want to know about spending behaviour, but she was used to her husband's unpredictable behaviour. "Ma, Pa. Come and join us. Sarah has something about psychology and people's buying behaviour."

They gathered around the dining table as Sarah took out her laptop to show some slides.

"The other day as part of pastoral care at my junior college, we had a guest professor from NUS Business School who came to talk to us about sunshine days and shopping," Sarah started talking.

She opened the Powerpoint slides from the talk. Teng looked at the opening slide and was amazed. He couldn't believe what he saw.

"Professor Sumit Agarwal? He's the speaker?"

"Yes. He's the prof from NUS Business School who was the guest speaker. Why? You know him?" asked a puzzled Sarah.

"Of course, I know him. He was my passenger long ago and he advised me on how I should budget my revenue as a taxi driver so that I become more financially savvy," Teng said. "And you know what? Our neighbour Professor Sing knows him too. What a small world!"

"Yah lor! Singapore is so small. We cannot anyhow do something wrong. People are sure to find out," Ah Mah said.

"Well, Prof Agarwal studied how people spend on sunny days versus less sunny days. The 'sunshine effect' as it is called," said Sarah as she began explaining.

"Huh? You mean from studying taxi drivers then, Professor Agarwal is now studying sunshine and shopping?" Teng asked.

"Yah! Oh, and I did some background check on him. He's quite prolific. Not only did he study taxi drivers, he also studied how Singaporeans use their CPF and how they use water and electricity. He also studied

MRT and schools and how they affect property prices. And he doesn't just study Singaporeans. He also does research on China, India and America, too. In fact, the talk he gave is a research project he did in the United States," explained Sarah, feeling quite proud that a university in Singapore has such prominent professors.

"Shall I start?" asked Sarah. She waited for a while for everyone to settle down. Ethan and Ervin were quietly watching cartoons on TV.

"It is easy to imagine how mood can affect people's buying behaviour. On the one hand, people can simply spend more while in a good mood because they tend to be more optimistic and think in a heuristic manner."

> **[M]ood can affect people's buying behaviour.**

"Wait . . . What is 'heuristic'?" asked Siew Ling.

"'Heuristics' are shortcuts, used when making a decision or solving a problem. People learn from experience how to make decisions based on simple rules – simple rules that have been shown over time to be useful.

"Like for instance, many people tend to use price as an indicator of quality. High price means better quality. Or they use size to indicate quality. The larger a shop is, the more reputable is the shop. So they save time by making these associations instead of having to evaluate in detail the quality of a product.

"So in this case, some research has found that when people are in a good mood, they tend to rely on heuristics to make a decision. In which case then, these happy people tend to evaluate products as being far better despite a less detailed investigation of their true quality. When this happens, they rate the product far better than it actually is and spend more when they are in a good mood."

"Right on! That was Siew Ling that day," thought Teng, but he kept silent because he didn't want to start a quarrel with his wife.

Sarah continued. "On the other hand, sad individuals could also buy more things in order to cheer themselves up. In that case, shopping helps to induce a happy mood."

"Oh no! That could have been Siew Ling too," thought Teng. He's not sure which version of Siew Ling was on that day. He knew she was happy but he didn't know whether the happiness came before shopping or after shopping.

Sarah continued.

"Professor Agarwal found that on average, a typical consumer spends 1 percent more on relatively sunny days than less sunny days. Using American data, this translates to an increase of US$1.30 more daily or more than US$471 annually, just on credit cards alone!

"Now, you might ask 'Who are these people who are more susceptible to the sunshine effect?' Well, Prof Agarwal found that people with higher discretion on their consumption such as those with higher income and those in the middle-age group exhibited higher expenditure on good weather days. Women and married individuals were also more affected by better weather."

"That's me," said Siew Ling as she pointed a finger to herself. She thought it was quite funny.

Teng thought that his wife was closer to the truth than she realised. He chuckled silently.

> [P]eople are in a better mood when there is sunshine than when there isn't.

"Research in psychology has shown that people are in a better mood when there is sunshine than when there isn't," Sarah continued.

"Hmm . . . I think that day when Siew Ling went shopping was a sunny day. It was the first sunny day after days of rain," Teng tried to recollect. "This might just be it."

"But wait . . . Aren't we rational? How could we allow the weather to influence how much we spend?" asked Siew Ling. "Maybe these people buy more because when it's sunny, it gives them a chance to go out and buy more things. When it's raining, you cannot go out and so fewer things are bought and hence, there's less spending."

"Well, Prof Agarwal thought just like you did, and tested to rule out alternative explanations. He found that the number of purchases were the same on sunny and less sunny days. There's no difference.

"Instead, it's the dollar amount spent that varied. On sunny days, people spent more in money terms and not in terms of the number of items bought. So it's not that sunny days gave people more opportunities to come in contact with purchasing the products since there were about the same number of items bought regardless of weather," clarified Sarah.

"Maybe people look at the weather forecast. If there's going to be a thunderstorm for the next few days and I know I can't go out then, I will buy more now to stock up. There are some people who plan ahead," Ah Mah added.

Teng thought, "Hmm . . . This is *deja vu*. It sounds like the conversation I had with the young Grab driver at Pek Hio market. I was thinking about how wonderful it would be if my taxi company can provide us with weather information in advance so we can plan and know where to be when it rains."

"Ah Mah, you've got a point there. You can be Professor Ah Mah!" said Sarah responding to Ah Mah's counter-argument. Everyone laughed. Ah Mah particularly liked it when people stroke her ego.

"Prof Agarwal also anticipated what you were thinking. So he investigated such a possibility too. So let's imagine you, Ah Mah, are very disciplined and plan ahead. After checking on the weather forecast for the next few days, you change your shopping pattern to shop on the sunniest day during this time period. If the weather forecast for the next week is accurate and you planned ahead in this way, then we should see you buying more on sunny days consistent with the 'sunshine effect' and very little on the rainy days. This means that the increased purchases on sunny days will be 'reimbursed' by decreased purchases on poor weather days, right? This would make the total purchases for the week unchanged. Does that sound right?"

Everyone nodded. That made sense.

"Well, Prof Agarwal did not detect such a pattern. There was no 'reimbursement' purchases between the sunny day and the poor weather days.

"Also, don't you think it's quite hard to imagine that most people will be like Ah Mah who plans her shopping in such an extreme way and that weather forecasts are always accurate? How many people are like her? Ah Mah is one of a kind!"

Ah Mah felt even more pleased that Sarah thought she's unique. She was glowing.

"You know what, Sarah? Now that you've explained the 'sunshine effect', I think sometimes I'm affected by it," admitted Siew Ling. "Sometimes, when it's sunny, and especially after a period of lousy weather, I will feel so much happier. I will go shopping. Not so much as in buying more things because I'm quite careful with my money in that respect. But maybe I'm more willing to spend more on the same item.

"Like what happened last month. I brought Ethan out to buy a power bank and batteries. Not unusual things. But I was willing to spend more on them. I wasn't really comparing features and prices. I just thought if a brand carries a higher price, it is probably better quality."

Teng sighed with relief. He didn't need to be the bad guy to point out his wife's poor decision making. And he won't need to sleep in the

dog house that night, as the saying goes.

> **[W]hile good sunshine days increase shopping as people are more willing to spend more, it may not be a good shopping day because people engage in less careful thinking.**

Ah Mah added, "Retailers must be happy if there's more sunshine than rainy days. Shoppers are in a better mood and so are more willing to spend more. And Singapore is so sunny, although Christmas is during a rainy season."

"What else did Professor Agarwal say? I'm sure there must be some takeaways?" asked Teng.

"Yes, he did give some advice," said Sarah as she closed her laptop. "He said that while good sunshine days increase shopping as people are more willing to spend more, it may not be a good shopping day because people engage in less careful thinking.

"So we need to check ourselves whenever we're in a good mood so that we do not make decisions frivolously especially for big-ticket purchases. We need to evaluate more carefully against sound criteria."

"In other words, when the weather is sunny, we should be mindful how we spend and save for a rainy day," laughed Teng. He liked his own joke, even though no one seemed to care.

WANT TO KNOW MORE?

This chapter is based on Sumit Agarwal, Souphala Chomsisengphet, Stephen Meier and Xin Zou (2019), "In the Mood to Consume: Effect of Sunshine on Credit Card Spending," Working Paper, National University of Singapore, https://papers.ssrn.com/sol3/papers.cfm?abstract_id=3014541

5

Cherry Picking

Siew Ling organised a dinner get-together with the Sing family and Peter. Mrs Sing had been treating them to her home-cooked meals ever since they moved in. Siew Ling felt they should also reciprocate in hosting such dinners. And it's good too for Ah Kong and Ah Mah to have different people in the house to keep them mentally stimulated.

Because Professor Sing is from the Real Estate School at NUS and Peter is a real estate agent, the two have gotten along from the get-go. At such gatherings, there's always revelry over the hot topic of property prices. Who in Singapore wouldn't be interested in where the property market is heading?

Sometimes, both Professor Sing and Peter were like inseparable twins, agreeing with one another and singing the same tune. At other times, their views were so contrasting that they would be sparring with each other in a heated debate. But they always ended up with a camaraderie spirit.

Dinner was great. Mrs Sing, a fantastic cook, complimented Siew Ling on her cooking.

"Thank you. Ma helped me prepare this dish. It's one of Teng's favourites and so I have to learn to cook it right. I've got lots of practice on this one," said Siew Ling humbly as she looked at Ah Mah.

"The way to a man's heart is through his stomach," joked Peter. "So you must cook more of Teng's favourite dishes. Then he'll love you more."

Everyone laughed.

"Peter, how long have you been as a property agent?" asked Professor Sing, changing the topic.

"How long? Too long," joked Peter again.

"Seriously. How long?" asked Professor Sing again so as not to let the question go unanswered.

"Hmm . . . About 13-14 years," was the reply from Peter, feeling a little uncomfortable to be under scrutiny.

"We've been friends for the last couple of years. Let me be direct with you, friend to friend. How many properties have you bought ever since you became a property agent?" Professor Sing asked Peter, looking directly in his face.

"Huh? What are you asking?" responded Peter, pretending not to understand the question.

"You know, right? Property agents can also buy and sell properties on their own account," elaborated Professor Sing.

"Oh, that ah. Well ever since the Singapore Government came up with the ruling about taxing property speculation, property agents have been very careful that they don't just buy a property and load it off in the market soon after to make a quick buck," replied Peter, trying to deflect the question.

"I know of some agents who got caught. They had bought a handful of properties and sold them quickly, like some six months later. Then at the end of the year, they'd receive a letter from IRAS (Inland Revenue Authority of Singapore) that whatever profits they made were subject to income tax.

"They were shocked. Because they had bought and sold too often, their behaviour revealed that they were not genuine buyers but speculators. They were trading properties instead of living in them. And such speculation was ramping the market into a frenzy. The government wanted to curb property prices and so this taxation helped to weed out non-genuine buyers."

"Isn't that like buying and selling stocks? Some people trade and profit on stocks too. How would this be any different?" asked Ah Kong suddenly. Ah Kong is a man of few words. Between the two grandparents, Ah Mah is usually the chatty one. So people were quite surprised when he spoke.

"What you said is true, Uncle," replied Peter. "But buying a property involves huge sums of money and it affects housing affordability. We want Singaporeans to find this place liveable, both socially and economically. Otherwise, people will get disgruntled. Moreover, people need a roof over their head but we don't need virtual stock scrips."

"Eh, Peter. You still haven't answered my question. How many properties have you bought as a real estate agent?" said Professor Sing, refusing to let Peter get away without answering.

"Yah lah. Tell us. Why so shy?" urged Teng to get his friend to confess.

"Sigh ... Maybe a few only," came the evasive reply. "I don't have the capital to put down a deposit. Also, I believe in 'easy come, easy go'. If money can be made so easily, it will be squandered fast too. And with the government clamping down hard on speculation, I'm very careful not to just buy and sell.

"Anyway, these purchases were made so long ago. Now with a quiet property market and the world economy heading nowhere, I wouldn't dare to speculate.

"Prof Sing, why are you so interested in how many properties I've bought?" Peter tried to put the attention on the professor.

"Ahh ... I asked because I'm currently doing a research on real estate agents and the properties that they bought," explained Professor Sing. "You know, real estate agents are important."

"Of course, lah. Now then you know?" teased Peter, feeling a little smug that his job, viewed often by many as unprofessional with a tinge of dishonesty, is finally getting its due recognition.

> **Real estate agents are important because most buyers and sellers are not as knowledgeable as they are concerning the property market.**

Professor Sing explained. "Real estate agents are important because most buyers and sellers are not as knowledgeable as they are concerning the property market. So agents use their knowledge to close the information gap between potential buyers and sellers. For instance, they know what properties are available for sale and with this information, they can help potential buyers look for the appropriate houses and in the process, reduce buyers' search costs and improve matching between buyers and sellers.

"But people tend to view property agents as not very forthright. Because they are paid a commission for brokering a real estate deal, they may be motivated merely by commissions. If that were the case, they may close deals in the shortest time possible, even to the extent of not revealing full information to the parties involved in the transactions."

"Eh . . . I'm not like that," protested Peter, waving his hand to salvage his reputation.

"We're not saying you are, Peter. Or do you have a guilty conscience?" came Teng's tease with a somewhat judgmental undertone.

"But you know, I heard of this incident that I'm sure has happened many times before.

"My friend lives in an HDB flat. He bought a condo that he rented out. It's got a beautiful view because it is located on a very high floor. After a few years, there was a family crisis. His wife became ill and he needed money to cover her medical expenses. And since the market had appreciated, he said he might as well sell the condo and take the profit. So he got an agent to market the condo. He told the agent his asking price was $2 million, which was quite high for the condo but the market was trending up and so my friend added a premium to the price.

"Now, this agent was not honest. First, she said that there was this Indonesian guy who was interested in the condo. That got my friend excited because it's an Indonesian buyer. Rich. Can make more money, right?

"Then a few days later, she said the Indonesian wasn't interested anymore and she started pointing out how another unit was better than his unit, and that the Indonesian buyer is now interested in the other unit. Blah blah blah. That kind of deflated my friend's expectations because it seemed his flat has all these flaws that make rich buyers like the Indonesians not keen in buying. But I tell you, all this is a scam."

"What happened? Why is it a scam?" asked a quizzical Ah Mah.

"Over the next few days, the agent told my friend that the Indonesian had bought the other unit. So now my friend is upset because the big fish – the rich Indonesian buyer – had gotten away. In the meantime, she said she'll try her best to sell but she doesn't know of any other potential Indonesian buyer.

"After a week or so, the agent called up my friend, telling him to meet her at the downstairs coffeeshop at 11 AM. She did not tell him anything except to meet her. So my friend was clueless because he had already lost the potential Indonesian buyer. Anyway, he went.

"Guess what? The agent gave him, right in front of his face, a cheque for $180,000 – 10 percent of $1.8 million. And she said this cheque is from a Singaporean buyer keen in buying his condo for $1.8 million. The cheque is the security deposit. The Indonesian buyer is no longer in the picture but here's an interested Singaporean buyer. Take it or leave it."

"$1.8 million is quite good money isn't it? Did he take it?" asked an excited Ah Mah.

All this while when Teng was narrating the story, Peter was chuckling. He had heard this scenario pan out more times than he could remember.

"You know, it's so hard to reject pure hard cash that is right there in front of you. But I tell you, my friend is a very pious man. He told me he had prayed and prayed that God will grant him wisdom in managing his assets. He calls it stewardship.

"Somehow, despite wanting to sell and use the money to pay for his wife's medical bills, he sensed something was not quite right. Why, out of the blue, is there this Singaporean buyer whom the agent had never told him about? And he was also uncomfortable with being strong armed into accepting cold hard cash. My friend actually told the agent that he was not interested and turned down the hard cash."

"Hah? Turned down? I wouldn't," gasped Ah Mah.

"Yup, he turned it down. And you know what he told me? He told me

'You should have seen the look on the agent's face. It became black although she tried hard to hide it!'"

"Then what happened?" asked Ah Mah, hurrying Teng to complete his story.

"My friend told the agent that it is too low and he wouldn't sell it for anything less than $2 million – the original price that he stipulated."

"So that's the end, lah. The agent will not sell for him," Ah Mah interrupted.

"Ma, my story hasn't ended. There's some more," smiled Teng as he relished keeping everyone on the edge of their seat.

"That very same day at 4 PM, while my friend was in the hospital with his wife, the agent called him again. This time, she told him that she had found another buyer who was willing to pay $2 million for the unit – the exact price that he was asking for. Would he be free to meet her to collect the deposit?

"Of course, my friend met her and this time, he accepted the cheque. After all, this was the price he had set from Day 1 and he wasn't greedy. He wasn't interested in playing the market up.

"But guess what? He looked at the name of the buyer on the cheque and in subsequent documents. It was an Indonesian!

"So while my friend has no conclusive evidence about what really happened behind his back, what do you think happened?"

"Your friend was lucky and the agent found for him another rich Indonesian buyer?" volunteered Siew Ling.

"The original rich Indonesian man changed his mind?" suggested Ah Mah.

"Nope. No such luck. This is what my friend thinks. He thinks that the agent was trying to pull a fast one on him. There was indeed a rich Indonesian buyer. He was genuinely interested in the condo. There was no other unit that he preferred. This other better condo unit that the agent claimed is fake.

"But like what Prof Sing said, the agent has full information. She knows who's interested and who's not, but the seller and buyer do not. This agent was greedy and wanted to take advantage of the situation. Although my friend didn't tell her about his wife's ill health, she might have sensed somehow his urgency to sell. So she fed false information to my friend to deflate his expectations so that he would be willing to sell the condo at a lower price. Remember the proposed deal at $1.8 million?

"But you might say, 'Lower transacted price means less commission for her', right? Why should she do that? Well, she's not stupid.

"She fabricated about the Singaporean buyer. My friend thinks there was no genuine Singaporean buyer at all. If anything, that Singaporean buyer could be her husband or brother or whatever. A partner of hers, let's say.

"So now, there's this cheque but for a smaller amount than my friend really wanted. Remember, my friend had just lost the big fish. He's discouraged and getting more anxious. Probably knowing that my friend was desperate to sell, the agent set him up. She was banking that my friend would take the bait of a smaller selling price of $1.8 million after supposedly losing the Indonesian buyer.

"If my friend had taken the bait, her partner would have bought it for $1.8 million from him and sell it to the genuine Indonesian buyer for $2 million that very same day as a sub-sale. She would have profited $200,000 plus the sales commission, well above the 1 percent sales commission which she also has to share with the real estate agency. That's why she was so glum when my friend turned down the $180,000 cheque. She couldn't make an extra $200,000.

"As for the Indonesian buyer, he knows no better because he never met the seller. He was probably told the asking price was $2.2 million and getting it at $2 million was a steal. And my friend would not know any better either because he thought the Indonesian buyer was history and he was selling to a Singaporean. But behind the scene is this so-called Singaporean making a quick $200,000 by palming it off to the Indonesian within a day."

"Then why doesn't she sell the condo at $2.2 million and get a higher commission?" asked Ah Mah.

"Because that commission will still not be as high as the capital gains of $200,000, the difference between $1.8 million and $2 million. And she probably knew the price threshold that the Indonesian was willing to pay. $2 million was the max," explained Teng.

"Wow! What a crook! So deceptive," Siew Ling said. "No wonder people always say real estate agents cannot be trusted."

"Not me, not me. Not all property agents are like that. I'm honest." Peter protested again. "Teng, maybe you should become a real estate agent instead of slogging to pick up passengers," said Peter, trying to deflect the focus to Teng.

"You're crazy," Teng retorted.

"Teng, the story about your friend was what got me and my colleagues to study property agents and whether they exploit what they know. Shall I tell you what we found?" chimed in Professor Sing.

"We wanted to find out since property agents are more knowledgeable – they have more information about the property market than people like you and me – were they able to buy their own house at a larger discount than non-agent buyers. Any guesses?"

"I'm not even going to hazard a guess. I'm going to stay out of this," declared Peter, feeling the heat of the conversation.

"Aiyah! After what Teng told us, I would say property agents can con the sellers and be able to buy their own house at a larger discount than other people," Ah Mah said. She was quite flabbergasted with property agents by now, except for Peter, of course.

"For this study, we collected data not from one, two, or three sources, but five!" Professor Sing said as he lifted his fingers one by one to demonstrate the extensiveness of the study.

"The first dataset contains private non-landed housing transactions with information on unit size, tenure and address. The second data source contains demographic information of Singapore residents. We can then match the sellers in the first dataset with the second dataset to obtain information on their current home addresses. By comparing the transacted property address and the residential address of sellers we can tell whether a seller is an owner-occupier or investor.

"The third dataset covers all the licensed real estate agents in the public registry so we can match the names of the agents to the names of the buyers in the first dataset to identify agent-buyers and non-agent buyers.

"The fourth dataset is a collation of listings data from major portals in Singapore. And finally, the fifth dataset consists of records of law events in Singapore's courts. We merged this dataset with the first dataset to know who are involved in lawsuits."

"Huh? Why would lawsuits be relevant to this research?" thought Teng. "It's strange."

"In the end, we created a master file from these various datasets to give us almost 110,000 transactions.

"Now, for the findings. Auntie, you are absolutely right. Agents pay less than non-agents," said Professor Sing as he turned to Ah Mah. Ah Mah smiled. She's happy that she got it right. It looked like she's living up to the 'Professor Ah Mah' title that Sarah had given her.

"We found property agents benefitted from their full knowledge and were able to buy their own property at a discount steeper than those by non-agent buyers. Specifically, real estate agents paid almost 3 percent less for their own house than did other people.

"Here, take a look," as Professor Sing scrolled through his smartphone to find the chart.

[P]roperty agents benefitted from their full knowledge and were able to buy their own property at a discount steeper than those by non-agent buyers.

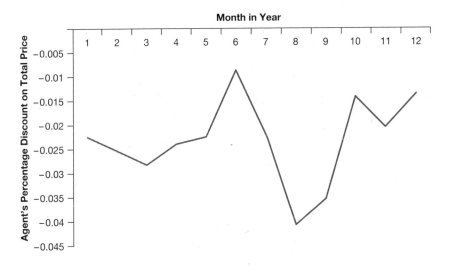

"Now, 3 percent may seem small but in absolute terms, it is a lot. If a property is say $1 million, an agent-buyer pays 3 percent or $30,000 less than if the buyer were a non-agent. $30,000! You can buy many things with $30,000.

"But the question is – how were they able to get that lower price?"

There was a momentary silence. The person who knew the answer, Peter, had vowed to keep quiet lest he incriminated himself. The rest at the dining table were novices, clueless as to how property agents could manoeuvre to get a better deal.

"Well, let's see how agents can capitalise on their informational advantage. First, agents can 'cherry pick' bargain deals from weak sellers. For example, agents can buy houses from distressed sellers who were involved in lawsuits and squeeze for a lower price."

"Ahh . . . So that's where the dataset on law events comes in. Clever," thought Teng. "These NUS profs are quite smart and creative."

Professor Sing continued, "We tested that but found no evidence that agents exploited this information to cherry pick such weak sellers. So agents were no different from non-agents in buying low purchase-priced properties which were involved in court cases.

"So where else can agents exploit? Well, there's another group of distressed sellers – those who face time pressure to sell their houses quickly, much like Teng's friend who wanted to sell his condo off to pay his wife's medical bills. His agent probably used that knowledge to tilt her bargaining power against him as a weak seller by bargaining down prices for personal property purchases. This is where we found it to be true. Agent-buyers paid lower prices relative to non-agent buyers when buying houses for own use from such distressed sellers."

"What scum bags! I'll have to tell my friend about your research and how this is exactly what his agent did to him," said Teng as he mentally noted that he should remember this.

Siew Ling, on the other hand, was telling herself, "Hmm . . . Knowledge is power."

Professor Sing continued, "We also found that they paid lower prices when buying houses for own occupation from individual-occupied and institutional sellers but not from investors. It appears that people with multiple properties, that's why they are called investors, seemed to be able to stand up against agent-buyers and not bow to their bargaining. I guess they have holding power. And perhaps being investors with multiple properties, they are more savvy and know the value of their property. They are less likely to be undersold.

"For owner-occupied sellers, perhaps they had bought another property to move into and needed to sell their existing property before moving in to the new one. So they were on somewhat of a time pressure. Or like Teng's friend, to sell it quickly to resolve a financial crisis.

"For institutional sellers, I think because the money is not personally theirs, they were more agreeable to let go at a lower price. But all in all, agents appeared to have stronger bargaining power than non-agents."

"So now, Teng, do you want to make a career switch? Real estate sounds quite lucrative, doesn't it?" mocked Peter again, jokingly of course.

"Now, where do these agents get their information from?" asked Professor Sing.

Perhaps, like many professors, Professor Sing enjoys answering his own question.

"One source of informational advantage is their access to a larger set of houses for sale in the course of dealings as agents representing potential sellers. In Singapore, real estate agents can source their listings either from open listings or exclusive listings. These agent listings are information exclusive to real estate agents.

"So agents can then use listing information which is not accessible to non-agent buyers to cherry pick cheaper houses. With this greater choice, we found that agent-buyers could bargain the price down by 1.8 percent more from the listing price."

> [A]gents can use listing information which is not accessible to non-agent buyers to cherry pick cheaper houses.

"I think these agents are part of the culprits in ramping up property prices. They buy them cheaper, but I think they sell them higher also," said Ah Mah as she cursed them. "Prof Sing, did you study agents when they sell their own house? Did they make even more money?"

"Unfortunately no, Auntie. We didn't study that, at least not yet. We're still writing this research for publication," replied Professor Sing.

"Did you find whether agents bargained for much lower prices when buying houses with unlucky addresses? I think they'll exaggerate about *feng shui* and hammer the price down. And later when they sell, they'll spin some story about *feng shui* being nothing," said Siew Ling as she recalled how she was affected by auspicious addresses when they were looking for a flat to buy.

"We didn't study that either but we can with our data. It's a good idea," said Professor Sing.

"Wait, wait. I'm not finished yet. We also found that sellers preferred to trade with non-agent buyers. I think they are wary of these tactics by agent-buyers. So the likelihood of transactions between agent-buyers and agent-sellers is higher."

"But how could the seller know that the buyer is not an agent?" quizzed Teng. "Look at my friend. The agent used her husband or brother as the buyer."

"True, there are these ways to mask the true buyer. So sellers need to be more careful who they are dealing with," said Professor Sing.

"Peter, next time when I want to sell my house, please don't sell it to an agent," pleaded Teng.

"How about conflict of interest?" asked Siew Ling. She had been absorbing what Professor Sing said, digesting each bit and thoughtfully going through them.

"That's a good point. So, in the banking industry, banks are the intermediaries between borrowers and depositors of funds. In the stock market, investors use brokers to execute their trades. Banks and brokers are intermediaries.

"In the housing market, we have appraisers who bridge the information gap between buyers and sellers. They provide an independent assessment on housing values used for the purposes of determining the loan quantum. Conflicts of interest may arise if appraisers relent to client (usually a bank) pressure by producing appraisal values that are the same or close to the contract price in return for repeated business from the same bank.

"For real estate agents, they should say they are interested in buying the property for themselves so that the seller knows he is selling to an agent who is better informed about the market."

"But why should that be necessary?" asked Siew Ling as she put up an argument. "Does it matter to you whether you sell your house to a teacher, a technician, a doctor, or even to a property agent? As long as you get a willing buyer at the price you are comfortable to sell at, then the buyer occupation shouldn't matter."

"But the property agent may con the seller because he knows the market better," argued Ah Mah. "So if the seller knows who he is dealing with, he may be more on his guard and not be bullied.

"Like at one time, banks were taking advantage of people's limited knowledge by selling them high-risk financial products. I was one of them. The bank lady was telling Pa and me how safe the product was and telling us all these complicated stuff. Luckily we didn't buy them because these were structured products and many turned out to lose money. A lot of old folks were pressurised into buying. That's why the government stepped in and warned banks not to engage in such hard sell practices."

"Sing, like what my mother said, you should also study how much agents sell their properties for," weighed in Teng. "Then, you'll have a more complete picture of how much property agents take advantage of our lack of information."

"Well, one study showed that agents sell their own houses for a premium of approximately 4.5 percent, while another found a premium of 3.7 percent. These were studies conducted in America. We might well do one in Singapore," concluded Professor Sing.

In China

"Let me briefly tell you another study," said Professor Sing as he seemed to be on a roll. "This one was done in China. It's not about real estate agents but it's about how people in general behave when the housing market boomed.

"This study was conducted by another colleague, Qian Wenlan, at NUS Business School. In general, land auctions are indicative of how hot the property market is. When the market is hot, auction prices go up.

"So, there were three cities in China in which record auctions were made – Shanghai, Hangzhou and Xiamen. Following this, local housing prices in these three cities experienced a monthly increase of 5 percent.

"My colleague found that when house prices increased, homeowners benefitted from a large windfall of wealth, which in turn, increased the appeal of leisure activities. People then began to realise how costly their time is. And so they started thinking about the opportunity cost of their time or effort spent on working."

"What is 'opportunity cost'?" asked Siew Ling.

Professor Sing explained, "'Opportunity cost' represents the benefits that a person may miss out on when choosing one alternative over another. In this case, the time or effort spent on working would mean the benefits of spending the same time on something else such as leisure activities are missed out.

"My colleague found this – people began to goof off. They shirked. They became less responsible at work and used work time for other activities not related to work.

"She found that for every 10 percent increase in house prices, employee shirking likelihood increased by 16 percent. After a rise in housing prices, some 60 percent of employees would use work time to take care of their personal needs."

> **After a rise in housing prices, some 60 percent of employees would use work time to take care of their personal needs.**

"How does she know that? How did she measure these non-work related personal activities?" Peter asked for the first time during this long discussion since the limelight was no more on Singaporean property agents.

"Ahh . . . She studied how they used their credit cards," answered Professor Sing. "She found that within a working day, non-work-related credit card spending was more concentrated in the early morning (9 AM–10 AM) and right before lunch (11 AM–12 PM).

"Hence, from such credit card use patterns, you could see that employees showed up late for work, took earlier lunch breaks, and left work earlier at the end of the workday. They also shirked more frequently during the later part of the work week when morale in general slowed down."

"Peter, you'd better do your job properly. Don't anyhow play play," said Teng as he took a jibe at his friend.

"She also found shirking behaviour to be more prominent among house owners, and particularly among owners of multiple properties. No such effect was found among those who rented their homes.

"Moreover, employees with lower work incentives such as those near retirement or in companies where the link between pay and performance is weak, had a stronger urge to shirk."

"So when the housing market is good, people slack," Ah Mah joined in.

"This sounds like the good mood theory that Sarah told us about. Prof Sing, you weren't here that day. But Sarah told us about how sunny days put people in a good mood and they start to spend more because they are not so particular about how they spend. Same here too, I think. People feel good when their house values increase and so they goof off from work and spend more time on leisure activities," elaborated Siew Ling, connecting the two studies together.

"Yah. And that study was done by your good friend, Professor Sumit Agarwal," jumped in Teng.

Tax Evasion

"Well, he has another one about China, too. Something about tax evasion and the property market. Let me try to recall," Professor Sing thought for a few moments as this wasn't his own research.

"In 2013, the China Government increased the capital gains tax of property transactions if the transacted units have a holding period of less than five years. Again, like Singapore, the China Government wanted to curb speculation."

"What is 'capital gains tax'?" asked Ah Mah.

"If you sell your property at a higher price than when you bought it, you make a profit. That profit is like income. So a tax on the profit is called capital gains tax because you gained on the capital which is the original price you paid for the property," explained Peter.

Professor Sing nodded that Peter was correct and continued, "To evade such taxes, buyers and sellers can report a lower registered price to the local tax authorities. Sumit found that after the increased capital gains tax was imposed, sellers reported a lower price to the tax authorities to the tune of 15 percent less! Just so to evade higher taxes."

"Looks like everyone is trying to cheat everyone," Teng laughed. He had heard of so many incidents of corruption and fraudulent practices in China. This is yet another.

"And despite the tax increase, it didn't deter everyone from buying properties," elaborated Professor Sing. "Sumit found that wealthy cash buyers were more likely to buy a house than buyers who needed financing. Why?

"Because buyers who are cash strapped and need financing want to report a higher purchase price so that they can secure higher bank financing. But sellers want to have lower reported prices to evade capital gains tax. So they would rather sell to wealthy cash buyers who don't need bank financing, and under-report the transacted price."

"But wouldn't this create wealth inequality?" asked Siew Ling, who seemed to be really thinking through on the impact of these findings.

"Exactly!" said a delighted Professor Sing. "If the housing market is rising and the wealthy are more likely to buy than the less cash-rich ones because of the need for financing, then the wealthy gets wealthier and the rest are left behind. That is a potential problem."

"Aiyoh! What if that happens to Singapore?" Ah Mah said. She had been hearing from people in the wet market that the income gap in Singapore is widening, that the rich are getting richer and the poor are getting poorer.

"Auntie, we don't have capital gains tax in Singapore," reassured Peter. "And in Singapore, you cannot anyhow register a price. If you get caught registering a different price from what you actually paid for, the consequences are severe. You know our Singapore Government. They will never let people get away with such fraudulent behaviour."

Professor Sing smiled as he thought, "My neighbours are certainly benefiting from research done by NUS, which is how it should be. I'm glad our research is useful."

WANT TO KNOW MORE?

This chapter is based on the following research: Sumit Agarwal, He Jia, Sing Tien Foo and Song Changcheng (forthcoming), "Do Real Estate Agents Have Information Advantages in Housing Markets?" *Journal of Financial Economics*, https://www. sciencedirect.com/science/article/pii/S0304405X19301229; Gu Qianlin, He Jia and Qian Wenlan (2018), "Housing Booms and Shirking," Working Paper, National University of Singapore, https://papers.ssrn.com/sol3/papers.cfm?abstract_id=3189933; Qian Wenlan, "When home prices rise, people goof off at work," *The Straits Times*, (24 March 2019), pp. B14–B15; Sumit Agarwal, Li Keyang, Qin Yu, Wu Jing and Yan Jubo (2018), "Tax Evasion, Capital Gains, and the Housing Market," Working Paper, National University of Singapore.

Pay, Lah!

Almost every day, when Ah Kong and Ah Mah bring Ethan back from kindergarten, they go through Nex, the shopping mall, to enjoy the air-conditioning. Sometimes, when Ethan is well behaved, they reward him by going to the ice-cream shop or the stationery shop to buy some small items.

Ethan was particularly well behaved that day. At the traffic light crossing, he held his grandmother's hand, hardened by years of hand washing clothes, wrinkled and blemished with sun spots. Yet, that hardened hand gave an assurance of dependability.

Ethan said, "Ah Mah. Hold my hand. You must cross the road carefully. Come, let me guide you when the green man light is on," as he reached out his plumpish hand to hold hers.

Ah Mah was so pleased. Her heart melted because she felt, just as she had done right with her son, she was now doing with her young grandson. It seemed an exchange of position – Ethan was so considerate to look after her, and not she looking after him.

"What a good boy, my eldest grandson. I'm so blessed," beamed Ah Mah with pride. To Ah Mah, a traditional Chinese woman, the eldest grandson is treated as her youngest son.

As they entered Nex, Ethan asked "Ah Mah, can we go to the bookshop today?" as he tugged his grandmother's warm hand.

"Why?" asked Ah Mah.

"I just want to go and see the things there. Please?" asked Ethan as he put on his most puppy-looking eyes.

"We just went there two days ago. Go again? There are no new things. Nothing has changed," growled Ah Kong. Ah Mah glared at him for being so impatient. After all, their grandson had been such an angel in looking after her.

Ethan looked at Ah Mah, held her hand even tighter and with his head slightly tilted to one side, pursed his lips just so slightly and gave the saddest look he could muster.

"OK. You're a good boy today. We'll go there just for a little while," said Ah Mah as she relented.

"Ah Mah! You're the best-est!" Ethan said with a gleeful smile and a little louder so that passers-by could hear how wonderful a grandma Ah Mah was.

Ah Mah was so happy. She loves adoration, especially in public.

But Ah Kong wasn't pleased at all. He felt his wife was spoiling their grandson. He knew that when Ethan was whispering those sweet nothings to her, there must be something up his sleeve. And his wife didn't realise she'd been had. This grandson had her wrapped around his little finger.

At the stationery shop, Ethan made a beeline for the eraser section. He looked at the ones with country flags printed on them. He had owned some of them. And there are the ones with the Captain America shield on them. He loves Avengers. He wants to be like Captain America although Spiderman seems to be another favourite. His best friend at kindergarten, Jay, likes Spiderman.

"Ah Mah, this eraser is pretty, isn't it?" asked Ethan as he held the one with Captain America's shield on it.

Ethan knows all too well that he shouldn't say outright that he wants the eraser. His mummy had scolded him many times before whenever he asked her to buy him something. So he found a way out. If he wanted something, he'd ask an adult whether she thought the item was cute or pretty or something good about it. And if the adult was agreeable and shared similar sentiments as he did, he'd hold on to it and admire it for as long as it took, and sometimes accompanied with a gentle sigh, before the adult said, "Ethan, do you like it so much? I'll buy it for you but you must promise to be a good boy."

Ka-ching! Ethan knew then that he had the adult in his pocket. He'd go home with the prized possession and he would not get a scolding from his mummy because the adult who bought it would say he didn't ask for it.

And so Ethan was going to put his charming skills to practice yet again. He described how well made the eraser was to Ah Mah.

"Ah Mah, see? The shield is exactly like the one in the movie. This is the shield shown in *Captain America: Civil War*. Captain America slammed down his shield and he left it there. It's a very special shield.

"And you see, Ah Mah, this eraser has very sharp corners. That will make it good for erasing because only the parts you want to be erased will be erased. The other parts are not affected. Then that won't mess up my writing. And the teacher will say I am a very neat boy."

The last sentence was intentionally added in because Ethan knows how much Ah Mah likes to boast to her friends about how good a student he is.

"How much is it?" asked Ah Mah.

"Only $1."

"OK. I'll buy it for you. But you must be a good boy. Do your homework first before playing," came the reply.

Ah Kong frowned.

At the cashier, the young lady asked Ah Mah, "Would you be paying for the eraser by PayLah?"

"Huh? What did you say?" Ah Mah strained her ear to understand what the lady was saying.

"Auntie, would you like to use PayLah to pay for the eraser?" asked the cashier again.

"What is PayLah?" asked Ah Mah. She looked at Ah Kong, but he shrugged his shoulders.

"Just pay, lah. Of course we'll pay, lah. Don't pay, how can?" he said, quite frustrated that his wife was spoiling their grandson again.

Ah Mah was somewhat confused. So she quickly took a $1 coin from her beaded purse to pay and left the store.

As they were heading home, Ethan, feeling a little guilty that he had caused Ah Kong to be upset with Ah Mah, said, "Ah Mah, PayLah is a new way to pay when you buy things. You put your phone to scan a QR (Quick Response) code and the money is paid from your bank account. You don't need to carry money. Many people use it now."

"Oh? How do you know all these things?" asked Ah Mah, curious that such a young boy knew such techie stuff.

"My best friend Jay has an older sister, Joy. Joy came one day to bring Jay home. And she was on her phone all the time. So Jay asked her what she was doing. And she said she was buying some things online and paying for them using PayLah."

Siew Ling was at home when they got back. As a retail assistant, she works in shifts and that day, her work didn't start till 1 PM.

"Hey! What have we got here? How was school?" Siew Ling gave Ethan a hug. "Ervin, come and say hello to *ge ge* (older brother)."

"Mummy, Mummy. Ah Mah bought me this eraser," said an excited Ethan as he took out the Captain America eraser from the plastic bag, having forgotten how much his mother doesn't like him asking others to buy him things.

"Another eraser? But you have so many already. Only last week I bought you one. What happened to it?" said Siew Ling with a stern tone underlying her voice.

"Lost," said Ethan as he quickly dashed to his room to avoid his mummy scolding him.

Somehow, Ethan is constantly losing erasers. Sometimes, he would say his friend borrowed them. Other times, he didn't even know what happened to them. Siew Ling had even resorted to buying a huge eraser so that it is not easily lost. But that didn't seem to help.

"I wonder where all these erasers go to? It can't be that they just disappear," thought Siew Ling.

Siew Ling dreaded how many of these stationery pieces Ethan would lose when he goes to Primary 1 the following year. Besides the auspicious address, another reason why Teng and she had chosen this flat was because it is near a primary school with credible standing. They are going to register Ethan soon for Primary 1 at this nearby primary school and were glad that after the first phase of registration, there were still quite a number of places left. Phase 1 registration is for children whose siblings are currently in the school they want to apply to.

The week before, she and Teng were having a chat about school registration before going to bed.

"Teng, did you read in the papers that there are seven schools with very limited Primary 1 places left after Phase 1? Thankfully, Ethan's school isn't one of them."

"Luckily Ethan wasn't born a year earlier," said Teng. "Last year, 22 schools were almost filled up after Phase 1."

"Really? Why?" asked Siew Ling.

"Dragon babies! There were 40,600 children born in the Year of the Dragon in 2012 compared to 38,000 applying for Primary 1 places in Ethan's year.[1] I remember when I was in primary school, Peter and I heard this news story about cohort size effect and how being born in the Year of the Dragon is not a blessing. In fact, because of the larger number of such babies, there's more competition for the limited number of places in choice schools. So class sizes are bigger throughout the years of their study and this doesn't benefit them. Yours truly is a Dragon baby and see what happened? I cannot quite remember the details but there was a study done in Singapore and the findings were not very encouraging for Dragon babies,"[2] replied Teng.

---

[1] Jolene Ang, "P1 places at 7 schools more than half-filled," *The Straits Times*, (6 July 2019), p. B1.

[2] For more on this research on the effect of cohort size on education and consumption, see Sumit Agarwal, Ang Swee Hoon and Sing Tien Foo (2018), *Kiasunomics: Stories of Singaporean Economic Behaviours*, Chapter 1 "Dragon Babies, There Are So Many of You," (Singapore: World Scientific Publishers). To read the academic article, see Sumit Agarwal, Qian Wenlan, Sing Tien Foo and Tan Poh Lin (2018), "Dragon Babies," Working Paper, National University of Singapore, https://papers. ssrn.com/sol3/papers.cfm?abstract_id=3032575. This research has also been published as a commentary; see Sumit Agarwal and Qian Wenlan, "Dragon babies, muted achievements," *The Straits Times*, (27 January 2017), https://www.straitstimes.com/opinion/dragon-babies-muted-achievements

"Well, at least Ethan is spared of this cohort size effect," felt a reassured Siew Ling. "And if Ethan gets to this school, it will help Ervin because he'll come under Phase 1 when he registers for Primary One."

PayLah

Siew Ling's reminiscence was jolted when Ah Mah recalled her shopping experience. "Siew Ling, when I was going to pay for the eraser, the cashier asked me whether I want to use PayLah. What is that?"

"PayLah is by DBS. Ma, you have a POSB account, right? Then you can set up payment using PayLah," said Siew Ling.

"You can do many things with PayLah. If you owe someone money, you can PayLah him. All you need is his phone number. Then you can transfer how much you owe him from your bank account to his bank account. There's no need to withdraw cash and give it to that person face to face. And PayLah is immediate too. So, it's very convenient.

"Or if you want to give someone money as a present, for instance, you want to give me $10 as a surprise, you can also use Paylah. It's like a mobile *hongbao* (red packet).

"And then of course for shopping purposes, you can use PayLah too. Shops have these QR codes which you can scan on your phone and pay for the merchandise. Even at my shoe shop, we are using QR codes now. More and more of our shoppers are using PayLah or some kind of mobile payment.

"In China, it's almost a cashless society. Everyone including grandpas and grandmas use WeChatPay and AliPay to buy things. When you go to the wet markets in China, you cannot pay using cash. They don't accept cash at all. You have to use mobile wallet. In fact, in some places like Alibaba's Hema supermarket, payment is by facial recognition! China is so far ahead in digital payment.

"So Ma, the shoe shop I work for has to keep up with the times. We also have PayLah facilities. Otherwise, we'll lose business."

"Is it safe or not?" Ah Mah asked. She's bewildered that money can be invisible, and sceptical that this mode of payment is safe. "How do I know that people won't take more from my bank account? What if they take all the money I have in the bank? My entire savings!"

"I don't know but everything is so high tech now. I suppose we need to be vigilant and always check that there are no suspicious transactions in our bank account," replied Siew Ling.

"You know, Siew Ling, I was so astounded that even Ethan has heard of PayLah. Of course he's a small boy and can't use it. But he more or less knows what it is. Stunning, isn't it?" Ah Mah said, "He said he learnt it from Jay's sister, Joy."

If Joy, a teenager, is using it and her six-year-old son knows about it, Siew Ling was curious how many Singaporeans are using PayLah or some kind of e-wallet payment services. She knows more and more of her customers are using them, but how many? And how are credit and debit cards affected? She'd have to ask Jothi her senior colleague when she gets to work.

Jothi was her friend who encouraged her to shop in Johor for better savings and even had numbers to back up her position that it pays to shop in Johor.[3] She knows so much about retail and shopping that she was promoted to manage a few stores of the shoe company. Maybe Jothi would also know about PayLah.

---

[3] For more on this research on how taxi drivers set targets, see Sumit Agarwal, Ang Swee Hoon and Sing Tien Foo (2018), *Kiasunomics: Stories of Singaporean Economic Behaviours*, Chapter 4 "To Johor, to Johor, to Buy That Nice Dress," (Singapore: World Scientific Publishers). To read the academic article, see Sumit Agarwal, Souphala Chomsisengphet, Qian Wenlan and Xu Weibiao (2018), "Tax Differential and Cross-Border Shopping: Evidence from Singapore," Working Paper, National University of Singapore, https://papers.ssrn.com/sol3/papers.cfm?abstract_id=3038550. This research has also been published as a commentary; see Sumit Agarwal and Qian Wenlan, "What shopping in Malaysia means for us," *The New Paper*, (23 December 2016), https://www.tnp.sg/news/views/what-shopping-malaysia-means-us

And sure she did. Jothi is the Miss Know-It-All when it comes to shopping. She told Siew Ling that she has a friend who is a consultant. Her consulting firm wanted to know the impact of mobile wallet on traditional payment methods such as credit and debit cards, as well as ATM (Automated Teller Machine) transactions. Then the consulting firm held a fee-paying seminar. Since the shoe company was contemplating whether or not to invest in QR code facilities, it had sent Jothi to attend.

Jothi educated her friend, "Singapore introduced its first QR code payment function in mobile wallets in April 2017. Before that, the mobile wallet facility was available but with no QR code payment. With the QR code technology, users can receive and make immediate payments by generating their own QR code on the mobile phone app. Buyers and sellers of merchandise can complete transactions by displaying or scanning QR codes. So essentially, this technology not only brings added convenience to consumers given the large smart phone ownership in Singapore, but it also reduces transaction costs especially for small and new businesses."

Siew Ling waited patiently as she was eager to know who they studied and the outcome.

"The company studied 250,000 Singapore consumers and their mobile wallet transactions including transaction amount and time. It also has information on debit and credit cards, and ATM transactions.

"This is what they found. The total amount spent on mobile wallet and the number of such transactions more than doubled within eight months after the first QR code payment was introduced. Essentially, mobile wallet was a success.

"Let me see if I have the graphs that my friend showed me. Ah . . . Here it is," said Jothi as she opened up her smartphone.

"The first graph shows the number of transactions involving mobile wallet on the left margin. There's also a corresponding number for ATM transactions on the right margin. The solid line is for mobile wallet while the dashed line is for ATM. The vertical line is when QR code payment technology was introduced.

"You can see that before the vertical line, prior to the introduction of QR code, the number of transactions via mobile wallet was somewhat flat. After that, there was a pick up that accelerated particularly in the fourth month and thereafter.

[M]obile wallet payment is being adopted at a rapid rate because of the QR code.

"Look at that for ATM transactions. It is almost at the same level throughout the 12 months, right? What does this tell you? While the number of ATM transactions remains flat, mobile wallet payment is being adopted at a rapid rate because of the QR code."

Siew Ling nodded. "This is interesting. Luckily our shoe shop has invested into the QR code. Otherwise, we will be losing sales."

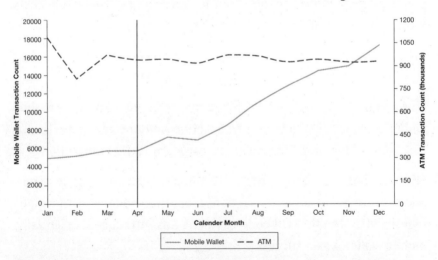

"Now, let's look at how much these transactions are valued at. Let me look for the graph on this," Jothi continued.

"Ah yes. This is the one. The pattern is similar. Again, the dashed line is ATM, the solid line is mobile wallet, and the vertical line is when

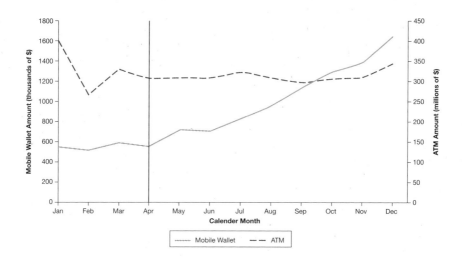

the QR code was introduced. The total value of the transactions for mobile wallet are indicated on the left margin, while that for ATM transactions are on the right margin. The total transactional amount incurred through mobile wallet is not big, but you can see it ramping up over time while that for ATM remains largely flat."

"This is similar to what's happening in Japan," added Siew Ling. She told Jothi that she had read in the newspapers about Japan's Internet commerce firm Rakuten trying to promote its QR code mobile payment system. When the baseball season started in Japan, fans found that the food and drinks stalls in the stadium did not accept cash. People were forced to switch to mobile payment. That resulted in a 20 percent jump in food, beverage and merchandise sales compared to the same period a year ago. The fans' spending habits changed.[4]

"Hmm . . . There seems to be some convergence in the findings and what happened in Japan. The consulting firm said that Singaporeans used the mobile wallet mostly for small-ticket transactions. That's why the cashier asked your mother-in-law whether she wanted to use PayLah for her $1 purchase.

"And it also said that on a weekly basis, the number of small-size

---

[4] "Japan bets on mobile payment to boost spending," *The Straits Times*, (4 July 2019), p. C2.

transactions valued at $100 or less increased by 114 percent. Those for large-size transactions or those more than $100 increased by 88 percent. Let me see whether I have the figures here. Ahh . . . Here they are."

Siew Ling studied them and observed that the number of smaller transactions galloped away with the introduction of mobile wallet services, more so than that for large transactions.

"What about for small companies like our shoe store? Do we benefit?" asked Siew Ling.

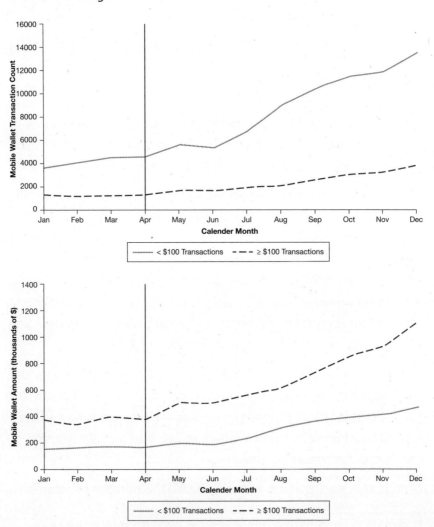

"It seems so," replied Jothi. "Compared to large merchants, small merchants experienced 3.5 percent more card sales amount during the nine-month period after the QR code payment was introduced.

"I'm not too sure about this next part but this is what the consultants said. They said something like if the increase in mobile wallet is from small-size transactions, might the spill-over effect on card sales be stronger among merchants selling products of smaller values?

"And they found that after the QR code introduction, these stores experienced a significant increase in monthly card sales amount by 7.4 percent."

"How about our store? How did it affect us?" asked Siew Ling.

"Would you say our store is new or old?" asked Jothi.

"The consultant found that among small merchants, newly established stores benefitted more than more established merchants. New stores saw card sales amount increased by 11 percent per month, while the established ones rose by only 2 percent."

"Perhaps the established stores have older customers who use cash rather than mobile payments. So they don't benefit fully from this new technology," contributed Siew Ling.

"Possibly. What's interesting is that the consultants think this new payment method with its convenience in enabling customers to pay at any place more easily, is able to bring traffic into retail stores especially stores that are less visible such as those operated by small new merchants," added Jothi.

> [T]his new payment method ... is able to bring traffic into retail stores especially stores that are less visible such as those operated by small new merchants.

"They found that customers who live in the same vicinity as the shops but have never spent there at all the year before QR code was introduced, actually went to these shops after QR code was implemented and increased their sales by 1.8 percent. Fascinating, right?

"And which sector do you think benefitted most from mobile wallet? Clothing stores? Electronic stores? Restaurants?"

"Restaurants?" Siew Ling hazarded a guess.

"You're right. Sales growth was highest for merchants of dining venues. Their total card sales went up by almost 13 percent," Jothi told her.

Pros and Cons of Mobile Wallets

"No doubt there are benefits to be had with mobile payments," said Siew Ling. "But I think as people cannot see or feel their money leaving their wallet when they buy things, they don't feel the pinch and may get carried away with their purchases. So people need to be more disciplined in their spending."

"You're right but maybe that's exactly what is needed for countries like Japan where the economy is deflationary," countered Jothi. "Japan's been experiencing a stagnant economy for decades. Its consumers are delaying spending because they think prices will get even lower. So if mobile payments can stimulate more spending, that may help to give the much needed lift to the economy."

"Didn't the Japanese Government increase the sales tax from 8 to 10 percent? Wouldn't that dampen purchases?" enquired Siew Ling, trying to understanding the Japanese Government's move given the deflationary economy.

"Yes," responded Jothi. "But the government offered points redeemable for future discounts to shoppers who use QR codes and other cashless payments for a few months after the sales tax was increased."

"That's somewhat like how some organisations like food courts are encouraging mobile payments. You get discounts when you use PayLah instead of cash," added Siew Ling.

Jothi nodded. "Currently the bulk, I think 80 percent, of transactions in Japan is in cash. That is the highest cash usage rate among developed countries after Germany. Do you know why? Because of low crime rates. Japanese are comfortable with carrying wads of cash. And having an ageing population doesn't help either as they are less receptive to technological innovations such as mobile payment.

"But the Japanese Government wants to change how Japanese pay. Going cashless such as using mobile payments can solve economic problems such as labour shortage and the falling profitability of Japanese banks."

"The consulting firm you mentioned studied transactional amounts. I wonder whether using mobile payment translates to profitability for the firms, especially smaller ones?" asked Siew Ling.

"You have a point there," agreed Jothi. "Typically there's a fee charged for using mobile payment. If a small firm already has low margins, then accepting mobile payments may eat into their profits.

"Mobile wallets are catching on in Singapore. A study by consulting company McKinsey showed that seven in 10 Singaporeans use a digital wallet and that the transaction volume is growing.[5]

"Many retailers realise that they need to change with progress. But installing the payment terminals is one thing. Training the staff to use it is another. I've heard of several cases where customers were made to wait quite long because the cashier staff doesn't know how to accept QR payments on their payment terminals. There was also

---

[5] Aw Cheng Wei and Marcia Lee, "Mobile wallet operators roll out time-saving measures to lure customers," *The Straits Times*, (8 July 2019), https://www.straitstimes.com/business/race-to-be-operator-with-fastest-mobile-wallet

one case where the customer had to teach the retail staff how to accept payments via PayLah. And in another instance, a customer said that marketing materials indicated that the shop accepts PayLah but the retail staff said it doesn't. That led to an argument between staff and customer. It's so ridiculous.

"The payment terminal provider, in this instance Nets, and the operator responsible for the mobile wallet must ensure that retail staff are trained so that customers are not kept waiting when making a payment."

"I agree," concurred Siew Ling. "But like it or not, when there's staff turnover, re-training has to take place. I also think these operators must make using the mobile wallet seamless. They should reduce the number of clicks needed to get the transaction done. Convenience is the key.

"But what I don't understand is, with Singapore being so small, why do we need to have so many operators of mobile wallets with more joining in. Besides PayLah, there's also GrabPay and FavePay. Do we need so many operators? Look at China. It's such a big country with everyone using the mobile wallet, and yet they have only two operators – AliPay and WeChatPay.

"You know, in our store, we do get mainland Chinese working in Singapore or even tourists from China buying from us. They use their AliPay or WeChatPay. So we have no problem here," said Siew Ling.

"But they told me that in China, until recently, the government doesn't allow tourists to open a bank account. And so even if a tourist has the WeChatPay app, they cannot transfer money from their home bank account to the mobile wallet to make their purchases. Instead, they have to get their Chinese friends to deposit money into their mobile wallet through the *hongbao* facility and they pay their friends in cash in return. Then they can use their mobile wallet to make purchases. So troublesome, isn't it?"

"Yes, that's what I've heard too," smiled Jothi. "But now AliPay is introducing a 'Tour Pass' programme for short-term visitors which allows them to download a version of the AliPay app. They can use a prepaid card service from the Bank of Shanghai that they can top up via their usual credit or debit card. And WeChatPay is following suit too in a partnership with Visa."[6]

Online Shopping

"Jothi, how about e-commerce? Do you think our retail shop will be able to survive given that so many online shops are sprouting out?" asked Siew Ling.

Siew Ling was concerned there were more and more online stores selling merchandise that one may not be able to find in a physical store.

"Besides Amazon, there's Zalora where you can buy shoes, Qoo10 and Lazada for all kinds of stuff and specialised ones like RedMart and Shopee for groceries. But the one I'm most interested in is Taobao from Alibaba. Its Singles' Day sale is so mind-boggling. The variety of merchandise and some of them are from well-known brands like L'Oréal and Kate Spade is so wide and the discounts so deep."

"Yes, I agree with you. Online commerce is a threat to the viability of physical stores," replied Jothi.

"But online stores are coming offline too. Look at Amazon. It's gone into Amazon Go. And Alibaba has expanded to physical supermarkets as in Hema. The thing is online stores is almost purely commercial. You go in, search for what you want, put it in your cart, pay and exit. It is very transactional. There's little entertainment to it – the joy of shopping is somewhat missing.

---

[6] John Detrixhe and Jane Li, "Travelers to China can finally experience its cashless economy like a local," www.qz.com (5 November 2019); "Alipay, WeChatPay open apps to foreigners visiting China," www.bloomberg.com (6 November 2019).

"On the other hand, physical shopping allows you to incorporate elements that make the shopping experience a lot more enjoyable and engaging. You can chitchat with the sales staff for more information, learn the story behind the brand and so on.

"Look at Singles' Day. Part of the reason for its success is because it went beyond being a commerce play. Alibaba gets its merchants like L'Oréal to put up booths for consumers to have a virtual reality trial of its cosmetics before they buy them online. That's a form of entertainment, isn't it? Putting the joy of physical shopping and integrating it with online purchase. And they even had Taylor Swift perform for them on Singles' Day!"

"I see . . . So for our shoe shop, we need our sales people to be more proactive and make the shopping experience for customers more rewarding," nodded Siew Ling.

"I've got to go soon but let me share with you this study on Taobao since you are so interested in this site," said Jothi.

"You know how much Chinese love bargaining, right? Whenever we can bargain and the harder we bargain, we often go away thinking that we've gotten a great deal.

"Taobao has a feature that allows buyers and sellers to haggle. Quite interesting, isn't it? It mirrors reality. Yet, we sometimes hear people complaining that they don't like bargaining because they don't know how to bargain and what the fair price for the product truly is.

"They also think that sellers intentionally inflate the prices to compensate for bargaining that will bring the price down to what they originally intended to sell the product for. Moreover, does bargaining work well for sellers? Do sellers make less profit when there's bargaining? We know it works well for buyers because they enjoy a lower price, but what about sellers?

"A study was conducted where the researchers came up with an experiment to see what could have happened to sellers' profits if bargaining were prohibited on Taobao. In reality, Taobao never stopped this bargaining feature.

"The researchers found that if prices were fixed and there was no bargaining, sellers' profits would be higher. But not all sellers enjoyed higher profits equally. What kinds of sellers do you think gained most from the 'no bargaining' rule?"

"Hmm . . . Sellers whose products are not of that good a quality?" guessed Siew Ling.

"You're right," replied Jothi. "The researchers showed that sellers with low reputation, or have high detailed seller ratings, and selling non-promotion products benefit more. So not having bargaining doesn't serve buyers well as the less reputable sellers benefit more from it. And so, Taobao was correct to have bargaining on its platform.

"Siew Ling, I really got to go because there's a meeting to attend. Nice talking to you. Catch up with you again soon."

WANT TO KNOW MORE?

This chapter is based on the following research: Sumit Agarwal, Qian Wenlan, Bernard Yeung and Zou Xin (2018), "Mobile Wallet and Entrepreneurial Growth," Working Paper, National University of Singapore, https://papers.ssrn.com/sol3/papers.cfm?abstract_id=3298266; Sumit Agarwal, "Mobile payments have positive impact on business growth," *The Business Times*, (13 February 2019), https://www.businesstimes.com.sg/opinion/mobile-payments-have-positive-impact-on-business-growth; "Singapore's small merchants benefit most from mobile wallet use: NUS survey," (13 December 2018), https://www.channelnewsasia.com/news/technology/singapore-s-small-merchants-benefit-most-from-mobile-wallet-use-11027628; Samantha Chiew, "Introduction of PayLah! boosts mobile wallet usage; fosters business growth for SMEs," *The Edge*, (13 December 2018), https://www.theedgesingapore.com/introduction-paylah-boosts-mobile-wallet-usage-fosters-business-growth-smes; Zhang Xu, Puneet Manchanda and Chu Junhong (2018), "'Meet Me Halfway': The Value of Bargaining," Working Paper, National University of Singapore, https://papers.ssrn.com/sol3/papers.cfm?abstract_id=2988631

7

Gotong Royong

A h Mah heard a commotion nearby. Men were shouting loudly, "Be careful. Don't drop the TV set."

"What's happening?" thought Ah Mah as she opened the front door slightly, just enough to stick her head out and see. A neighbour further down the corridor was moving out. The movers were ensuring that the furniture were not damaged in the moving process.

Ah Mah didn't know the neighbour. She only knew them by sight – a quiet Malay family of four consisting of two adult children and the parents. She hardly saw them. But she was inquisitive. Mrs Sing had also come out to see what was happening.

"Mrs Sing. Good morning. Do you know this neighbour? Where are they moving to?" asked Ah Mah.

"They are moving to Woodlands. With two full-grown children, the parents will be retiring soon. So they needed a cheaper place. And they told me that because Woodlands is near Johor, they can do their shopping there. That would be cheaper, especially when they are retired," replied Mrs Sing.

"Yes. Because the Malaysian ringgit is weaker, many Singaporeans go there to shop. Last time, when Teng and Siew Ling lived in Woodlands, they would go to Johor every weekend to buy their groceries. They told me that the things there are 10 to 25 percent cheaper depending on what they are,"[1] added Ah Mah.

"I heard that too. But now that Malaysia has the Sales and Service Tax, I wonder whether the savings is as much as before, though I still hear of people going there to shop," Mrs Sing added.

"Do you know how much they sold their flat for? And who did they sell it to?" asked Ah Mah.

Mrs Sing didn't know. Ah Mah thought to herself that she would make it a point to know the new neighbour.

The weeks that followed were noisy. Renovation works were carried out in the flat by the new neighbour whom no one had yet to see. The lifts were covered with cardboard to protect the floor and inside walls from scratches when carrying debris and new tiles. The hacking and drilling were making Ervin cry, and giving Ah Kong and Ah Mah a headache.

Even Sarah complained because her exams were around the corner and given that her unit was closer to the renovated flat, the pounding was amplified. Ah Mah boiled some herbal tea for her to be able to concentrate better when studying. She treated Sarah like her granddaughter.

---

[1] For more on this research on Singaporeans' shopping in Johor, see Sumit Agarwal, Ang Swee Hoon and Sing Tien Foo (2018), *Kiasunomics: Stories of Singaporean Economic Behaviours*, Chapter 4 "To Johor, to Johor, to Buy That Nice Dress," (Singapore, World Scientific Publishers). To read the academic article, see Sumit Agarwal, Souphala Chomsisenghet, Qian Wenlan and Xu Weibiao (2018), "Tax Differential and Cross-Border Shopping: Evidence from Singapore," Working Paper, National University of Singapore, https://papers.ssrn.com/sol3/papers.cfm?abstract_id=3038550; Sumit Agarwal and Qian Wenlan, "What shopping in Malaysia means for us," *The New Paper*, (23 December 2016), https://www.tnp.sg/news/views/what-shopping-malaysia-means-us

"Sarah, years ago when there was construction going on to build the community centre, Ah Kong and I would shut the windows and turn on the air-conditioning. That lessened the noise and the cool temperature made us feel better too. Less irritable. Less moody. You should do that too especially since you need to study for your exams," advised Ah Mah.

"But you must remember this – once the renovation is over, please go back to how you used the fan and not the air-con. Don't get too comfortable and make turning on the air-con a habit. Teng told me that many people tended to continue to use the air-con needlessly even after the construction noise was over. Then, you'll be wasting energy."[2]

"Thanks, Ah Mah. But I think I'll stay longer at school. I'll study in the library. Not only is it cool and quiet, but also seeing other people study will motivate me to study too. Otherwise, when I'm at home, I'm afraid I may not be disciplined enough and get distracted from studying," said Sarah.

As the renovation quietened down, Ah Mah knew that the new neighbour would be moving in soon. She wondered whether they would be Chinese or Indian, or Malay like the previous neighbour.

Ethnic Integration Policy

As a multi-racial society, HDB has an ethnic integration policy (EIP) to ensure racial integration. With 80 percent of the population living in HDB flats, the

HDB has an ethnic integration policy (EIP) to ensure racial integration.

---

2   For more on this research on the effects of construction on utilities consumption, see Sumit Agarwal, Ang Swee Hoon and Sing Tien Foo (2018), *Kiasunomics: Stories of Singaporean Economic Behaviours*, Chapter 14 "Mama, Don't Forget to Switch on the Air-Con", (Singapore: World Scientific Publishers). To read the academic article, see Sumit Agarwal, Satyanarain Rengarajan, Sing Tien Foo and Derek Volmer (2015), "Effects of Construction Activities on Residential Electricity Consumption: Evidence from Singapore's Public Housing Estates," Working Paper, National University of Singapore, https://papers.ssrn.com/sol3/papers.cfm?abstract_id=2371314

government takes a strong position on maintaining a balanced mix of ethnic groups within a block and in a neighbourhood. Hence, in 1989, the EIP was introduced to prevent the formation of racial enclaves and to foster harmonious living among ethnic communities in public housing estates.

Block quotas and neighbourhood quotas were established in the allocation of new flats, and revised in 2010 as the population mix changed.

Population Composition and Ethnic Quotas in HDB Flats

Ethnic Group	Population Composition		Maximum Ethnic Limits			
			From March 1989		March 2010	
	1989	2010	Neigh-bourhood	Block	Neigh-bourhood	Block
Chinese	77.8%	74.1%	84.0%	87.0%	84.0%	87.0%
Malays	14.2%	13.4%	22.0%	25.0%	22.0%	25.0%
Indians	7.0%	9.2%	10.0%	13.0%	12.0%	15.0%

The New Neighbours

Ah Mah noticed a young Malay couple coming in and out of the renovated unit. "Ahh . . . So they are our new neighbours."

They didn't seem to have any children, just the two of them.

Wanting to strike up a conversation, Ah Mah knocked on their door one Friday evening with some curry puffs in one hand, and towing Ethan in the other. Having a child around usually helps to break the ice.

She found out that this is Johan and Fadhilah's first home. They had bought it from the resale market instead of directly from the government because they liked the Serangoon neighbourhood.

She very much wanted to ask them how much they paid for their flat as that would give her an indication of how much Teng's flat is worth.

Ah Mah was *kiasu* in that regard. She wanted to ensure that Teng did not lose out by overpaying for his flat. But she didn't know how to ask the new neighbours without seeming to be rude. Little did she know that she could find about the sale price of a unit from the HDB.

Ah Mah invited them for tea – a *gotong royong* of sorts where she'd also invite the neighbours, Professor Sing and his family as well as Josie and Sarah, hoping someone somehow would ask the important question of how much they paid for their flat.

Tea

Ah Mah introduced Johan and Fadhilah to the neighbours.

"Josie, I haven't seen you for so long. Sarah has been a very good girl. She's been studying very hard even when the renovation was going on," said Ah Mah.

"Yes, Auntie. I'd been on work trips. Thank you for keeping an eye on Sarah when I was away. Your herbal teas are wonderful," said a tired Josie.

"Since taking on my new role in the NEA, I've been travelling to different cities to study their pollution standards. My recent trip was to China. I've so many stories to tell you. One day, I'll invite you and Uncle for lunch and we can have a cosy chat. There are some Chinese cities that are so polluted. It's worse than the Singapore River in the old days before it was all cleaned up."

"Oh! So sorry for the noise from the renovation," Fadhilah offered when she overheard that the neighbour was disturbed by the renovation noise.

"No worries. Renovation is to be expected when someone buys a new place. Anyway, I spent most of my time studying in the library instead," said Sarah.

They soon found out that Johan works in a bank and Fadhilah at the HDB. In fact, Fadhilah volunteered that they knew the unit was going up for sale because the previous owner had called the HDB to enquire about the EIP and how that might affect the sale of the unit.

"I was very fortunate," said Fadhilah. "The previous owner called up with this enquiry. It just so happened my colleague who would usually take the call was out for lunch and I was covering for her. I had to explain to him about the transaction price, appraisal value and COV."

"What is COV?" asked Siew Ling. She recalled vaguely that Peter had explained this term to her when they were looking for a flat.

"COV stands for Cash-over-Valuation. It is the difference between the transaction price and appraisal value," explained Fadhilah. "I have here some of the statistics about COV and transaction prices. They're not the latest but they do give some idea of valuation. It's useful to know when you are selling your house."

Fadhilah showed Siew Ling a graph from her smartphone.

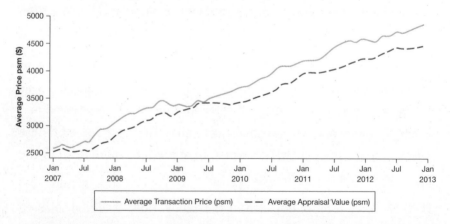

"The solid line is the transacted price. The dashed line is the appraisal value. The difference between the two lines is the COV. Can you see in mid-2009 where the solid and dashed lines are close to each other? That means the COV is negligible."

"Does it mean that if I sell my flat, I'll also get the same COV as you did?" asked Siew Ling further.

"Not necessarily. The buyer and the seller negotiate on what the COV is. Hence, it is unique for each property transaction," was Fadhilah's reply.

"In our case, because of the EIP, there were some considerations," jumped in Johan.

"How so?" asked Professor Sing. He was curious because as a professor in real estate, he wanted to understand deeper how such schemes influence the property market.

"Well," paused Johan. "The EIP is a great scheme for ethnic integration. It's wonderful to have the quota set so that every block has a good mix of different ethnicities, which it should be for a harmonious multiracial country like Singapore.

"But by limiting the supply of new housing units to an ethnic group in a neighbourhood or a block, it inadvertently imposed a constraint on buyers from that ethnic group in the secondary market, while potentially creating housing premiums to sellers of the affected ethnic group."

Seeing a somewhat blank look among some of his neighbours, Johan continued.

"Let me explain. For instance, when a housing block with a concentration of Chinese residents has reached the maximum limit of 87 percent, then a prospective Chinese buyer will not be allowed to buy a resale housing flat from a non-Chinese seller. Why? Because doing so will tilt the balance above 87 percent. This is called binding Chinese quotas.

"So what can a Chinese buyer do if he really wants to live in that block? Well, he can buy a resale flat from Chinese sellers in the block so that the quota will not be breached. This will mean that the Chinese sellers have leverage – there is demand for their flat as the buyer cannot buy it from a non-Chinese. And so, the price is jacked up and the flat is sold at a premium."

Most of the neighbours gave a slight nod to show that they understood.

"So in your case, the previous owner is also a Malay. Did it affect you? Was the quota reached? Did you have to pay a premium?" asked Ah Mah, as she slowly inched to find out how much was paid for the flat.

"We were very fortunate. Fadhilah, tell them about the COV. You know this better than I do," said Johan as he directed his wife to explain.

Since young, Fadhilah has been meticulous and methodical in how she does things. She would organise her clothes in her cabinet very systematically. For folded clothes, the recently washed ones would be placed at the bottom of the pile and not at the top, or else they would always be worn as Johan tends to just pick what's on top to wear. Mugs in the kitchen cabinet are arranged from short to tall. Some may even describe Fadhilah as having OCD (Obsessive Compulsive Disorder). This trait is carried over to her work as well.

"So I work in the HDB, right?" said Fadhilah slowly. "Well, when we were looking for a flat, I did some homework. My colleague in the Transactions Department told me she thought that in HDB blocks where there are many Chinese residents, there also appears to be a high volume of Malay sellers selling to Malay buyers. This is contrary to what Johan just mentioned – if a block has many Chinese residents but it has not reached the limit yet, you would expect Malay sellers to want to sell to Chinese buyers so that they can sell at a higher price, right?

"Instead, my colleague said she thought almost 90 percent of Malay sellers sold their homes to Malay buyers. This means that Malay sellers were willing to accept COV discounts to trade with Malay buyers."

> **Malay sellers were willing to accept COV discounts to trade with Malay buyers.**

"Like in our case," smiled Johan, happy that he had paid a lower COV for the flat.

"During my lunch break, I would calculate the value of this COV discount. On average, an HDB flat is about 97 square metres. So I *agak agak* (estimate) the average cost of an average unit of that size. With the help of my colleague, we estimated that the COV discount for Malay sellers was about $6,000," Fadhilah elaborated.

"Having this information was useful to us because then we know Malay sellers tended to sell at a COV discount. And knowing how much the average COV was, we told ourselves we shouldn't overpay for the unit we buy. So we bargained and reached a great price, at least that's what we think."

"What if one of us had sold the flat to you? Would you still pay a lower COV by buying from a Chinese seller?" asked Professor Sing.

"Unlikely. Malay buyers are unlikely to enjoy COV discounts when buying homes from non-Malay sellers. So luckily I didn't buy the flat from any of you," laughed Fadhilah sweetly. "That's why when I heard that the previous owner was selling and he's a Malay and he wanted to sell to a Malay family, my ears perked up and I was excited."

"Then, how about Chinese sellers? Do they sell to Chinese buyers at lower COV too?" asked Teng as he wanted to protect the value of his flat.

"Relax, relax. You are OK," laughed Fadhilah when she saw the look of concern on Teng's face.

"Teng is like that. He's always worried about property prices. He was even concerned about whether HDB depreciates faster than private properties," said Siew Ling as she recalled Teng pestering Peter for more information about old HDB and depreciation.

"Of course! Like what Peter said, a house is not only for consumption. It's also for investment. And for us, this is a very big investment," defended Teng.

Fadhilah continued. "I completely understand. Well, I was quite a *kaypoh* (busybody). I wanted to know whether this pattern also applies to Chinese buyers. So whenever Johan was working overtime, which is often, I'd also stay back after work to churn out the numbers, just for comparison's sake. Again, these are just estimates.

"Based on my calculation, it looks like Chinese buyers pay an additional COV of $95 per square metre in Chinese quota blocks, and an additional COV of $115 per square metre if the block was subject to the neighbourhood-level Chinese quota.

"So, if the average appraisal valuation is say $4,000 per square metre, then the COV premiums are estimated to range from 2.4 to 2.9 percent."

"What if there is no quota?" asked Professor Sing.

"For blocks without binding Chinese quotas, that means the 87 percent limit has not yet been reached, Chinese buyers would still pay a premium but less. Remember that those with a binding quota paid $95 more on COV. Well, for those without a binding quota, their additional COV was $66 where there is a high concentration of Chinese. The lower the concentration of Chinese, the lower the additional COV I suppose," answered Fadhilah.

"While I was doing my homework on HDB prices, I chanced upon this graph published by a real estate company. You might be interested in this. It shows the average COV and ratio of COV to transaction price from 2007 to 2013."

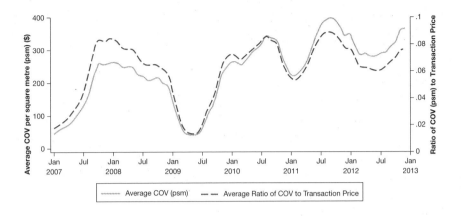

"I'm curious. Where did you get your data from?" asked Professor Sing. His research instincts were prompting him to verify the data.

"If I recall correctly, I think these were public housing resale transaction data from the Singapore Real Estate Exchange, a commercial real estate data company representing 16 leading real estate agencies here. It had information on appraisal value, COV and housing characteristics such as address, postal code, floor, unit size and so on," elaborated Fadhilah.

"Aiyoh! Fadhilah and Johan are our guests, but you all are asking them so many questions. They have no time to eat," cried Ah Mah.

"It's alright, Auntie," smiled Fadhilah. "It's understandable that people are interested in property prices. And I'm from the HDB. I get these questions all the time."

"Yah. My wife is very popular at get-togethers. People are always asking her about the HDB. Me, I'm just a banker. Not very interesting," teased Johan.

"You know, I was quite surprised that there was a very high level of transactions between sellers and buyers from the same ethnic group. It need not be the case. Even my colleague from the Transactions Department who helped me was surprised too. Here, take a look at my rough sketch," said Fadhilah as she showed another graph from her smartphone.

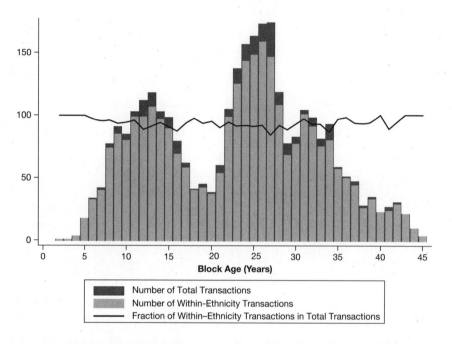

Number of Total Transactions
Number of Within-Ethnicity Transactions
Fraction of Within–Ethnicity Transactions in Total Transactions

Almost 100 percent of transactions are conducted between sellers and buyers of the same ethnicity.

Almost 100 percent of transactions are conducted between sellers and buyers of the same ethnicity, regardless of the age of the unit.

"This is your own sketch?" asked a surprised Siew Ling at how detailed Fadhilah is. "It must have taken you a long time to do this up."

"I told you I have quite a few free evenings when Johan works late. So I occupy myself doing this. I have Excel files with all these data.

Anyway, my colleague was very helpful and gathered some data for me too," was Fadhilah's reply.

"Hmm . . . I wonder why our previous neighbour sold their flat to you? It's not that we don't like you. Please don't be mistaken," Professor Sing quickly added, just in case his new neighbours were offended.

"What I meant is they could have waited to sell their homes to Chinese buyers instead, especially since the quota had not been reached. Then they wouldn't be selling their house at a discounted COV and make more money instead. Strange."

"I see your point, Prof Sing," responded Johan. "As a finance person, I'm curious too."

"I think I may know why," said Sarah, who had been keeping quiet but going through her mind the psyche of these sellers. She was trying to apply what she had read in psychology to the selling phenomenon.

"Perhaps there's a bias. Although the units are the same when HDB sells them brand new, the renovations and decorations made to them may appeal to certain groups of people. No offense, but maybe Chinese buyers don't fancy how the place was done up when they see a Malay home. So knowing that it's difficult to sell to Chinese buyers, a Malay seller may not bother to sell to them. Instead, he sells to a Malay buyer because it's easier."

"That's what I thought too but my colleague said she didn't think so," responded Fadhilah. "She reminded me that non-Malays also included Indians. Yet, Malay sellers still prefer to sell to Malay buyers and at a COV discount.

"Instead, she told me that probably, there's something to do with housing search not being an easy process. We don't buy and sell houses all the time. Perhaps maybe two or three times in our lifetime. As such, we are not experienced and are likely to incur high costs in finding a suitable home.

"So what would help make the search for the ideal home more seamless? Perhaps the community – the ethnic social environment where people speak the same language and come from similar educational backgrounds. These ethnic social networks could have improved the matching of sellers and buyers from the same ethnic group. And this may have encouraged within-ethnicity transactions."

"And perhaps real estate agents specialise in ethnic groups, too," Professor Sing chimed in. "For example, agents can create customised real estate Web portals that serve only a selected ethnic community. They maintain a client base consisting of buyers and sellers from the same ethnic group. They also reach out to the networks of other agents servicing the same ethnic group."

"Wow, Professor Sing! You read my colleague's mind," exclaimed Fadhilah. "She told me exactly what you just said – that agents could have been the reason behind high within-ethnicity transactions.

"She said that it seemed real estate agents specialise in servicing a selected ethnic group. And when they have a high ethnic concentration in their customer base, they tended to be less competitive and work in a large agency company.

"And she may be right because before we bought this unit, we were looking around and the agents interested in helping us find a flat were Malays. They seemed to know which units are owned by Malays. They knew the Malay community well.

"And I suspected that their clients seemed older too. Whenever we see a unit, the sellers were old people. Don't you think so, Johan?"

Johan nodded in agreement. He was contented to let his wife do the talking.

"I shouldn't complain because it worked well for us as buyers," continued Fadhilah. "But these agents indirectly contributed to a higher volume of within-ethnicity transactions via their ethnic social networks, which comes at the expense of their seller customers because of the lower COVs."

"So when we sell our house, we shouldn't be using a Malay agent. He may not get us the best price," Johan reminded Fadhilah.

"Then I should introduce you to Peter our friend who is a property agent," recommended Teng. "But hey! Why are you talking about selling when you've just bought your place?"

Everyone laughed.

WANT TO KNOW MORE?

This chapter is based on Sumit Agarwal, Choi Hyun-Soo, He Jia and Sing Tien Foo (2019), "Matching in Housing Markets: The Role of Ethnic Social Networks," *The Review of Financial Studies*, Vol. 32 (10), pp. 3958-4004, https://academic.oup.com/rfs/advance-article/doi/10.1093/rfs/hhz006/5305593

CHAPTER 8

Thy Neighbour's Misfortune

"Teng, I like that the government has ethnic integration plans for the HDB," said Siew Ling thoughtfully one day, shortly after the welcome tea Ah Mah had organised for Johan and Fadhilah, their new neighbours. "It's good for all to be familiar with one another's culture, and especially for Ethan and Ervin. They'll learn to appreciate Singapore's diverse heritage."

"I agree. If it's all Chinese neighbours around us, then the kids only know about Chinese New Year. Now with Johan and Fadhilah just a few doors away, the boys can learn about Hari Raya when they celebrate. You know, we should have gotten to know better our previous neighbour. We hardly talked to them," replied Teng.

"They were very quiet, though. They kept to themselves all the time. Sometimes, I even wondered whether the flat was occupied," sighed Siew Ling with a tinge of regret that she didn't try hard enough to know their previous neighbour. But she thought Johan and Fadhilah were more engaging and personable. And hopefully, they would be seeing each other more often.

Ah Mah joined in the conversation. "Talking about neighbours, did you hear about the uncle who lives upstairs on the 4th floor?"

"You mean the one who's still working but soon to retire? About 60 years old? Kind of on the skinny side and somewhat hunched?" asked Siew Ling as she tried to recall her neighbours living the floor above.

"That's right. That's the one," Ah Mah nodded. "I heard he's in financial difficulties. I think he's been made a bankrupt!"

Ah Mah started to relate how she got to know of this unfortunate incident. "In fact, some time ago, I thought there was something wrong already because he seemed hagged and I could hear quarrels from his flat. But I didn't think much about it.

"Then the other day when I was at the market, the lady from whom I always buy my *toufu* asked me whether I live in Block 102. I thought it strange that she asked but I replied yes. Then she told me that one of my neighbours just became a bankrupt. She said that the uncle had lost all his money. His wife is so sad. She cried to the *toufu* seller."

"Oh no! How could this have happened?" asked a concerned Siew Ling.

"Apparently, the uncle is a compulsive gambler. Not only did he spend a lot of time in both casinos as well as gambling on 4D lottery and going to the horse races, he was also very much into speculating in the stock market," Ah Mah said.

"Hmm . . . Come to think of it, I recalled overhearing him tell another neighbour about horse racing – win, place, tierce bets. I didn't understand what these were," remarked Siew Ling.

"Let me explain to you," volunteered Teng. "These are different kinds of bets. A 'win' bet means you bet that the horse will win. If the horse comes in 2nd or 3rd, you lose your bet. A 'place' means you bet that the horse will come in either 1st, 2nd or 3rd. So long as the horse finishes in any of these positions, you win your bet."

Teng paused for a moment to see whether his wife and mother understood.

"So it's harder to win a 'win' bet than a 'place' bet. I'm *kiasu*. I would bet a 'place' than a 'win'. Does it mean that the money is higher for a 'win' than a 'place' bet?" asked Siew Ling.

"Definitely. And it's called 'dividend' not money. Dividend is the return you get when you win," corrected Teng. "Now, for 'tierce'. A 'tierce' is when you bet on which are the first three horses that will finish the race in the correct order. So if you bet Horse A will come in 1st, Horse B comes in 2nd and Horse C comes in 3rd, they must finish in exactly that order for you to win your bet."

"Wow! That is so tough. It's almost impossible to win. So the dividend must be very high for tierce bets," responded Ah Mah. Ah Mah has been doing her own bit of social gambling. She'd occasionally go to the Singapore Pools outlet next to the market to place a 4D bet.

"How do you know so much about horse racing?" asked a stunned Siew Ling. She had never before heard Teng talk about gambling, let alone horse racing.

"Don't worry, dear. I learnt it from my passengers. When they win at the races, they take taxis home! So on some race days, I would be at the Turf Club waiting for these 'winning' passengers," reassured Teng.

"These passengers told me that more people bet when there are more horses in a race. Some races have eight horses, some 10 horses. I guess different people have different favourite horses and so when there are more horses, people have more opportunities to bet.

"More people also tended to bet in later than earlier races. Maybe some got to the Turf Club later and so missed the first few races. Or they were just getting warmed up and betted small in the earlier part of the day and started to bet more later. Or some won in the earlier races and that gave them confidence to bet more in later races. Or they lost in earlier races and to make up for the losses, they betted even more in later races."

"Or, the Turf Club wants people to stay there longer and continue betting and so they put the more exciting races at the later part of the day," quipped Siew Ling.

"Interesting, right?" smiled Teng as his wife never ceased to amaze him. "Of course, if the race is competitive with more horses that are of similar good quality, like they had finished in the top 3 in their last race, more bettors would bet. All these mean more revenue for the Turf Club.[1]

"Come to think of it, the uncle upstairs seems to fit the profile of a heavy gambler. Some of my passengers bet a great deal.

"There was once this man, about 55 to 65 years old. He was in my taxi. Now, he might have been exaggerating. But he told me that in a year, he would have betted almost $300,000! That's like don't-know-how-many-times my earnings! It's out of this world. And yet, when I look at how he dressed and talked, I didn't think he had that much money to spend."

"Don't you think betting on horse racing and buying 4D and so on can lead to bankruptcy? If so, why does the government still allow them to operate?" asked Siew Ling.

"Well, if people want to gamble they will gamble, no matter what. By hook or by crook, they'll find a way to gamble. And now, there's illegal gambling available, especially online," answered Teng.

---

[1] Sumit Agarwal, Ang Swee Hoon, Jussi Keppo and Song Changcheng (2018), "Impact of Race Characteristics on Revenue," Powerpoint presentation to Turf Club.

"If there is no legal gambling such as through Turf Club or Singapore Pools, people will just go to illegal bookies and the consequences can be even worse. Remember those *Ah Long* (loan sharks) who sprayed paint on the doors and walls of people who owe them money from gambling?

"So having these legal operators actually soaks up part of the illegal market. And that's good because the earnings from Turf Club and Singapore Pools are channelled to fund sports, education and community development."

"Yah, Teng, I remember seeing some sports events that were sponsored by Singapore Pools. And I think charitable organisations like Club Rainbow also benefit from them," said Siew Ling. "But regardless, people shouldn't get carried away with gambling."

"Ma, what else do you know about the uncle?" asked Teng.

"Well, I don't think he earns much. But I think he spends more than he makes. The women neighbours were talking about him in the void deck below. Some men about the same age as the uncle's age also joined in. I heard one of the aunties said that she had noticed he betted on almost anything – even on whether the person who comes out when the lift door opens is a man or a woman. Like what you said, if someone wants to gamble, he will gamble no matter what. There are so many stories I've been hearing about him from these women," said Ah Mah.

"Ma, it seems like the women are the ones gossiping about it," observed Teng, thinly veiling his disapproval of gossips.

"Well, we women socialise more. So we know what's going on and are more attuned to what's happening. You men are quieter and quite blur about what's going on," was Ah Mah's retort.

"Teng, this reminds me of Muthu. He also became a bankrupt but not because he gambled away his money but because he wanted to get rich quick. So he took a lot of risks. All his businesses went bust and he got played out by his partner. Remember?"[2] as Siew Ling reminded Teng of his primary school classmate. Teng, Peter and Muthu used to be tight.

Teng was solemn on hearing yet another case of bankruptcy involving someone he actually knew. It was a disturbing reminder of how fortunes can swiftly turn if one is not careful.

Bankruptcy in Singapore

Singapore has very strict rules regulating bankruptcy. Bankrupt individuals need to pay back their debt under government supervision. They are also prohibited from consuming anything beyond subsistence needs for an extended period of time. Hence, going on vacation, traveling by taxi or buying luxury products are prohibited unless consent is given by the creditors.

Personal bankruptcy is also public information as this is published in the Government Gazette. This implies the possibility of social stigma when an individual is made a bankrupt. In Singapore, where traditional Asian values run deep, bankrupts are often labelled as irresponsible spenders.

As such, bankruptcy has severe consequences. Not only do bankrupts lose almost all their assets, but post-bankruptcy, they also have very little to spend.

---

[2] For more on this research on bankruptcy profiling and behaviour in Singapore, see Sumit Agarwal, Ang Swee Hoon and Sing Tien Foo (2018), *Kiasunomics: Stories of Singaporean Economic Behaviours*, Chapter 7 "Muthu, Don't Be Reckless," (Singapore: World Scientific Publishers). To read the academic article, see Sumit Agarwal, He Jia, Sing Tien Foo and Zhang Jien (2018), "Gender Gap in Personal Bankruptcy Risks: Empirical Evidence from Singapore," *Review of Finance*, Vol. 22 (2), pp. 813-847, https://www.researchgate.net/publication/326877992_Gender_Gap_in_Personal_Bankruptcy_Risks_ Empirical_Evidence_from_Singapore. This research was also published as a commentary, see Sumit Agarwal, Sing Tien Foo and Zhang Jien, "Gender gap in bankruptcy risks: Its meaning for policy at home, at work," *The Business Times*, (6 December 2016), https://www.businesstimes.com.sg/opinion/ gender-gap-in-bankruptcy-risks-its-meaning-for-policy-at-home-at-work

One of the few assets that bankrupt individuals in Singapore can keep is their main residence if it is a public housing flat. They can continue living in the HDB flat and maintain social ties with their neighbours.

Social Interactions

And such social ties can be easily maintained in Singapore especially in HDB flats. Housing estates have shared amenities such as schools, wet markets, food courts, clinics, libraries and sports and recreational facilities where people socialise. The Singapore Government also fosters community bonding in HDB towns by providing facilities and community spaces for residents to mingle and interact.

A survey found that among HDB residents, almost all (97.8 percent) wanted to maintain good neighbourly relationships.[3] They interacted by striking up casual conversations, shopping together, borrowing/ lending household items, helping to buy groceries and even looking after each other's children. The survey also indicated that 75 percent of these interactions took place among neighbours living in the same block, usually along the common corridor, lift lobbies and the open space on the ground floor of each block.

The Study

Given such cohesive neighbourly ties among HDB residents and the social stigma associated with personal bankruptcy, might there be peer influence of a bankrupt neighbour on the spending patterns of residents living in the same block? In other words, might there be a social multiplier effect?

A team of professors and their PhD student from NUS Business School wanted to investigate this possible social multiplier effect on residents

---

[3] "Public Housing in Singapore: Social Well-Being of HDB Communities," *HDB Sample Household Survey 2013*, Housing & Development Board, https://www.singstat.gov.sg/find-data/search-by-theme/ households/households/external-sources

living in the same block as the bankrupt. They studied the spending behaviours of residents over a two-year period before and after their neighbour's bankruptcy.

Several datasets were used. The bankruptcy data on personal bankruptcy cases were obtained from the Supreme Court of Singapore. The second dataset was a unique proprietary dataset on Singaporean residents including gender, ethnicity, age and residence. The last dataset was also proprietary with information on individual consumption using their chequing accounts, credit cards and debit cards.

Over 1,600 bankruptcy cases were studied together with 17,000 of their neighbours living in the same block. The professors studied their spending patterns before and after the bankruptcy occurred to see whether their neighbour's bankruptcy affected their expenditure.

The Findings

The NUS Business professors found peer effect to be at work. Compared to their average spending during the 12 months and two months before the bankruptcy occurred, people living in the same block as the bankrupted individual spent almost 3.5 percent less per month on their credit and debit cards after the bankruptcy incident. Both credit card and debit card spending saw similar decreases.

This is unlike people living in nearby blocks within 100 metres from the bankruptcy-hit block. The professors found that for such residents, there was no change in their expenditures. They do not live in the same block and therefore, the peer effect was negligible.

> [M]ore than 20 percent of the neighbours living in the same block as the bankrupt individual decreased their average monthly spending ...

Moreover, relative to people living further away in other blocks, more than 20 percent of the neighbours living in the same block as the bankrupt individual decreased their average monthly spending by up to 5 percent of their pre-bankruptcy monthly income when they heard about the bankruptcy.

Women and Age Cohort

Who are these same-block neighbours who were affected by a neighbour's bankruptcy?

The professors thought that perhaps neighbours who were more sensitive to or aware of their neighbour's dire situation were more likely to be affected. These people were more active in social interaction directly or indirectly with the bankrupted neighbour.

They identified two types of such more sensitive neighbours: (1) women, who are usually more socially minded than men and thus engage more actively in the neighbourhood; and (2) neighbours around the same age as the bankrupted individual, specifically plus or minus four years, as they are likely to have closer social ties or stronger peer pressure together.

Indeed, the professors found that these same-block neighbours were more affected by the bankruptcy. Women living in the same block decreased their expenditure by 7 percent more. In contrast, men in the same block did not experience any change in their card spending.

Similarly, among neighbours who were four years older or younger than the bankrupted individual, their spending went down by 7 percent, which is 6 percent more than neighbours less close in age to the bankrupt.

Again, these findings support that there was peer effect and that the social multiplier took place.

Private Residences

While the above findings concerned HDB residents, the NUS Business professors also studied bankrupts whose main residence is a private property. According to the law, unlike those who live in HDB flats and can continue to do so upon bankruptcy, such private-residence bankrupts have to move out and liquidate their residence. Moving out means their social connections with their neighbours living in the same private block would be diminished. In which case, the peer effect observed among HDB residents may be negligible among private property residents.

Indeed so. The professors found that expenditure did not decrease for neighbours of bankrupted individuals from the private housing market as there was no peer effect given that the social connection among the neighbours with the moved-out bankrupted individual has diminished.

Keeping Up with the Joneses

The NUS Business professors also wanted to assess the psychological motivation underlying peer effect in such spending behaviour. They studied the neighbours' purchases of visible products and non-visible products. Visible products are those that are conspicuous where others can see such purchases. This includes apparel, cars and jewellery. They also studied the value of each single purchase to assess conspicuousness.

If the neighbours were, as the saying goes, keeping up with the Joneses, then when a neighbour became bankrupt and had less to spend, the other neighbours would likewise spend less on both conspicuous and less conspicuous items in line with the bankrupted neighbour to keep up (or in this case, keep down) with him.

Their results showed that 'keeping up with the Joneses' was at work. Neighbours proportionately reduced their spending on conspicuous

or status-driven purchases as well as non-visible purchases just like their neighbour after he went bankrupt.

> '[K]eeping up with the Joneses' was at work.

Ah Mah and Her Friends

Ah Mah met the neighbours the next day. It was their *tai chi* lesson held at the void deck as it was raining. The *tai chi* lessons were attended by a group of women who used these lessons as a way to socialise and catch up on happenings in the neighbourhood. A few retired men also participated in these lessons.

In between breaks, they gathered to talk about the bankrupted uncle. He never joined them at *tai chi* because he was busy spending his time at the casinos, but the older men knew him as he would interest them to buy lottery tickets or join him at the casinos.

"I feel sad for his wife. I saw her the other day. It looked like she'd been crying. Her eyes were all puffed up. He's so irresponsible to leave his wife in debt. And at this old age, he should have known better," said the first woman neighbour.

"Hey! Please don't say like that. The family is already ashamed of his bankruptcy. We shouldn't make it worse for them," said another woman neighbour.

"Thankfully the law doesn't require him to sell his HDB flat. Otherwise, where will he live? At least with the flat, he can still live in this community," said a third woman neighbour. This neighbour is savvy and the most affluent of them all. Although she lives in a flat, she has a private property that she rents out. Among the women, she would be the one who spends most on brand name clothes, bags and shoes.

"Whatever it is, we must remember to curb our spending. I think this uncle's bankruptcy is a timely reminder to us to be careful of how we spend our money," Ah Mah said.

"I'm one step ahead of you," teased the first woman neighbour. "Now, every time I go to the wet market to buy my meat and vegetables, I'd think twice whether I am spending unnecessarily."

"Me too," added the second woman neighbour. "The other day, I had the urge to buy 4D. But I stopped myself when I thought of our bankrupted neighbour. I think I saved myself $10 every week so far."

Ah Mah thought to herself, "I should try not to buy 4D. I don't want to get addicted to it and find myself spending more than I have."

"Aiyah! These are small purchases," joined in the third woman neighbour. "The other day, I was at Paragon and I saw this beautiful handbag. It was quite pricey at over $1,000. And it wasn't even leather. But it had this brand name on it. I really loved it. But I kept thinking about bankruptcy. And that stopped me from buying it. My heart was quite torn."

Everyone agreed. The women said they seemed to have tightened their belt in light of the uncle's bankruptcy. They wondered who else knew about his bankruptcy. The younger residents didn't seem to be aware of or interested in what's happening. In fact, they were quite nonchalant.

"The other evening, when my children came home from work, I reminded them to be more careful in the use of their credit cards. I find my children are quite the spendthrifts. Even though they are working, they ought to save more," said the first woman neighbour. "But do you know what they said when I told them about the bankrupted uncle. They said, 'The uncle is so much older than us. We're different from him. This won't happen to us.' So arrogant."

"Yes, true true. I think the young people cannot relate to the uncle and recognise that they could become a bankrupt too. Only people in the same generation as the uncle will empathise with him and learn from his misfortune," agreed the second woman neighbour.

"You are right," joined in a male neighbour about the same age as the bankrupted uncle. "We used to chit chat every now and then. There was a group of us, about the same age, hanging around in the evenings drinking some beer. We would talk about a lot of things and sometimes, he would try to get us interested in gambling.

"Now that we know about his misfortune, I'm sure it will hit us hard. It could have happened to any one of us. I think the rest of us who hung out together would be more watchful of our expenses so that we don't fall into a similar fate."

"You know, I think we should help each other by reminding one another not to overspend," suggested the first woman neighbour.

"That's a great idea," chimed in the second woman neighbour. "When you see me buy unnecessary things like lottery tickets, please remind me of our bankrupted neighbour so that I won't get carried away. I think having each other around to influence us to be watchful of our expenses may be more effective than just self-reminders."

And with that, they all agreed and continued with their *tai chi* lesson.

WANT TO KNOW MORE?

This chapter is based on Sumit Agarwal, Qian Wenlan and Zou Xin (2017), "They Neighbor's Misfortune: Peer Effect on Consumption," Working Paper, National University of Singapore, https://papers.ssrn.com/sol3/papers.cfm?abstract_id=2780764

Like Father, Like Son?

With the two bankrupt cases of Muthu and more recently the neighbour etched in his mind, Teng was in a somewhat pensive mood. There were too many things bothering him – the economy, his takings, daily expenses. He felt his mind was perpetually running on a hamster wheel. He had brushed these concerns aside only to be irritated by a persistent gnawing that these issues could potentially hurt his livelihood.

Just the other day when he was reading the newspapers, there was an ad by a local bank headlined "60% of parents in their 30s find it tough in meeting both their parents' and children's needs." Teng didn't need to be reminded of that. He knew he could potentially have a financial problem. He just wasn't sure how to avoid it.

For one, he was concerned that his mortgage interest might be caught up with rising interest rates. Although the interest rate hike possibility now appeared remote compared to a few months ago, Teng knew only too well that the world economy hung on a delicate balance.

His taxi-driving future also looked dim. With fewer people flagging down cabs at the kerb and the pending distance-based road charges, Teng thought he would probably be cruising less to pick up passengers to save costs. But this would affect his daily takings. And there was the occasional haze like the one in August that threatens business and tourism. He might have to take up those SkillsFuture courses that Peter had been talking about to prepare himself for another job.

Looking at the economy, Teng wasn't encouraged either. The United Kingdom is mired in the Brexit conundrum, the EU is floundering, China's economy is slowing down, and the United States, amid its political crisis, has its on-off disputes with China and North Korea. And added to this are the tensions in the Gulf, and the unrest in Hong Kong. Negative outcomes of any of these events could have a crushing effect on the economic system. Singapore's GDP (Gross Domestic Product) growth for the first two quarters of 2019 came in lower than expected and narrowly missed a technical recession in the third quarter. The general consensus is that the forecast will be revised downwards for the year.[1]

Teng recalled hearing a news report about mortgage rates while driving along the PIE (Pan Island Expressway). Although it was a research conducted in China, he remembered he was struck by its findings. The researchers found that when China suddenly reduced interest rates which in turn, reduced the interest expenses of mortgagors, this 'windfall' news led to increased credit card spending. Even cash-constrained individuals spent more.[2]

---

[1] Janice Lim, "Economists downgrade 2019 growth forecast for Singapore: MAS survey," *Today*, (12 June 2019), https://www.todayonline.com/singapore/economists-downgrade-2019-growth-forecast-singapore-mas-survey; Seow Bei Yi, "Q2 growth slumps; full-year recession not expected, says Heng," The Straits Times, (13 July 2019), p. 1; Sue-Ann Tan, "Singapore narrowly dodges technical recession as economy grows 0.1% in Q3: Flash data," *The Straits Times*, (14 October 2019), https://www.straitstimes.com/business/economy/singapore-narrowly-dodges-technical-recession-as-economy-grows-01-in-q3-flash-data

[2] For more on this research, see Sumit Agarwal, Deng Yongheng, Gu Quanlin, He Jia, Qian Wenlan and Ren Yuan (2019), "Mortgage Debt, Hand-to-Mouth Households, and Monetary Policy Transmission," Working Paper, National University of Singapore, https://papers.ssrn.com/sol3/papers.cfm?abstract_id=3298878

Teng had told himself that if it were him, he would be more disciplined. He would not spend all the loan-payment savings enjoyed from an interest rate cut, should that ever come about. The economy is way too uncertain and fragile, shifting between growth and recession like a pendulum.

"This 'windfall' reduction in interest rates in China seems similar to cash bonuses that the Singapore Government had given to its citizens," Teng thought. Both were surprise announcements that its citizens did not anticipate.

He recalled not too long ago when the Singapore Government gave out cash bonuses to adult Singaporeans. At that time, an election year, adult Singaporeans received a one-time payout ranging from $600 to $800 depending on their income and annual home value in what was called the Growth Dividend Programme. It represented a significant income bonus of about 18 percent of monthly median income at the time. A total of $1.5 billion was given out.

How times have changed. How Teng has changed. Young and carefree then, he was quite impulsive and had even encouraged Siew Ling to spend the 'windfall' from the Growth Dividend Programme ahead of receiving the actual cash.[3] Now, he holds a somewhat different perspective.

The gnawing reminder came back and Teng remembered that his HDB flat may be depreciating as it ages. After Peter had shared the findings that HDB flats do not depreciate as fast as private leasehold properties, he had made a mental note to check how old his flat is. Yet he had

---

[3] For more on the research regarding the effects of the Growth Dividend Programme on Singaporeans' spending, see Sumit Agarwal, Ang Swee Hoon and Sing Tien Foo (2018), *Kiasunomics: Stories of Singaporean Economic Behaviours*, Chapter 5 "Gentlemen, Start Your Engines," (Singapore: World Scientific Publishers). To read the academic article, see Sumit Agarwal and Qian Wenlan (2014), "Consumption and Debt Response to Unanticipated Income Shocks: Evidence from a Natural Experiment in Singapore," *American Economic Review*, Vol. 104 (12), pp. 4205-4230, https://www.aeaweb. org/articles?id=10.1257/aer.104.12.4205. This research was also published as a commentary, see Sumit Agarwal, "Government rebates: Spend or save?" *The Straits Times*, (8 June 2013), https://www. straitstimes.com/singapore/govt-rebates-spend-or-save

not got around to doing it. His procrastination had seen more and more of these seemingly minor but important issues pile up. Teng also wanted to know how much of his mortgage loan was outstanding. He wanted to be prepared should there be a sudden turn of events.

Being a *kiasu* father, Teng wondered how he could get his family one step higher in the social ladder. How could he provide a better life for Ethan and Ervin? Would his sons have more opportunities than he had in terms of studies? Career? Property ownership? What could he do to give them a springboard in life? Do families similar to his ever move up the social ladder, even if it were just one step at a time?

The Social Leveller

The Singapore Government is mindful of the need to tackle social inequality. It wants everyone to continue to progress. One social leveller is education. Among senior Singaporeans in their 50s, over 60 percent do not

> **[W]ith a better educated population, individual progress is by meritocracy.**

have more than a secondary school education.[4] But Singapore has transformed its education system to benefit the younger generation. Primary education is compulsory. The quality of education is unquestionable. From the MOE (Ministry of Education) perspective, every school is a good school. And with a better educated population, individual progress is by meritocracy.

But the nature of meritocracy makes safeguarding social mobility more challenging. For example, parents who have done well will engage private tutors for their children to ensure that they do better.

---

[4] "To tackle inequality, ensure everyone is progressing: Tharman," *The Straits Times*, (26 October 2018), https://www.straitstimes.com/singapore/to-tackle-inequality-ensure-everyone-is-progressing-tharman

Parents who have not done so well will find the odds stacked against their children doing better in life.

The MOE has identified three issues arising from Singapore's progress that could be potential stumbling blocks to mobility: (1) material progress becoming more difficult for the middle class, (2) risks of stratification becoming entrenched in successful families who pass down these privileges to the next generation while the less privileged families find it harder to uplift themselves, and (3) segments of Singaporeans becoming more socially distant along socio-economic lines.[5]

The NUS Talk

Teng had discussed these issues with Siew Ling before. Both were honest with themselves. They were more than aware of the harsh reality of not being able to afford all the privileges they wanted.

But there were times when Teng felt he needed a third party's perspective. Peter had always been his go-to confidant. Growing up together as classmates since they were six years old and coming from a similar socio-economic station in life, Peter could empathise with Teng.

Knowing his friend's concern, Peter called him up one day. "Teng, I read in the papers that NUS is holding this talk on wealth mobility. It's titled 'Like Father, Like Son? Inter-generational Housing Wealth Mobility.'"

"Hey! That sounds exactly like what was concerning me. I don't want Ethan or Ervin to be just like me. I want them to be better off than me," said an excited Teng in a more hurried tone.

---

[5] Than Yuen-C, "Parliament: Tackling inequality is national priority, says Ong Ye Kung," *The Straits Times*, (15 May 2018), https://www.straitstimes.com/politics/parliament-tackling-inequality-is-national-priority-says-ong-ye-kung

"This is at NUS? Can we attend? We did not graduate from there," said Teng as he was reminded that he and Peter had only 'O' level academic qualifications, nowhere near the smart brains from NUS.

"It's OK. The advertisement says it is open to the public. We are members of the public, right?" Peter responded. "And anyway, such research should benefit everyone, not just selected people."

"You are right. It's good to know what the professors have found and that they wanted to share their insights with the society," agreed Teng.

"And Teng, was the professor you had as a passenger years ago . . . the one who advised you about budgeting and financial planning . . . is his name Sumit Agarwal?" asked Peter. "He's one of the speakers!"

"Wow! It would be nice to meet him again. Sing, my neighbour from NUS, had told me that Professor Agarwal also does research on China and India. Now, he's doing research on wealth mobility too?" remarked Teng as he felt what a good fortune it was to have met Professor Agarwal. "Can I bring Siew Ling along for the talk? How do we sign up?"

Housing Wealth Mobility

Teng, Siew Ling and Peter arrived early at the Hon Sui Sen Memorial Auditorium next to the NUS Business School. They wanted to get good seats. And knowing how sprawling NUS is, they wanted to be sure that they wouldn't be late, although Teng had assured the other two that as a taxi driver, he had driven through the NUS campus many times and he knew where the auditorium was.

The auditorium filled up quickly. Some chairs had to be added at the back and along the aisles to accommodate as many people as possible. It seemed that almost all who had registered for the talk had shown up. The attrition rate was quite low.

"I think everyone is interested to know whether their children will do better than them," whispered Siew Ling to Teng. "Luckily we came early," as she saw ushers asking the audience to move to the centre seats so that latecomers can easily find empty seats at the sides.

The talk began on the dot at the time stated in the advertisement. An emcee instructed the audience to post questions on the Pigeonhole Live app. Pigeonhole Live is a mobile, real-time question-and-answer tool that allows the audience to post and vote for questions using their smartphones.

"Good afternoon, everyone," began Professor Agarwal. "Thank you for coming this Saturday afternoon as we share what my co-researchers and I have found concerning a topic that I believe is very important and close to our hearts – wealth mobility. In other words, how do our children fare in terms of wealth compared to us parents? This is what is termed inter-generational wealth mobility.

"With the permission of my colleague, I'm going to tell you this true story to start off this talk. Over lunch one day, my colleague Swee Hoon mentioned that she came from a humble background. Both her parents did not complete their PSLE (Primary School Leaving Examination). Her father was a daily-rated worker, holding down three jobs to feed his homemaker wife and three kids. They lived in a small three-room flat at Commonwealth. As the kids grew up and expenses mounted, and her father became less able to handle three jobs, all five of them would sleep in one room and rent the other room out for extra income.

"Since then, Swee Hoon and her brothers have come a long way. All of them received a tertiary education, sponsored in part through scholarships and bursaries, and the help of generous relatives. They may be poor, but they are certainly not short on brains. Each of them became a professional, well established in their careers. They and their respective families no longer live in a three-room HDB flat. They are comfortable. And they certainly have progressed.

"So that got me thinking. Obviously for Swee Hoon and her siblings, they have moved up compared to their parents. There was inter-generational upward mobility. And as responsible parents, we want to see our children grow up in a better environment than we had. We want to see them receive better education than we had, have better career prospects than we had, lead a more comfortable life than we have enjoyed, and so on. We want the best for our kids.

"But does upward wealth mobility occur for everyone? Are there only some Singaporeans who become better off? Or does the next generation become worse off? What would encourage upwardly mobility for the next generation?"

Teng and Siew Ling were particularly glued on what Professor Agarwal had said so far. This was exactly what Teng wanted to know. He could totally identify with the professor's colleague. Would Ethan and Ervin have a more comfortable life than he had? He hopes so.

Professor Agarwal continued. "Let me also be clear about what I mean by wealth mobility. Wealth consists of many factors – liquid assets such as cash, and less liquid assets such as stocks, cars and properties. Specific to our research, we studied housing wealth mobility.

"You might ask why only housing wealth mobility. For one, wealth is a very personal and confidential matter and we do not have data concerning those parts of wealth that are private and cannot be observed.

"Property, on the other hand, is visible and there are available public data to assess its value. Notwithstanding this, property in land-scarce Singapore is expensive. Most Singaporeans have to take up a mortgage loan to buy their property with loan periods of 20 to 30 years. This means that most of their savings and salaries during much of their working life is poured into the property. As such, property makes up the bulk of a Singaporean's wealth, and in all likelihood would be a reasonable indicator of overall wealth."

Teng nodded. He understood the rationale.

The Data

To measure housing wealth, Professor Agarwal and his colleagues studied all residential property transactions in both the public and private housing markets from 1995 to 2018, adjusting the transaction price to 2014 Singapore dollars to account for inflation. The data also included each resident's gender, age, ethnic group, housing type and address.

They focused on the 1965-1984 birth cohorts – people born during this period – to identify parent-child pairs not residing together as well as those residing in the same address. The age difference between parent and child ranged from 18 to 45 years.

The Findings

"We generated heat maps for children's housing wealth distribution conditional on whether their parents came from the bottom 60th, 60th to 80th, or top 20th percentile ranks," said Professor Agarwal as he elaborated on the analyses.

He thought he had the audience in his hands. They seemed riveted and wanted to know whether they fell in the category of upward mobility. But he took pleasure in milking the moment.

"Come on. Hurry up," thought Teng. He couldn't be bothered how Professor Agarwal got the data or how he analysed it. He trusted that the data were correctly analysed. Otherwise, why would the professor dare to share it in a public talk and risk his reputation.

Siew Ling tightened her grip on her handbag, anxious and excited.

Not to hold his audience in suspense any longer, Professor Agarwal spoke slowly but clearly, with the authority of someone who knew his research inside out.

"Let me show you the overall findings. This concerns parents and children who do not live together. The bottom horizontal axis is the percentile of the parents' housing wealth. And the vertical axis is the percentile of the children's housing wealth when they no longer live with their parents. Now, what does 'percentile' mean? If you are at the bottom percentile, say 20th percentile, it means 80 percent of your cohort is richer than you in terms of housing wealth."

Professor Agarwal's eyes spanned the audience to make sure they understood. Then he continued. He flashed the first graph onto the screen.

"In the figure, the straight line at an angle of 45° means the parent and child remained the same in their respective housing wealth. That means there is no upward or downward inter-generational mobility.

"The curvy line is our findings of where children's housing wealth stands relative to their parents."

A few in the audience gasped. Professor Agarwal could hear murmuring. Obviously, some of the parents knew how to interpret the findings. Others were still at a complete loss.

"You can see from the figure that to the left of the 60th percentile at the bottom, the curvy line is above the straight 45° solid line. This means children's housing wealth is higher than their parents.

"These are children who grew up in grassroots families – families where the parents are in the bottom 60th percentile of housing wealth. They demonstrated the greatest upward mobility in housing wealth."

> **[C]hildren who grew up in grassroots families … demonstrated the greatest upward mobility in housing wealth.**

"Yes!" said Teng underneath his breath, with a slight fist bump on the arm of the chair. He was relieved.

Professor Agarwal paused, waiting for the audience to absorb the information. "Remember my colleague Swee Hoon? She and her brothers are the children in this group. They came from the bottom 60th percentile of parents but have made good, even better than their parents.

"This finding is consistent with an earlier study showing that among children born to parents in the bottom 20 percent of incomes, over 14 percent reached the top 20 percent of income. This is almost double that observed in the United States (7.5 percent), and above that found in the United Kingdom (9 percent), Denmark (11.7 percent) and Canada (13.5 percent).[6]

"Now, I want to compare the grassroots wealth mobility pattern with that of Scandinavian countries where the pattern is similar, and see if we can draw some insights. In these countries, there is high equality of opportunities.

---

[6] Raj Chetty (2015), "Improving Equality of Opportunity in America: New Evidence and Policy Lessons," *The Boston Foundation*, https://www.tbf.org/-/media/tbforg/files/forum-presentations/chetty-oppor-tunity-and-education-slides.pdf; *Ministry of Finance*, https://www.mof.gov.sg/Newsroom/Speeches/The-Economic-Society-of-Singapore-SG50-Distinguished-Lecture-by-Deputy-Prime-Minis-ter-and-Minister-for-Finance-Tharman-Shanmugaratnam

"So we looked at Singapore and asked ourselves where these opportunities are to move up for the less privileged?

"Remember that I earlier said we used heat maps to see geographic patterns. Interestingly, we observed an association between the geographic distribution of inter-generational housing wealth mobility and public housing policies. Let's take a look at this heat map."

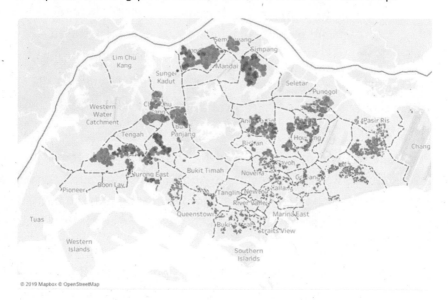

"This is a heat map of where parents in the bottom 60th percentile rank live. Most of the children born of these grassroots parents who enjoy upward mobility grew up in new urban areas on the outskirts of the city. Specifically, these estates are Punggol and Pasir Ris in the northwest and Jurong West in the west."

"Aiyah! Why not Serangoon," muttered Teng silently. He wanted to maximise and ensure that both his sons would live in a bigger and better house than the current flat in Serangoon.

Professor Agarwal explained.

"Recall that we studied parents born from 1965 to 1984. So when they became parents in the 1980s or 90s, the Singapore Government was promoting quality public housing with subsidies in these areas.

By providing such subsidised housing, the government is actually undertaking social engineering programmes to facilitate these children's ability to surpass their parents who had benefitted from the public housing scheme.

"Another mobility opportunity is the Married Child Priority Scheme. This scheme increases the chances of a flat applicant getting a flat if the married child and the parents can live together or close to each other to help look after one another. This scheme also helps children climb up the housing wealth ladder. Other schemes such as subsidised BTO (Build-To-Order) HDB flats also assist in giving a leg up to children of grassroots parents to be upwardly mobile.

"Now, how about the people from middle income and the elite class?

"Let's start with the top 20th percentile. We found that for children born to these parents, there is high inter-generational persistence in housing wealth. Children of the rich typically remain living in central regions where the rich traditionally locate and have a high co-residence rate with their parents.

"Now for children born to middle-income families, defined as parents in the 60th to 80th percentile ranks," paused Professor Agarwal as he took a deep breath. This is where the knife is stabbed in and twisted. "We found that they are worse off than their parents."

There was clearly a sharp and louder gasp from the audience and the chattering started again. As he stood there cutting a solitary figure against the backdrop, the audience began to quieten down as they knew Professor Agarwal had more to say.

"Less than 50 percent of children born to middle-income parents who live in private residences ended up living in private residences. Again, we compared this downward wealth mobility pattern to that of other countries and found that it is an echo of the pattern found among middle-income children in the United States.

"So, what happened? Why was there upward inter-generational mobility among the lower-income segment but not among the middle-income segment?"

Professor Agarwal gave a pregnant pause for effect.

"There are at least two possible explanations. I shall first deliver what one might say 'the bad news'.

"Earlier, I had mentioned that for those in the lower percentile of housing wealth, new town areas was a way to give them a booster so that the next generation, their children, could move upwards. We think that these new town areas may possibly witnessed downward mobility for children from middle-income families, perhaps because of a lack of excellent quality public schools. Let me explain.

> **[N]eighbourhoods with schools that have below-average academic scores have the highest level of inter-generational mobility.**

"We analysed by matching the academic admission scores of all public secondary schools to the 82 postal sectors in Singapore. We found that neighbourhoods with schools that have below-average academic scores have the highest level of inter-generational mobility. Sounds strange, right? But if you look at Singapore's educational system, you'll find the standard is generally high. Singapore has one of the best education systems in the world. Therefore, children from poor families residing in these neighbourhoods benefit as long as there are public schools in their vicinity.

"Then we looked at neighbourhoods where there are several schools with very high academic scores for admissions. Children living in such neighbourhoods have the highest level of inter-generational persistence in housing wealth. This is likely due to upper-income families living in good neighbourhoods with great schools that help them to maintain their economic standing. So with excellent education and similar peers they meet in school, the well-heeled children were able to maintain their parents' wealth standing. Here, take a look at this heat map for where the top 20th percentile live.

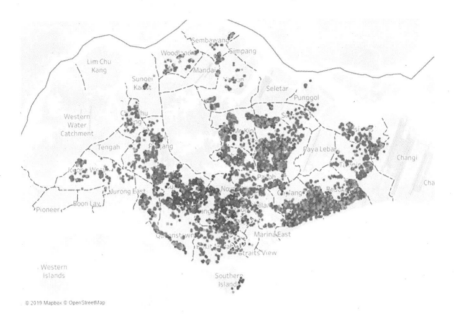

© 2019 Mapbox © OpenStreetMap

"They are concentrated in the central area where most elite schools are located – schools such as Singapore Chinese Girls' School, Anglo-Chinese School, Nanyang Girls' School, Raffles Girls' School and so on.

"Now, for children born to middle-income parents. They are less likely to live in the neighbourhoods where the high net worth class is living. They probably live in the outskirts of elite neighbourhoods, a little too far away from the high-quality public schools for their children to attend.

"Therefore, they are likely to go to neighbourhood schools where grassroots children attend. There are more grassroots children which makes the cohort larger, and hence competition is more intense. This makes the probability of middle-income children succeeding over grassroots children lower. Together, this inhibits middle-income children from keeping pace with their parents' wealth. Here's the heat map of where they live."

There was a flurry of whispers as the audience digested the information. There were more similarities in the housing location between the grassroots and middle-income groups.

The tension was high in the auditorium.

Professor Agarwal understood that what he had presented may take a little longer to digest, not just technically but also from a social implication perspective.

Teng, on the other hand, was racing to the time when Peter had once told him about property prices near choice schools.

"Eh, Peter. You had told me before about housing prices near good schools. What were the findings?" whispered Teng, well aware that he was adding to the decibel in the auditorium.

"Houses located within one kilometre from a choice school are sold at over 2 percent premium, and those within one to two kilometres at an 18 percent premium compared to houses located two to four kilometres away,"[7] rattled off Peter who seemingly is a property-prices robot.

"Ahh . . . That must be in the central region where there are many private landed residences and elite schools. They go hand in hand. People want their kids to go to these schools and will pay a princely sum for a property near these schools. Therefore, property prices near choice schools go up," thought Teng as he put two and two together.

When the audience quietened down, Professor Agarwal prepared to deliver the good news.

"Remember I had said there were at least two explanations why the middle class children fared worse than their parents? This second explanation is the good news.

"Among you parents who are from the middle-income bracket and you despair because you think your children are going to do worse . . . There is a light at the end of the tunnel. Let me elaborate.

"Now, by show of hands, how many of you bought an HDB as your first property?"

There was a sea of raised hands. Almost everyone has an HDB flat as their first property.

Professor Agarwal smiled. He could feel he was going to win the audience over.

---

[7] For more on this research on the effect of choice school location on property prices, see Sumit Agarwal, Ang Swee Hoon and Sing Tien Foo (2018), *Kiasunomics: Stories of Singaporean Economic Behaviours*, Chapter 15 "Boy Boy, Go to a Good School," (Singapore: World Scientific Publishers). To read the academic article, see Sumit Agarwal, Satyanarain Rengarajan, Sing Tien Foo and Yang Yang (2016), "School Allocation Rules and Housing Prices: A Quasi-Experiment with School Relocation Events in Singapore," *Regional Science and Urban Economics*, Vol. 58, pp. 42–56, https://papers.ssrn.com/sol3/papers.cfm?abstract_id=2380761. This research was also published as a commentary, see Sumit Agarwal and Sing Tien Foo, "How school proximity affects house prices in Singapore," *The Straits Times*, (17 December 2015), https://www.straitstimes.com/opinion/how-school-proximity-affects-house-prices-in-singapore

"And rightly so for several reasons. With income not exceeding the threshold set by HDB and hence there's limited personal savings, an HDB flat is the most affordable option as the first property. Moreover, as Singapore citizens, you want to enjoy the full benefits of government subsidy when you buy your flat directly from HDB. And don't forget, if you were an HDB owner, you are allowed to purchase a private property subsequently but not the reverse. These are valid reasons for buying an HDB flat as your first home."

Some people in the audience nodded, though there were still others, probably from the middle-residence wealth bracket, who remained glum.

Professor Agarwal carried on.

"Well, your children are smart. It may well be that the middle-income children intentionally on their own accord buy an HDB flat instead of a private property. So it seemingly looks like they fared worse than their parents. But no. They purposely bought an HDB flat because they know it makes the most sense. They are being rational. They want to reap the benefits that I mentioned earlier – government subsidy and the opportunity to buy a private property thereafter.

"And therefore, although we see a drop in inter-generational property wealth for the middle-income segment, it may well be because of the favourable circumstances of owning an HDB flat as their first property rather than a real downward wealth mobility."

It was remarkable how the auditorium suddenly became a lot less tense. You could feel a sense of relief in the air.

"So if we buy this second explanation, we can actually see progression for both grassroots and middle-income segments while the high-end segment remains as they are."

Professor Agarwal could feel he had gotten the audience on his side. He felt good.

"One last bit before we welcome questions from the audience," said Professor Agarwal, mindful of the time, and trying to move the talk forward.

"We also studied inter-generational housing wealth mobility and cross-class marriages. If people marry someone from a different socio-economic class as themselves, what does it do to their children's mobility? Here's the finding in a pictorial form of a map.

"In this map, inter-generational mobility and cross-class marriage are measured by colour and by height of the bar. The lighter the colour, the higher is the mobility across generations. The higher the bar, the higher the probability of cross-class marriage. We found that inter-generational mobility is associated with a higher possibility of cross-class marriages."

Then, Professor Agarwal looked at the questions projected on the screen. These were questions posted and voted by the audience using the Pigeonhole app. He took the highest voted question first.

"We need to answer the questions that you have posted. The most popular question is: 'What can be done to help middle-income Singaporeans move upward?'"

"Well," began Professor Agarwal, "Like I said, I don't think middle-income Singaporeans are downsliding in their wealth mobility. It is very likely that young Singaporeans, being very pragmatic, would buy an HDB flat as their first home to benefit from the generous government subsidy. So in effect, they are progressing because there's substantial savings from the subsidy which they can use for a private property purchase in the future.

"The next question says: 'Why did you use 60th percentile and below to denote grassroots? Shouldn't the less privileged be the 20th percentile and below? Singapore doesn't have so many less privileged families.'

"Indeed, you are right," said Professor Agarwal, acknowledging the audience's point. "Singapore is in a privileged situation where there are not many families or people living from hand-to-mouth as in other countries, including those in developed economies. About 80 percent of Singaporeans live in HDB flats. Of these, three-room flats make up about 24 percent and four-room flats 42 percent. So we wanted to study this group of HDB residents and see whether their children upgrade eventually. The top 20 percent of HDB flat owners – those living in five-room and executive flats – would be considered in the middle-income range with some private property owners. All in, I think this is a fair categorisation of housing wealth given Singapore's unique housing situation.

"Here's an interesting question: 'There are areas in Singapore that were previously unpopular and houses were going for a song. Then they became hugely popular. Tiong Bahru, for instance, is a great example. It has transformed from an old people's community to a trendy yuppie enclave. How is that accounted for in your study? The adjustment to 1984 prices accounts for inflation but not these shifts in lifestyle.'

"Yes, I've been to Tiong Bahru and it is a swanky place now," laughed Professor Agarwal. "The market there is great. I tried the *chwee kway* there and I like the *kueh dadah* from Glacier."

The audience laughed as Professor Agarwal seemed to be quite familiar with Tiong Bahru.

"To answer the question . . . Yes, property prices in Tiong Bahru have escalated as the area attracts a younger segment who is willing to pay for the lifestyle that the location offers. And if the prices have risen together with lifestyle and yet, the younger generation is still willing to pay, it says well about progress. Remember that we have adjusted the prices to 2014. So any differences in prices are likely to be reflective of demand. So if the children can afford higher-priced HDB flats better than their parents during their time, then they have moved up.

"Let's move on. The next question asks: 'What future research will you be doing to find out more about inter-generational wealth mobility?'

"We want to follow up with the adult children and see how they progress five years, 10 years down the road. Particularly for the middle-income segment, we want to explore whether these children bought a second property while having an HDB flat and become multiple property owners. We want to know whether they cashed out after living in an HDB flat for five years and upgraded to a bigger flat or a private property, which would be suggestive of them transferring the subsidy from the government to private property purchases. These would be suggestive of upward mobility.

"Because time is running out, we'll take the last question: 'Besides education, are there other ways to level the social classes?'

"Education is a key driver in progress. Beyond that, I would say a bold attitude to persevere and never give up. Be hungry and don't get too complacent. Also, the ability to spot opportunities and a willingness to take calculated risks can also help to level social classes. We've heard numerous cases of individuals who had little formal education but had the foresight to see the next big idea and were willing to take that plunge."

The talk drew to a close. Many in the audience came up to Professor Agarwal for clarifications to questions that they were too shy to ask despite having the Pigeonhole app available. He patiently answered their questions.

"Let's hang around for a while," urged Teng. "I want to say 'hello' to Professor Agarwal."

When the crowd thinned out, Teng approached him.

"Professor, I'm Teng. Thank you very much for your talk. I don't know whether you remember this, but we met some years ago when you took my taxi years from Farrer Road to NUS."

Professor Agarwal's memory raced back to that time and with a cheeky and I'm-going-to-surprise-you smile, he said, "You were the one whom I shared my study about taxi drivers in Singapore, right? The study on financial planning and budgeting? I'll not forget that because that was one of my first research projects in Singapore. And you were so interested in hearing my findings. It's so nice to see you again."

He nailed it. Teng was stunned that the professor could recall such an innocuous chance meeting. "No wonder he's a professor," Teng thought. "I can't even remember my children's birthdays."

"I hope you're doing well. My neighbour, Professor Sing, knows you. And another neighbour who is studying at a junior college said you gave her class a guest lecture on sunny days and shopping," said Teng as he went through the pleasantries.

"Oh wow! Such a small world. That's fantastic!" said the very amiable professor. Looking at Siew Ling, he asked, "And is this your wife?"

"Yes, this is Siew Ling. I'm still driving a taxi but have also signed on as a Grab driver. I now have two boys – six and two years old."

"Wow! I just had a baby boy," beamed Professor Agarwal who could not contain his excitement.

"Congratulations! Your first son?" Siew Ling asked.

"Yes. And we call him Sid," said the professor with a broad smile on his face.

"Hah! And he's not born in the Year of the Dragon so there's no cohort size effect," joked Teng as he thought about their opportune first meeting. "He's born with parents who have made it."

WANT TO KNOW MORE?

This chapter is based on Sumit Agarwal, Fan Yi, Qian Wenlan and Sing Tien Foo (2019), "Like Father Like Son? Social Engineering and Intergenerational Housing Wealth Mobility," Working Paper, National University of Singapore.

Smoke Gets in Your Eyes

As promised, Josie arranged to have lunch with Ah Kong and Ah Mah. It's her way of saying thanks to her neighbours as Ah Mah had been boiling herbal soups for Sarah when Josie was away. Josie had been on work trips for the last several months studying how other cities are tackling their environmental issues and learning their best practices.

Sitting at a quiet corner in the renovated Crystal Jade Palace restaurant were Ah Kong, Ah Mah and Sarah. Sarah had taken Grab to bring the two elderly neighbours to meet her mother for lunch at Orchard Road. Ah Kong and Ah Mah hardly venture out of their Serangoon area as the estate is self-contained with all the amenities that they needed.

"Mum is late again. As usual," sighed Sarah.

She had gotten used to her mother's busy schedule. In some ways, that worked well for Sarah as she gets her independence to manage things by herself. Today being a working day, she wasn't surprised that her mother was late.

"She's probably caught up in some meeting," Sarah thought, so familiar with her mother's tardy appearances at social functions.

Her mother was a high achiever first at the LTA, and recently at the NEA. Josie had taken up golfing to break the glass ceiling with new contacts. In fact, it was at golf that she met senior management from various government organisations including the NEA whom she began to hobnob with.

Her golfing activities took a notch higher when she heard about the perks of golfing especially for women wanting to climb the corporate ladder. She had heard from her friend that a study by NUS showed that golfing as a social networking tool may give women additional social capital to be accepted in predominantly male corporate boards.[1]

Sarah entertained Ah Kong and Ah Mah with stories of her school life. As usual, Ah Mah kept asking her whether she has a boyfriend and how important it was to have one or she might be left single when all the eligible young men are already taken up. This has been a recurring topic during Chinese New Year and whenever they meet up for dinners at any of the neighbours' home.

She was relieved when Josie showed up.

"So sorry, so sorry. My meeting ended late and the traffic outside Takashimaya is horrendous. I hope you didn't wait too long," apologised Josie profusely.

---

[1] For more on this research on how golfing is related to directorship, see Sumit Agarwal, Ang Swee Hoon and Sing Tien Foo (2018), *Kiasunomics: Stories of Singaporean Economic Behaviours*, Chapter 12 "Lady, Do You Want to Tee off?" (Singapore: World Scientific Publishers). To read the academic article, see Sumit Agarwal, Qian Wenlan, David M. Reeb and Sing Tien Foo (2016), "Playing the Boys Game: Golf Buddies and Board Diversity," *American Economic Review*, Vol. 106 (5), pp. 272–276, https://www.aeaweb.org/articles?id=10.1257/aer.p20161033. This research has also been published as a commentary, see Sumit Agarwal and Qian Wenlan, "Golf buddies and board diversity," *The Straits Times*, (8 March 2018), https://www.straitstimes.com/opinion/golf-buddies-and-board-diversity

"Aiyoh, Josie! You've been working way too hard. You've gone thinner," said Ah Mah. "I need to make the double-boiled chicken herbal soup for you. It will bring colour to your face."

"You've been traveling so much. Is it all business trips?" enquired Ah Kong.

"Yes, it's all for work. Recently, I went to China and spent two months there," replied Josie, as she looked through the menu to order the dishes.

"Oh . . . So you had time for sightseeing and shopping too, I suppose," said Ah Mah.

"Auntie, I wish that was the case. Then I'd have enjoyed my trips more," replied Josie. "But no. I was so occupied the whole day every day, and moving from one city to another. I was free only during the weekends but that's when I need to rest and recharge for the following week."

"Anyway, China is so polluted. Some places were so bad that I didn't want to go out if I could avoid it," Josie continued.

Josie is a pro-environmentalist. She refuses to drive to work but instead takes public transport wherever she goes.

"It's that bad?" Ah Kong raised his eye brows. "I've heard of the smog in Beijing during the winter months but I didn't think other cities were affected too."

"Uncle, do you know that one study found that more than 80 percent of Chinese are regularly exposed to pollution levels deemed unhealthy by the U.S. Environmental Protection Agency? And another estimated that air pollution kills about 4,000 people in China a day or about 17 percent of all deaths in China!"[2] voiced out Josie.

---

[2] Robert Ferris, "China air pollution far worse than thought: Study," *CNBC*, (18 August 2015), https://www.cnbc.com/2015/08/18/china-air-pollution-far-worse-than-thought-study.html; "Air pollution in China is killing 4,000 people every day, a new study finds," *The Guardian*, (14 August 2015), https://www.theguardian.com/world/2015/aug/14/air-pollution-in-china-is-killing-4000-people-every-day-a-new-study-finds

"Really? Then how come some people say they went to Zhangjiajie where the movie Avatar was filmed and they tell me that the air there is so fresh and crisp," asked Ah Mah. Her friends had been regaling her about Zhangjiajie and she had hoped to visit there one day with Ah Kong.

"Auntie, China is so big. There'll always be some places where the air is clean. If the whole of China is polluted, then I think we're in seriously big trouble," said Josie with a nervous laugh. "Come, let's order the dishes first. Then we have time to talk."

"Wah! So terrible," said Ah Mah. "Thankfully in Singapore, we have limited pollution except for the occasional haze. We had a slight haze when you were away."

After ordering the food, Josie continued. "I was in Beijing and several places in Zhejiang and Hebei to study their environment and pollution controls. It was also to help their Ministry of Environmental Protection (MEP) as an independent body to assess their pollution control system."

The first dish came – cold meat cuts. As an environmentalist, Josie did not order shark fin soup. Instead, watercress soup was served.

"Auntie and Uncle, please eat," said Josie as she took some of the char siew pieces with her chopsticks and gave them to the old folks.

"Your job sounds interesting. And something that you are passionate about," said Ah Kong.

"Please tell us what you did in China. Spending two months there is a very long time," added Ah Mah.

"Oh! It was an eye opener for me," said Josie as she began chatting about her recent trip. "We always take for granted cleanliness and pollution-free air in Singapore. Over there, it's a totally different story.

"In fact, as part of the independent body to help the MEP assess their environmental pollution, I had to do some inspections for them. It wasn't just meetings in air-con rooms. I had to be on the ground and monitor their air quality."

"Mum, you mean you actually had to take air and water samples and test them?" asked Sarah.

Josie nodded. She was there to learn as well and what better way to learn about the environment than to get down on one's knees and do the job of monitoring yourself.

The second and third dishes came. There was a plate of sweet and sour spare ribs and a plate of yam basket with crispy rice vermicelli and stir-fried chicken dices. This was quickly followed by a vegetable dish. Josie asked that the e-fu noodles be portioned for them.

As everyone was eating, Josie began to tell about her stint in China.

Josie Prepares

Josie's visit to China was several months in the making. While she was there to learn about environmental standards, there was a special project arrangement where Josie was also needed to serve as an independent entity to assess the effectiveness of China's monitoring system in curtailing pollution, specifically industrial pollution.

She had been liaising with her contact at MEP – a young man called Rui Yuan, who arranged all her site visits as well as help her collect data for the independent report. In other words, in China, Rui Yuan was her right-hand man whom she depended on so she could accomplish her tasks as well as she could.

In their correspondence before her trip, Rui Yuan had told her that according to the World Health Organization, exposure to 20 μg/m^3 of sulphur dioxide (SO_2) on a 24-hour average may lead to negative health consequences. But, in many parts of China, especially those in northern China, the hourly average of SO_2 is above 20 μg/m^3. So one of the objectives of her trip was to study the pollution situation in China, specifically how much do factories contribute to pollution.

During her career at LTA, she had read some reports on air pollution as transportation could result in pollution from vehicle emissions. Hence, Josie was somewhat familiar with SO_2 as well as other pollutants.

"Rui Yuan, before I arrive in China, I need you to do the following for me. I understand MEP has monitoring stations installed in various parts of China?"

"Yes, Mrs Leong," was Rui Yuan's answer. He addresses her formally by her married name as she is his senior. "We have about 1,600 such stations. They record the level of pollutants on an hourly basis."

"And what kinds of pollutants do they measure?" asked Josie.

"There's SO_2, $PM_{2.5}$, PM_{10} and other toxins like carbon monoxide (CO) and nitrogen dioxide (NO_2)," replied Rui Yuan.

"Good. Do you have the AQI (composite Air Quality Index) measure as well? If you have, that's good. I'll need the hourly measurements of these pollutants for the last two years. I don't think I'll need the measures for CO and NO_2."

Drawing from her experience at LTA, Josie knew that because industrial sites tended to have a higher density of road networks and vehicles, it was difficult to separate whether these pollutants were from the factories or vehicles. Moreover, there were issues regarding how sunlight might have a chemical effect on NO_2. Hence although measures on CO and NO_2 were available, they may not be useful in studying industrial pollution.

"Rui Yuan, I also want you to count the number of factories located within a three-kilometre radius of each monitoring station and the number of factories in the SO_2-intensive industries. These would include factories in the production and supply of electric power and heat power, metal-related industries, raw chemical materials and chemical products, and petroleum processing industries," instructed Josie.

She wanted to assess the relationship between industrial intensity and pollution.

While it is expected that industrial areas would have higher pollution than residential areas, might there be other differences such as time of day that one would not expect?

Thus she reminded Rui Yuan, "Remember also to collect the pollution index every hour, even when the factories have shut down."

What other information would she need to make a comprehensive and compelling report? She wanted to make a deep impression not only on the MEP but also to her bosses at the NEA.

"Mrs Leong, you might want to consider the time when the sun sets in various parts of China. Unlike Singapore, we have four seasons here. Our winter has very short daylight hours. That might have a possible chemical effect. Do you want me to collect the daily sunset time of each monitoring station?" offered Rui Yuan.

"Smart thinking. That would be excellent," appreciated Josie. But more than that, Josie had other ideas too. She was mindful of horror stories she had heard about malpractices. She was thinking whether it was possible that these factories engage in suspicious activities where pollution was concerned when the sky had gotten dark. Hence, readings after the sun has set may come in useful.

"Hmm . . . Rui Yuan, thus far, the data is from MEP's monitoring system as well as sunset times from your meteorological office. How easy is it to get information on hospital visits?" asked Josie as she ventured to get additional information. She had a certain hypothesis that she wanted to test but wasn't sure whether the information was available.

"I can try," said Rui Yuan. "These hospitals can be quite co-operative especially when I say we're from the MEP and explain to them the rationale for wanting the information."

"Hmm . . .," thought Josie for a short while before instructing Rui Yuan further. "In that case, I want info on as many hospitals as you can get and from as many cities as possible. The info should include for each day, the number of patient visits, classified as whether it was an outpatient or an emergency visit, and what the visit was about – pollution-triggered respiratory diseases including pulmonary disease, bronchitis, asthma, and lung cancer; or other ailments such as diabetes. Of course, please also collect the usual demographic characteristics like patient's age and gender."

Rui Yuan worked tirelessly to get the data for Josie. While data from the monitoring stations were relatively easy to get as they were from the MEP, it was a challenge to secure information from the hospitals. He had six months to collect the data before Josie arrived in Beijing.

He knew Josie would be pleased with the pollution data he had collected so far.

He managed to obtain hourly pollution data from almost 1,600 national monitoring stations in China on the pollutants that Josie wanted – SO_2, $PM_{2.5}$, PM_{10} as well as AQI. He had also tabulated the number of factories within a three-kilometre radius of each station and counted the number of factories in the SO_2-intensive industries which included production and supply of electric power and heat power, metal-related industries, and petroleum processing industries.

The MEP had also installed monitoring devices in factories. So Rui Yuan managed to collect these monitoring data from 150 factories in various cities in Hebei province, and another 180 factories in Zhejiang province.

The hospital data were tricky to come by. He wasn't sure whether he could get the data ready for Josie by the time she arrived. He had written to the administrators in 50 hospitals in 33 cities, informing them that this was a government project to assess China's pollution standards and that an independent body had been called to help out. He also laid out the benefits of the study such as knowing how pollution might influence different illnesses. This information would in turn help hospitals in managing their manpower and medical supplies to treat various ailments. Rui Yuan even visited as many of these administrators as he possibly could to get their co-operation.

Just two weeks before Josie arrived, Rui Yuan managed to get all 50 hospitals to give him the data. Now, he had two weeks to put the data together to show Josie.

Josie Arrives

No sooner had Josie stepped off the Singapore Airlines plane at Beijing Capital International Airport, she was fast at work; first, meeting the senior management at the MEP and then meeting with Rui Yuan to review the information he had gathered for her.

As she had also wanted to visit the factories, Rui Yuan had arranged for the first visit the following day.

On their way to the first factory in the morning, a chemical factory that makes raw materials for the production of writing instruments such as crayons and highlighters, Rui Yuan updated Josie that he had conducted some preliminary analyses and found that in winter, the SO_2 level is higher in the north, while during summer, SO_2 is higher in the south.

"Rui Yuan, at each place we visit, I want you to note down the emission levels of the various pollutants at that time. Do this unobtrusively. Don't make it obvious," instructed Josie.

As she visited the factory, she was well aware that the factory management was prepared for her visit. She was given a warm welcome with a flower bouquet. Importantly, she observed how spick and span the factory was. And everyone, all the way from the manager down to the cleaners, smiled and greeted her. There were no signs of pollution infringement. Everything seemed satisfactory and in good order.

She had a similar experience with the second factory, a petroleum refining company. The impression she had was that everything was compliant with environmental and safety regulations. And so it was also with the rest of the factories she visited over the next few days.

And the pollutant readings that Rui Yuan obtained at each visit were within the range expected of an industrial site. All seemed too good to be true. Josie was sceptical.

Josie was aware that even in Singapore, when people knew a person of importance was going to pay a visit, they would have their place spruced up to create a good impression. She remembered Sarah and her classmates had to clean their classroom and go through a grooming session on what was proper school uniform and acceptable hair-do the week before the Minister for Education visited the school. It just wasn't reflective of day-to-day going-ons in school.

She thought she would have to make surprise visits to these factories to get a better sense of the reality.

Josie Finds

In the meantime, she poured through the data that Rui Yuan had meticulously gathered for her. She thought for a start that she'd just do a simple plotting of the pollution levels for SO_2 throughout the day and night.

And what she saw stunned her.

With the horizontal line representing the number of hours before and after sunset, '0' means the time when the sun sets and '-1' means

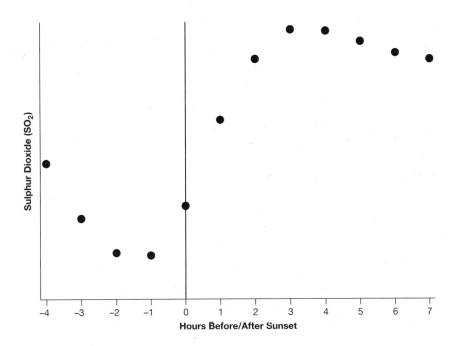

one hour before the sun sets while '1' means one hour after the sun has set – in other words, when it was dark. Josie was stunned that there was a very evident spike in SO_2 level when night fell.

It was apparent to her that the SO_2 levels were significantly higher after the sun had set than before.

> SO_2 levels were significantly higher after the sun had set ...

"There seems to be some mischief going on here," thought a suspicious Josie.

"But I shouldn't jump to conclusions. It is possible that weather conditions, winter heating or industrial characteristics of the city may have resulted in higher SO_2 after sunset. Lower temperature after sunset, for instance, may have affected the dissipation of pollutants. I should pay a surprise visit to these factories at night to verify."

And Josie did just that. She and Rui Yuan spent the next couple of weeks making spot checks at these factories. Some three to four hours after the sun had set, they stood outside the factory, with the N95 particulate respirator mask covering their nose and mouth, measuring the various pollutant levels.

"%#!?*," cursed Rui Yuan as he saw the readings. "These guys are polluting the air in the dark. They are cheating us."

As a dedicated MEP employee, Rui Yuan has a strong sense of honour and doing right by the environment to help his countrymen. He felt a sting of betrayal that these factories were cheating not just the government body but also the people.

"We need to remain calm. There's no point in making a hue and cry about it but without any concrete evidence," said Josie so that Rui Yuan would not get too worked up. "We have the past data you gave me as well as the current data. Just make sure that the evidence is properly documented for my report.

"Now, we need to rule out other explanations for the increase in pollutant levels. For instance, the atmospheric conditions may affect pollutant readings."

"What should we do then?" asked Rui Yuan, who was bent on nailing the culprits.

"Well, we'd also need to collect SO_2 readings before and after sunset in a nearby station that is located in a non-industrial area. Then, both stations would have similar atmospheric conditions because they are in the same locality. That way, if there is a difference in readings before and after sunset at the monitoring station at a factory as well as at the residential area, then we know it's due to atmospheric conditions.

"But if there's differential readings at the factory station but not at a nearby residential station, then we can infer that the difference in findings between the two stations is due to one being in an industrial area and the other isn't."

"Ahh . . . Now I get it," Rui Yuan said, nodding his head and understanding how the data were to be analysed.

"Do we have such data from a nearby monitoring station that is in a non-industrial area?" asked Josie.

Thankfully, the massive data that Rui Yuan had collected included these non-industrial stations as well. But Josie wanted to measure the levels herself on top of the data Rui Yuan had previously collected for her. That meant spending time at night at different places near the targeted factories.

Josie began studying pairs of monitoring stations in the same city – one in an industrial area and the second in a non-industrial area – and compared whether their SO_2 readings differed. And for good measure, she also compared $PM_{2.5}$, PM_{10} and AQI readings as well.

"Rui Yuan, you won't be happy with what I found," Josie told Rui Yuan a few days later. "Our suspicions are confirmed. In residential areas, there was no difference in emission levels before and after sunset.

"But in industrial areas, there was evidence of increases in emission levels after dark, just like the graph I found earlier. Here are the results:

Pollutant	Reading (4 hours after sunset vs 4 hours before sunset)
SO_2	16% increase
$PM_{2.5}$	7% increase
PM_{10}	10% increase
AQI	9% increase

"And mind you, the ozone levels in these areas dropped 20 percent after sunset.

"This is how the SO_2 levels looked before and after sunset for the stations in industrial and non-industrial areas," said Josie, showing Rui Yuan another graph plotted on her computer screen.

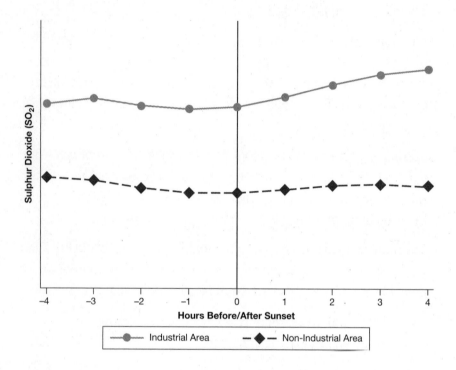

"You can see from the graph that the SO_2 levels in the non-industrial areas are somewhat flat during the four hours before and after sunset. But the SO_2 levels in industrial areas, while higher than in the non-industrial areas during working hours in the day, should have tapered by nightfall when the factory shuts down. Instead, we see a spike after sunset," said Josie with a raised eyebrow as she explained the graph that she just plotted.

Rui Yuan was fuming. "Does this confirm that the factories increase pollution levels in the disguise of the night?"

"It does look like it. There is disguised pollution, especially in areas where

There is disguised pollution, especially in areas where there are small factories.

there are small factories. It seems that small factories are the culprits," elaborated Josie.

"I'm sorry to say, Rui Yuan. I think the real level of pollution is likely to be higher than the disguised pollution that we've just observed. I had controlled for factors such as winter heating, traffic, different industrial electricity prices within a day, and atmospheric chemical reactions that may have influenced the readings."

"Sigh! And we have these factory inspections and they come to nought?" fumed Rui Yuan. "Or have our inspectors been bribed?"

Rui Yuan was becoming cynical after being disappointed by what the data showed.

"Well, there are so many factories that not all can be inspected," said Josie to quell Rui Yuan's disappointment. "And among those inspected, these factory owners are clever. They know how to evade detection like the way they did a spring-cleaning and gave me such a wonderful reception when I visited," said Josie. "These planned inspections curb disguised pollution only temporarily – only during the stay of the MEP officials. After the MEP officials have left the site, the polluting-causing activities resumed. So you need to have more unexpected visits, even at night."

"Well, that's easier said than done. There's the issue of manpower. These inspections are conducted in the day; getting checks conducted at night cannot be done all the time," acknowledged Rui Yuan, citing the constraints.

Why Pollute?

While Josie's investigation had yielded these discrepancies between what was found by inspectors in the day and what occurred at night, Josie wasn't satisfied. For her report to be comprehensive, it must also include reasons why companies resorted to pollution. Could it all boil down to pure greed?

> [D]isguised pollution was likely to be a consequence of economic downturn.

The next day, Josie asked Rui Yuan to collect more data.

"Rui Yuan, please get me China's GDP and other economic numbers. This should be relatively easy to obtain. I want to study whether there is a relationship between GDP and pollution. Actually, why don't you run this test for me? It's quite straightforward."

Rui Yuan obliged. It appeared that such disguised pollution was likely to be a consequence of economic downturn. When a business experienced poor revenue during a downturn, it would be pressurised to find ways to cut costs. One such way is not to maintain safety standards as these incur costs. Hence, these factories compromise on pollution standards.

"This is what I found. A one percentage decline in GDP growth rate in the previous year increases the magnitude of disguised pollution in the current year by 9 to 14 percent!"

Josie shook her head. "Greed," she thought.

Consequences

Now that she had the pollution levels covered and the reason explained, the next step was to detail the consequences: how does the pollution affect workers and people living near the factories? Do the higher levels of toxins make people sick?

"Ahh . . . That's why you wanted me to collect the information on hospital visits," said Rui Yuan as he understood better now why Josie had sent him on the demanding and laboured task of collecting the hospital data. "Before we analyse the data, let's visit some of these hospitals. Perhaps the doctors and patients there can give us some insights," suggested Josie.

She didn't want her report to be filled solely with hard numeric data. Soft but in-depth insights from interviews with the medical staff and patients would complement her hard findings for a balanced and comprehensive review.

Josie and Rui Yuan visited three hospitals and spoke to numerous doctors and nurses, and a few patients who were willing to talk about their illnesses.

"We've been noticing a spike in the number of patients coming down with bronchitis and asthma ever since more factories opened up in our city," observed one doctor. "But we don't know for sure whether it is due to the factories. If you have evidence of that, that would be good for us. The local government can do something about it. As of now, our hospital is overrun with such patients. We don't have enough staff to look after them."

"It can get quite crazy at times," informed a nurse. "A family can come in with breathing difficulties. There was one family, I remember. The father worked for one of the factories making iron ore and copper pipes. He was coughing and coughing. By the time he came to see us, he was already in an advanced stage of lung cancer. And his two young boys were asthmatic. It's quite a pitiful sight as the mother seemed to be quite weak too. I don't know what will happen to them when the father is no longer around."

Josie had a heavy heart when listening to these interviews. She knew that she had to include her findings that cities with more disguised pollution also have a higher mortality rate. By tracking the number of hospital visits over time as emission levels changed, Josie found that higher levels of SO_2 drove up hospital visits for respiratory diseases by 16 percent.

She was disturbed by the findings. But nothing could prepare her for what she found next – the increase in respiratory diseases was particularly stark for young people below 18 years old. Respiratory diseases went up by more than 40 percent for young men and 30 percent for young women.

Josie was more determined than ever that her report should highlight the health and ultimately economic consequences of pollution on the city and its residents.

Lunch Continues

"Aiyoh! This is so bad," Ah Mah cried as Josie finished telling them what she found about pollution in China. Ah Mah was thinking about her two precious grandsons.

They had finished eating the main dishes and were about to start on the dessert.

"It's like killing people for the sake of making a profit," Ah Mah continued. "In fact, it reminds me of the pollution in Pasir Gudang."

"Pollution in Pasir Gudang? What happened?" Josie asked. She had been in and out of Singapore so frequently that she couldn't keep track of what's going on in this region.

"This is in Johor," answered Ah Mah as she related the event. "It was found that toxic chemical waste was being illegally dumped into the river in Pasir Gudang. More than 4,000 people were treated for shortness of breath, nausea and vomiting after inhaling the toxic fumes. Students, canteen workers and even an environment inspector were hospitalised. Over 110 primary and secondary schools were closed for two weeks because of this incident."[3]

"The waste they threw into the river was marine oil waste which emits flammable methane and benzene fumes," added Sarah. "And there

---

[3] Yiswaree Palansamy, Emmanuel Santa Maria Chin and Ben Tan, "Two incidents of pollution in Pasir Gudang affected thousands: Here's what we know so far," *The Malay Mail*, (13 July 2019); "Pasir Gudang pollution needs firm action," *The Straits Times*, (6 July 2019), p. A37.

was a massive clean-up and inspections of other sites to see whether chemicals had been stored illegally or dumped."

"But that's not all. We thought that was the end of it but the pollution continued," updated Ah Mah. "A few months later, some more students complained about breathing difficulties and vomiting, some were even hospitalised. And schools were closed again. Apparently, this second incident was not related to the first incident, but it's still pollution."

"And there was the case of a 12-year-old boy who developed myokymia which causes parts of the body to tremble, apparently after exposure to pollution from the river," added Sarah.

"This is like what I found – pollution and health hazards especially amongst the young," thought Josie.

"So what is the Johor government doing about it?" asked Josie.

"Well, the newspapers reported that the government said they'll need a long-term plan to resolve the pollution issue," Sarah told her mother. "But for a start, they will not be approving any more applications for the construction of new chemical plants in Pasir Gudang. And these factories have to adopt schools near their operations and equip the schools with gas detectors. And a massive inspection is underway to shut down chemical factories operating illegally."

"Sarah, do you know whether NUS teach ethics in business?" asked Josie. She had always thought that ethics should be a mainstay in the curriculum especially for students taking business. After all, as industry captains of tomorrow, they should have a moral compass to put public safety first.

"I heard from my seniors in NUS Business School that they do," responded Sarah.

"That's good. Businesses should be responsible. They cannot allow profits to override public interests," opined Josie. "I have friends at the URA and JTC (Jurong Town Corporation) who used to tell me that Singapore has very good town planning. We have distinct industrial areas, buffered from residential areas to ensure that pollution, if any, is minimised for residents."

"And perhaps identify high-risk chemical factories and locate them furthest away from the rest of Singapore," suggested Sarah.

"And of course, our regulators are very strict on adhering to emissions standards and safety. So that's comforting to know," said Josie as she paid for the lunch.

She had to run off for her next meeting and left Sarah to bring their elderly neighbours home. While riding in the car back to her office, Josie reflected that she had learnt much from her two-month stint in China.

WANT TO KNOW MORE?

This chapter is based on Sumit Agarwal, Qin Yu and Zhu Hongjia (2019), "Disguised Pollution: Industrial Activities in the Dark," Working Paper, National University of Singapore, https://papers.ssrn.com/sol3/papers.cfm?abstract_id=3359404

Pick a Card, Any Card

J osie's trip to China was an eye-opener not only in terms of pollution standards and monitoring, but also daily living.

She had completed her report on how effective China's monitoring system was in curbing pollution. It included not only her findings on pollution measurements during and after working hours but also what she thought were possible factors contributing to the pollution despite monitoring measures. And for completeness, Josie also provided data and analyses on how the pollution affected residents' health.

She was pleased with her report and after spending almost two months in China, she was looking forward to going home.

Despite having heard about the prevalent use of mobile or e-wallet throughout China, Josie was nonetheless still amazed at the way it has become part of the fabric of daily living. People, young and old, are using WeChatPay and AliPay for purchases not only in modern department stores but also in wet markets to buy fruits and fish. She thought this was where Singapore had to play catch-up.

Josie recalled an earlier work trip she had made to India. She noted that to some degree, there was a similar embrace of the mobile wallet in India. In an attempt to flush out black money and combat tax evasion and counterfeiting, Indian Prime Minister Narendra Modi had implemented without notice a demonetisation scheme in which old notes of 500 and 1,000 rupees became invalid. For a heavily cash-based economy, this sudden stripping of the legal tender status of existing notes and the prolonged unavailability of new notes disrupted the economy.

But when Josie was in India, she found that this disruption was a blessing in disguise. The drying up of cash led to a rise in payment digitisation using e-wallets and debit cards. She learnt from her Indian colleagues who were previously infrequent card users that they began using debit cards more because it was a good substitute for cash.

While shopping, she noticed Indians transferring cash into their digital wallet and then using the e-wallet to pay especially for small-value purchases with the QR code or the retailer's registered smartphone number. To her amazement, payments could also be made offline without requiring active Internet connection. With such convenience, Josie understood why the less sophisticated Indian consumers and retailers benefitted the most from digitisation.

She made a mental note that she should ask Rui Yuan, her China counterpart, about mobile wallets in China before she flew back to Singapore.

Mobile Wallets

Rui Yuan had been a great help to her project. Ambitious and eager to learn, the young man was seldom discouraged. Josie had given him tons of work to do before she arrived in Beijing. He accepted all his assignments willingly, no matter how insurmountable they appeared to be. Collecting data from hospitals was particularly challenging but Rui Yuan was hardworking and resourceful. He managed to get hold of the information and that proved to be very useful for Josie's project.

"Rui Yuan," she told him. "I marvel at how widespread and effective WeChatPay and AliPay are. I see not only working adults using them but the old folks as well. It's so convenient and people don't have to carry cash around."

"Yes, Mrs Leong, almost everyone is using it. Like what you said, without the need to carry cash, it's not only convenient but it is also safe. You don't have to fear being robbed," replied Rui Yuan.

"But that would mean everyone needs to have a smartphone," observed Josie.

"That's not really a problem. We have so many local brands – Huawei, Xiaomi, Oppo, Vivo. Cheap and good too, if not better than iPhone. One study found that 98 percent of people with smartphone use these smartphone payment systems," said Rui Yuan with a sense of pride for his national manufacturers.

"Hey, Rui Yuan. I have a joke about Huawei," said Josie, a little distracted when Rui Yuan mentioned Huawei. "It's a true story. Huawei once had a promotion in Singapore. It was selling its smartphone at $54 to senior Singaporeans above 50 years old. Well, they didn't expect it to be so popular. Many uncles and aunties queued way before the Huawei shops were opened. Thousands went away disappointed because only a few smartphones were available at each store and they didn't manage to buy one.

"So the joke is this . . . Do you know what Huawei stands for?"

"It means 'Chinese Achievement'," came Rui Yuan's prompt reply.

"Aiyah! Remember that this is a joke," sighed Josie at Rui Yuan's very earnest response to what the name Huawei means. "Huawei stands for <u>H</u>ow <u>U</u>ncles and <u>A</u>unties <u>W</u>aited <u>E</u>agerly and <u>I</u>n the end, got nothing."

"Funny," said Rui Yuan. "Do Singaporeans like to make such jokes using acronyms?"

"More than you realise," came Josie's response. "But another characteristic of Singaporeans is they are *kiasu* – afraid to lose out. These uncles and aunties are elderly and yet they would queue up, some as early as 8 AM even though the stores open only at 10:30 AM. They didn't want to lose out on the deal.

"But sorry for the Huawei interruption. What were you going to say about smartphone payment systems?" as Josie asked Rui Yuan to continue his explanation.

"Oh yah! As I was saying . . . Using smartphone payment is not just convenient for consumers, but also for the retail stores. More and more shops have stopped accepting cash. From retailers' perspective, one of the problems with cash is counterfeiting. Counterfeit currency is rampant here. So mobile payments do away with that problem. And not accepting cash eliminates the problems of keeping it safely and depositing it in the bank at the end of each working day. All these save costs."

"But what about the elderly? I can't imagine my grandmother being able to use the smartphone. What if she gets cheated into paying more than she should? Or what about young kids? Parents need to teach them financial discipline and to keep track of their daily expenses," voiced Josie who thought of the days when she trained Sarah to keep a notebook of her daily expenses so that she can track her spending. Now, with such virtual payments, the pinch of seeing cash coming out of one's own pocket is gone and spending may not be as prudent.

"I agree. That's an issue," replied Rui Yuan. "You've seen the Hema supermarkets, right? That's Alibaba's futuristic supermarket chain that combines online and bricks-and-mortar shopping. It used to be that Hema customers could only pay for items using Alibaba's AliPay either through smartphones or at self-checkout counters in the stores. But people started complaining because the very elderly with no smartphones or tourists who have no local bank accounts to pay using AliPay cannot shop there. So I heard that some Hema stores now have installed cash registers."

"How about credit cards then? Can't they use credit cards? Although I guess usage would have decreased with the convenience of mobile payments," asked Josie as she thought how in Singapore, credit card use is on the decline because of the popularity of mobile wallets and tighter regulations to curb excessive debt.

"I think so too but you know, in stores that don't accept cash, I think they still accept credit cards but using a smartphone is still the primary mode of payment," said Rui Yuan.

The Godfather

"You know, I've this true and somewhat bizarre story to tell you," said Rui Yuan. "Years ago, before mobile payments existed, credit cards were the rage and everyone tried to get a credit card especially for overseas purchases when they travel. Well, something happened to my neighbour.

"My neighbour is like me, then a junior person working for the local government. But he's up and coming. To be fair, he's very good at his work and he has a way of sweet-talking to people. He's adept at developing *guanxi* or networking connections. So he had a 'godfather' in his organisation – a senior bureaucrat who mentors and protects him.

"Now at that time, the anti-corruption campaign was just about to start or had just started. There were a few cases of high-ranking officials being caught for bribery and being on the take."

Josie was well aware of corruption that existed at various levels, although the Chinese Government had time and time again engaged in efforts to clamp down on such practices.

"These various parties that had been bribing government officials had to be even more creative in their ways to transfer money to them without either side getting caught," continued Rui Yuan.

"Now, my neighbour didn't know how elaborate these set-ups can be. After all, he was still a relatively small fry, though his career path looked promising.

"At the urging of his godfather the senior bureaucrat, he applied for a credit card. Now, when you apply for a card, you need to fill in your occupation, age, annual salary and so on. Unknown to him, his application was specially earmarked by the bank. Why? Because he's an up-and-coming government official."

"Uh oh! I can see where this is going," thought Josie. "But how did the bank bribe him? What was the mechanism?"

"Well, my neighbour received his brand new credit card. There's a spending limit which is a portion of his annual salary. He actually thought the credit limit given to him was quite generous. He thought it ought to be lower but since the bank gave him a higher limit, he just accepted it. But despite the generous limit, he was very careful in how much he spent on his card.

"Then one day, while having lunch with his godfather bureaucrat, the senior bureaucrat asked my neighbour to pay for the lunch using the credit card. He thought, 'OK, he forgot his wallet and he'll pay me back his share later.'

"But that didn't happen. The senior bureaucrat didn't pay my friend back. The next day, the same thing happened again for lunch. And again, the following day and so on. Worse, as weeks went by, his godfather would bring him out after work to wine and dine, and got him to use his credit card again to pay. His credit card bills were mounting.

"His godfather became even more outrageous in his spending and got my neighbour to pay for almost everything using his card. It started with the lunch, escalated to dinners including wine, and even included shopping!

"Hold on . . . You mean his mentor, this so-called godfather who is a senior bureaucrat, was making use of your friend and getting him to pay for his personal expenses with your friend's credit card?" asked a stunned Josie.

"That's right, Mrs Leong," nodded Rui Yuan. "And there's more. Once, they had a quick lunch because his godfather said he needed to go and run some errands. He told my neighbour to go along with him. Guess where they went? To a high-end jewellery shop! And he didn't just buy gold. He bought a diamond necklace with matching diamond earrings. And told my neighbour to pay using his card.

"Of course my friend was frantic. He could not go on footing the bill for him, even though this man was his mentor. My friend was in a tight spot. But the senior bureaucrat 'ordered' him to use the card for payment. My friend just paid. On their way back to work, sensing my friend's panic, the senior bureaucrat reassured him that all would be well. But of course, how could you feel good when you know you have busted way past your credit limit?

"The expenses just kept piling. After the jewellery purchase, there were purchases for a Louis Vuitton handbag, then a Chanel bag, a Prada bag, an Hermes bag and other brand name items. All these for the bureaucrat's wife and daughter. And all the time, the senior bureaucrat just smiled and told my neighbour not to worry."

Disguised Corruption

Rui Yuan continued recounting his neighbour's card-spending spree.

"One day, the credit card bill came. Of course, my friend couldn't pay the full amount. He became indebted to the bank. And the interest rate for late payment was ridiculously high. My neighbour was still harbouring the thought that his godfather bureaucrat would one day pay for the purchases incurred."

"Hah! He can kiss his money goodbye. I think he's been scammed by his godfather!" said Josie. "Rui Yuan, have you seen the movie 'Godfather' starring Marlon Brando? Your neighbour's godfather is like that movie character."

"Well, my neighbour didn't know what to do. He was exasperated. On the one hand, he's indebted to his mentor for bringing him up the career ladder; yet on the other, he can't be footing his luxurious expenses forever. The bills came and he defaulted each time. He would have been declared a bankrupt sooner or later.

"So my friend was just about to blow the whistle on his godfather mentor. Then his godfather let him in on a secret."

Rui Yuan paused. Josie was excited. Rui Yuan continued.

"His godfather bureaucrat told him very calmly, 'Don't worry. I've made even more of such purchases on my own credit card. I also couldn't pay. But don't worry. You don't have to pay either. All will be good.' My friend didn't know what to do. Should he trust his mentor who had taught him so much and knew the ropes?

"Remember I said earlier that this was about corruption? This is how it works. With the central government closing in on corruption especially among government officials, how can corruption take place while looking seemingly legit?

"Well, look at the banks. They need support from local governments for their operation and growth. Local governments are an important source of deposits; banks want them to deposit money with them. But the banks cannot offer explicit bribes to government officials with the central government embarking on the campaign to clean out corruption. But what if the banks can creatively engage in disguised corruption without getting caught?"

"Ahh . . . Clever. So the banks are using credit card as a conduit for bribery?" asked Josie.

> [B]anks are using credit card as a conduit for bribery.

"That's right, Mrs Leong. Our credit card system at that time had very little transparency and governance. It could potentially be used as an implicit bribe to government officials," said Rui Yuan.

"By extending overly generous credit lines?" interrupted Josie.

"Exactly, but there's more to it than that," Rui Yuan nodded.

"Like what you've guessed, my neighbour received an overly generous credit limit than what non-government credit card holders with similar income would have gotten. And he told me that he bet his godfather bureaucrat had an even higher limit relative to non-officials because of his seniority and hence, clout in making decisions in favour of the bank. So the overly generous credit limit allowed him to spend more and buy whatever he needed.

"Then, he defaulted on his payments because of the string of massive purchases made on the card. Usually, when you can't pay, the banks will come and haunt you. They'll be calling you day and night, and haul you to court to pay. I've even heard of cases where people have to sell their house to pay their debt.

"But in my neighbour's case, like what his godfather had said, the bank was very lenient to him even though he became a delinquent in his credit card payment. My friend couldn't and didn't pay his bills for months. So his credit card privileges were stopped, but not for long.

"Instead, he was given preferential treatment. One day, to my neighbour's surprise, the bank just 'forgave' him of the debts he had accumulated and reinstated his card to active status again. And all this happened very fast. The suspension of his credit card was only temporary."

"What?" Josie couldn't believe what she had just heard. "You mean the bank not only gave him a higher credit limit than it would otherwise to non-government officials, but also easier delinquency terms on top of that?"

"That's right," replied Rui Yuan, nodding his head. "Essentially, the corruption works by allowing him to use the card to buy whatever he wanted even beyond busting the generous credit limit. He got away without paying, simply by defaulting. And the bank wrote it off as part of its bad debts.

"My neighbour's godfather bureaucrat had a much higher limit on his card but had apparently crossed his spending limit several times before. So the bank had told him he should tone down on his purchases and not make it so obvious that there's corruption going on. So he recommended my friend to apply for a credit card and used his card to buy more stuff that he wanted, knowing that my friend would likewise be 'forgiven' of his debt by the bank."

"That is so cunning," thought Josie but knowing full well that different countries have different ways of dealing with businesses, and that such disguised corruption may not be consistently prevalent throughout China.

"But won't the losers be the regular man on the street who is not a bureaucrat? He would not be able to receive a credit line as favourably as that of a government official," asked Josie.

"Sadly, yes. But perhaps that's a blessing too as he won't be spending so much," came the reply. "Anyway, when the crackdown started rolling out in full force and there was more stringent governance, banks began to engage less in corruption. Otherwise, the consequences will be dire.

"My neighbour tells me that his credit card limit has since been cut down. And his godfather bureaucrat now doesn't ask him to charge his expenses to his credit card anymore. I think the delinquency rate and reinstatement likelihood have been curbed too after the clamping down."

Josie was glad to hear of this as transparency helps in business dealings. It is another step that China has to overcome to show that it is worthy to be an economic giant.

"I never knew that on this trip, I would have learnt not only about disguised corruption but also disguised pollution," thought Josie as she reflected on her pollution report.

After two months in China, Josie was ready to go home.

"Rui Yuan, when you come to Singapore, call me. I'll be your tour guide," said Josie as she bade farewell to her new friend.

WANT TO KNOW MORE?

This chapter is based on the following research: Sumit Agarwal, Debarati Basu, Pulak Ghosh, Bhuvanesh Pareek and Zhang Jian (2018), "Demonetisation and Digitisation," Working Paper, National University of Singapore, https://papers.ssrn.com/sol3/papers.cfm?abstract_id=3197990. This research was also published as a commentary; see Sumit Agarwal, "India's demonetisation drive: A necessary jolt towards a more digital economy?" *Forbes*, (1 September 2018), https://www.forbes.com/sites/nusbusinessschool/2018/09/01/indias-demonetization-drive-a-necessary-jolt-towards-a-more-digital-economy/#7c9b635c3dc3; Sumit Agarwal, Qian Wenlan, Amit Seru and Zhang Jian (2018), "Disguised Corruption: Evidence from Consumer Credit in China," Working Paper, National University of Singapore, https://papers.ssrn.com/sol3/papers.cfm?abstract_id=3152892. This research was also published as a commentary; see Sumit Agarwal, Qian Wenlan and Zhang Jian, "Pick a card, any card: Cloaked corruption in China," *The Straits Times*, (6 January 2016), https://www.straitstimes.com/opinion/pick-a-card-any-card-cloaked-corruption-in-china

My Own Boss

After hearing that Peter had benefitted from SkillsFuture training by taking up courses on personal finance as well as insurance, Teng and Siew Ling had been toying with the idea of how they could improve themselves. They had thought of learning some computer programming but were deterred when they saw the books they would be using. They could barely master English and to learn a computer language seemed forbearing. They wanted something where the learning curve was not too steep but the 'yield' in terms of putting the new skill to good use was fast and high.

The fashionista in Siew Ling thought that perhaps a course on costume jewellery making or fashion designing might well be her cup of tea. She could sell her hand-made jewellery or designs online. Or perhaps accounting. Siew Ling knew some accounting as she had to do that as part of her job in managing the shoe store. Perhaps a SkillsFuture module on accounting would help her not only at work but also in managing her household budget. And who knows? She might even venture into helping some small mom-and-pop businesses in their accounting. Given her shift hours in the retail line, she could spend the morning hours when she's not at work in the shoe store to help out and earn some extra money.

"Teng, look at this," nudged Siew Ling as she clicked on her computer while working from home. "There's this HOS (Home Office Scheme) that the government is encouraging to foster entrepreneurship. I didn't know that it was set up so long ago . . . 2001! That's almost 20 years."

"What's this scheme about? Singapore has so many of these schemes and they have these acronyms that don't make it easier to know what they are about," remarked Teng.

"HOS is Home Office Scheme. It's to help small businesses to operate from homes," explained Siew Ling. She understood where Teng was coming from. Singaporeans use acronyms way too often. At times, she also found it difficult to follow the acronyms used for places and programmes.

Her friend had joked once, "In Singapore, GST rebates are deposited into your CPF from which you can pay for your HIP HDB flat but not for COE on a car with an IU for driving on AYE into CBD where LTA has installed ERP, and that's not to be confused with ECP."

That got everyone going, "What???"

Siew Ling continued. "It says that HOS is particularly suitable for start-ups that wish to minimise time and costs in setting up an office. Apparently, you can register online and entrepreneurs can start operating almost immediately."

"And so? How's HOS relevant to us? We're not entrepreneurs," shrugged Teng as he didn't understand why his wife pulled him to the computer to read about HOS.

"Not yet. I know it's premature but I'm thinking ahead," explained Siew Ling. "If I, say, take up accounting courses under SkillsFuture,

I'm wondering whether I should set up a business at home to do some accounting work for small businesses like the provision shops or the hairdressing shops in the neighbourhood. I think the uncles and aunties managing these shops need a hand."

"You mean you are thinking of quitting your sales job at the shoe store?" raised Teng's voice a little tad higher. He was stunned.

"No, lah. I'll still keep my retail sales job. But since I'm already doing some accounting for the shoe store and with this training from SkillsFuture that I hopefully will do soon, I'm thinking maybe I can start a small side business doing accounting after completing the course. I'll do this business during my spare time of course," said Siew Ling.

"Hmm . . ." Although Teng was quite taken aback initially, he was warming up to the idea. He remembered the young man from NUS who was a Grab driver in-between jobs. He had mentioned the new distance-based car charges that would put a damper on his taxi cruising. And together with the downward trend of flagging taxis from the kerb, Teng anticipated his taxi returns would be affected. He also recalled what Professor Agarwal had said at the public forum on inter-generational wealth mobility. Perhaps if they plan ahead and either he or Siew Ling embarks as an entrepreneur from home, that might provide a leg up for Ethan and Ervin to do better than both of them.

As though reading his thoughts, Siew Ling advised, "Teng, you should also think of a possible sideline that you can do to augment your taxi earnings." She thought that it might well be Teng and not her becoming a home-based entrepreneur. "Think of what interests you and then sign up for the relevant SkillsFuture courses."

"First things first, one step at a time. We need to register for the SkillsFuture course and do well. Otherwise, this HOS is a no-go," cautioned Teng.

"I've already registered for a three-month course on Intermediate Accounting. And there's an advanced course after that which I'll sign up for after I complete this one," replied Siew Ling as she informed him that she was mindful of the steps she needed to take.

"And I'll ask around for advice from people who may have attended such courses and find out what it was like. I'll take it slow. It might all well be a pipedream but having a start-up business is a possibility I'm thinking of exploring."

Hari Raya Puasa

The fasting month of Ramadan ended and Johan and Fadhilah invited their neighbours, friends and family for the festivities, especially since this is the first year in their new house. It would be a house warming as well as a New Year celebration.

Similar to the Chinese New Year, Hari Raya Puasa is a time of bonding where the young and the old put on new clothing in similar themes or colours. Muslims also visit their friends and family.

Fadhilah's mother had come a few days earlier to help her with cooking and baking for a buffet spread of delicious beef rendang, satay and chicken curry. She simmered the food on the stove over a couple of days so that the beef and chicken had absorbed the spices and were tender. The neighbours had been tempted by the waft of aromatic spices. Ethan, always the hungry one, had asked several times whether it was time to go to the neighbour's house. He couldn't wait to taste the food.

And then there are the sweet *kueh* – dollops of *bahulu* and *dodol* for that quick sugar rush. Fadhilah and her mother had painstakingly stirred coconut milk with rice flour in a big wok for nine hours straight to get the thick, non-sticky, deep golden-brown delicacy in *dodol*. It was a labour of love. And the *bahulu*, a traditional Malay sponge cake, was perfect to complete the meal.

Decked in similar lime green outfits, both Johan and Fadhilah looked so co-ordinated. It was a change to see Johan not in his neatly pressed long-sleeved white shirt that he wears to work but in a loose tunic *baju melayu* and sarong wrapped around his hips. Fadhilah was resplendent in her *baju kurung* – a loose knee-length blouse worn over a long skirt, with a diamond studded brooch pinned in the middle of the neckline.

"Hi, Teng and Siew Ling. Thank you for coming," greeted Fadhilah as she welcomed her guests. "Come, let me introduce you to my mother and my sister."

As Fadhilah's mother could only speak Malay and Teng and Siew Ling weren't fluent in this language, they left it to Ah Kong and Ah Mah to converse with her. It is unfortunate that most of the younger generation are not able to speak Malay like the older folks.

Growing up, Ah Kong and Ah Mah had to speak the main Chinese dialects of Cantonese, Hokkien and Teochew to survive, and Malay as well to the Malay community. Few were conversant in English. They had no choice but to learn each other's language to be able to communicate.

But now, the emphasis in school is for the Chinese to master Mandarin while English is for everyone. Hence, people of different ethnic backgrounds have a common language in English and there has been less urgency to learn each other's dialect or native language. While Teng and Siew Ling can still speak Hokkien, their dialect, it is lost on Ethan and Ervin. They could possibly understand the dialect but can't speak it as they are always speaking in English or Mandarin.

Fatimah

"Teng, Siew Ling, this is my sister, Fatimah," as Fadhilah introduced a younger version of herself. Siew Ling thought the resemblance was quite uncanny.

Before Fatimah could start a conversation, Johan pulled Teng away to introduce him to his friends, leaving Siew Ling with Fatimah.

She soon learned that Fatimah worked from home. Having graduated with a diploma in design, Fatimah worked for a design company for a few years but decided to strike out on her own when she found her skills were very much in demand but her employer wasn't interested in giving her the raise she thought she deserved.

"It was not an easy decision. I had a steady job with a steady income. But the working hours were crazy because the clients would keep on asking for me to be their designer. So my boss kept on piling project after project on me," said Fatimah as she shared her experience with Siew Ling.

"I really love designing and so I put a lot of time into each project. But my boss was accepting all kinds of projects and I had no choice but to do them. He was getting all the revenue because of my skills but I had to put in so many hours to ensure that the designs were well done. I was overworked.

"And when I told my boss that there were way too many projects and I couldn't work overtime every day, he told me to cut corners by spending less time on my designs so that I can complete as many projects as possible. But that was so difficult for me because I always put my heart and soul into my designs. I didn't want to compromise. But my boss was only interested in profits.

"So after several months of soul searching, and weighing the pros and cons, I took the plunge and quit my job. There went my job security."

"Wow! That must have been very tough. And very brave too," empathised Siew Ling.

"Oh definitely," said Fatimah in between biting onto a stick of satay. "But there's a silver lining.

"Before I quit my job, I had already thought of setting up my own design company so that I can make my own decisions and choose what projects I want to do.

"I was encouraged that the design industry is becoming important in Singapore. Do you know that because Singapore wants to be an innovation-driven economy, the government has established this thing called Skills Framework for Design that runs programmes to improve design skill? It's organised by SkillsFuture and Workforce Singapore."

"SkillsFuture again?" thought Siew Ling. Is this a coincidence? Perhaps she and Teng should seriously look into signing up for courses sooner than later.

Fadhilah continued. "But starting your own business is risky and can be very costly – rental, buying equipment and there's no guarantee of revenue coming in.

"Moreover, I live with my mother. My father passed on many years ago. My mother is a home maker. As the only single daughter, I have to look after her. It wasn't easy especially for lower-income people like us."

"So how did you manage?" enquired Siew Ling.

"Have you heard of HOS?" asked Fatimah.

The moment Fatimah asked that question, Siew Ling was clued in. "Was this yet another sign from the higher beings? First, SkillsFuture, and now HOS."

"Please tell me more. I'm interested," Siew Ling said with an appreciative smile.

"HOS helped me quite a bit," Fatimah explained. "I registered myself as an entrepreneur doing design work. This way, as a home-based entrepreneur, I can use my residential address as the office address.

It is quite easy because almost immediately, I could start operating already. And I didn't have to worry about the expiry of my home office authorisation as the permit is valid as long as the business remains in operation.

> **[T]here are quite a number of such home-based businesses now after HOS started. Most are in computer programming and consultancy services.**

"I must say I'm a bit of a *kiasu*. I was initially afraid of failure. HOS helped me to be more confident in starting up my own business and be willing to take risk.

"Apparently, there are quite a number of such home-based businesses now after HOS started. Most are in computer programming and consultancy services. People can work from home for these projects. For me, I can design from home. All I need is my computer, software and a normal printer."

"So you save on rental?" added Siew Ling.

"Not only rental, but equipment costs too. Because I work from home, I'm more mindful as I don't have much space. So I don't buy office equipment unnecessarily. If I need to make large prints or mount them on boards, I just go to the photocopying and printing services at Queensway. So my fixed costs are lowered," explained Fatimah.

"And being my own boss, I can work on my own time. I'm fortunate that I had built my reputation as a designer when I was working for my previous company. So the clients know me from back then. When I started my own business, these clients gave me small jobs first because they weren't sure whether I could handle big projects without the support of a big organisation. Anyway, I let my work do the talking and now my business is thriving."

"What kinds of business does HOS accept? I'm sure there are some rules on that," enquired Siew Ling.

"Well, because the business is operating from your home which is residential, it cannot disturb the peace in the neighbourhood. So it's a 'No-no' to restaurants and of course, massage parlours," laughed Fatimah at the thought of having a massage parlour next door to one's flat.

"Do you think your business is as profitable as your previous workplace?" asked Siew Ling.

"Well, my previous boss also started his own business. But he had to pay office rent and had all these other overheads. I remember him telling me how some of his friends who also had the traditional start-up structure didn't survive. So I would say that start-ups that went through HOS have a comparative financial advantage because of lower overheads. Chances of survival would probably be higher than if you had gone the traditional route of renting office space," answered Fatimah.

"Also, I think I'm more productive with my HOS start-up. I know what projects work well for me and so I pick those to do. Together with the cost savings, it makes the business less risky.

> **Together with the cost savings, it makes the business less risky.**

"But I think what I enjoy most is creativity. As my own boss, I get to experiment ideas in design. Whether I'm showering or watching Netflix, or just simply lying down in bed, I'm thinking of ways to be innovative to see my business succeed.

"In fact, I think in a couple of years, if my business continues to grow like the way it has been in the last two years, I will probably venture into another business. I'm now doing a lot of visual storytelling but after establishing a name for myself, I may also go into design consulting. I think I've been bitten by the entrepreneurial bug!"

Both ladies laughed. Girl power.

"Truth be told, I'm thinking that perhaps in the future I might set up my own business at home," confessed Siew Ling.

> [T]he risk of failure is lower than if you were to start a business by renting office space instead of working from home.

"Well, if you have a great idea and you are focused on it, HOS offers a great scheme to save costs. For me, the timing was great because design is something Singapore is in to. I would think that the risk of failure is lower than if you were to start a business by renting office space instead of working from home," advised Fatimah.

"I have a friend who started his own business too from home under HOS. For some reason, his business failed despite lower costs. But guess what? He picked himself up and tried again. He learned from his failure, made some adjustments, and applied for HOS again. The second time was a charm. He succeeded. I think because the house is always there whether you run a business or not, it motivates you to try and try again until you succeed as the financial penalty is a lot less. So, HOS actually makes entrepreneurs more resilient to failures."

"Hmm . . . And I guess should the business fail, the 'loss of face' is not too critical because unlike setting up an office space where it is so public, running a home business is quite discreet. So if a business fails under HOS, it will probably be less of a social embarrassment compared to having to close an office in a public area," contributed Siew Ling.

"Yes, I think so too. The cost of failure is low both financially and socially," nodded Fatimah in agreement.

"Hey, I heard you have two young kids and your in-laws live with you. So you'll be familiar with the many commitments involving young kids and old folks.

"Well, for me, starting my business from home not only means I have one less thing to worry about – costs – but I also have the flexibility to attend to household matters. Sometimes, I have to bring my mother to the polyclinic for various health matters. Having said that, I need to be disciplined with good time management.

"And this flexibility is consistent with the 'gig' economy, isn't it?"

"Gig economy?" thought Siew Ling. "What's that?" She didn't want to appear ignorant to Fatimah but will have to ask Professor Sing for what that means.

She will also have to tell Teng about what Fatimah had shared and discuss with him further when the time is right about running their own business. But from now till then, many things can happen.

The 'Gig' Economy

Siew Ling spotted Professor Sing near the kitchen with Teng. She asked him what 'gig' economy is.

"Ahh ... It's where temporary jobs are created and companies work with contracted employees for short-term stints. 'Gig' is a slang for 'a job for a specified period of time.' It offers flexibility in working hours," explained Professor Sing.

"In fact, a 'gig' economy can benefit women and narrow the gender wage gap. Work can be divided into smaller parcels and people can choose their preferred timings and place to work. So women who have to look after their children and take care of household chores can choose a pattern of work that suits their circumstances."

"Ahh ... That's why Fatimah said HOS offers flexibility like a 'gig' economy," as Siew Ling made the connection.

Professor Sing continued. "You know, I think jobs like Teng's – taxi driving or even Grab driving – is flexible because people can choose what time to work and where to drive. And so, it would be suitable for working mothers. They can plan their working patterns around their personal commitments."

"Oh yes! We have a few women taxi drivers and I noticed they are quite particular about what time they drive. Some of us say they are so fussy," remarked Teng.

"Really?" asked a curious Siew Ling. "How so?"

"I don't know why, but they seem to like to drive at midnight. Isn't that a more dangerous time for women?" said Teng.

"Singapore where got dangerous?" replied Siew Ling in her Singlish. "I go to the 7-Eleven store at midnight and nothing has happened to me."

"Ahh . . . Do you know why these women prefer to drive so late at night?" asked Professor Sing.

"Because they've already finished all their household chores which their husbands didn't help at all," said Siew Ling, taking a jibe at Teng's no-housework-for-me attitude.

"Yes, that's one reason but the other is because midnight driving is more lucrative. The fare is more expensive and therefore they can earn more money in a shorter period," explained Professor Sing.

"Hey, we women are smart OK," laughed Siew Ling. "We know how to make full use of our working time. Don't play play."

Chinese New Year

After the Hari Raya party, when Teng and Siew Ling were getting ready to go to bed, Teng turned to her and said, "Siew Ling, when we celebrate Chinese New Year next year, we must also celebrate it with a bang. Look at Johan and Fadhilah. They went all out to have so much food. And they had so many people in their home. And they decorated their house so nicely. We must do the same. Have more noise. We should buy beer too. Not just good food. During Chinese New Year, there must be drinking and gambling. That's the tradition."

Siew Ling isn't too pleased. For the last several years, she had kept their Chinese New Year celebrations clean and wholesome because of their two young children. While there are festivities, there had been no gambling or drinking. She was hesitant with Teng wanting to have alcohol included in their get-together.

"Never mind. I'll have the next few months to work on changing his mind. Maybe he'll even forget about it," thought Siew Ling. She will find a way.

It was 9:15 PM. The kids were already in bed, exhausted from playing and eating too much at their neighbour's house. Ah Kong and Ah Mah were flat out tired too.

Only Teng and Siew Ling were sitting on their sofa watching the news programme before going to bed. Teng was yawning. The news was coming to a close before the Sports news was due to start. The newsreader, Melanie Oh, reported a study on alcohol consumption in Finland.

She read, "Recent research by the National University of Singapore studied the relationship between alcohol consumption and health and social harms."

"What's this? Hmm . . . It seems like I don't need to do much to convince Teng to change his mind," thought Siew Ling as she gave Teng a nudge to make sure that he was paying attention to the news.

The newsreader continued.

"Using data from Finland, the NUS study reported that when the Finnish Government increased allowances in travellers' tax-free import of alcohol, municipalities near the Russian and Estonian border where tax-free alcohol is available experienced significant increases in alcohol consumption and drunk driving. It also saw increases in epilepsy and asthma."

Siew Ling interrupted, "Are you listening?"

"Shh . . .," as Teng shut her off so he could hear the rest of the news.

The newsreader continued.

"There was also a marked increase in impulsive crimes such as assault, aggravated property damage and manslaughter. Further, the researchers found that employment, voter turnout and vocational education were lower after the tax-free alcohol import was raised."

"Eh, Teng, listen," asked Siew Ling. "It looks like there are many ill effects of too much drinking. Do you still want beer during Chinese New Year?"

"Uh . . . I guess not," yielded Teng. He knew better not to argue with his wife.

WANT TO KNOW MORE?

This chapter is based on the following research: Sumit Agarwal, Sing Tien Foo, Song Changcheng and Zhang Jian (2018), "Workplace Flexibility and Entrepreneurship," Working Paper, National University of Singapore, https://papers.ssrn.com/sol3/papers. cfm?abstract_id=3136792; Sumit Agarwal, Cheng Shih-Feng, Sing Tien Foo, Sultana Mahanaaz (2019), "Explaining the Gender Wage Gap of Singapore Taxi Drivers," Working Paper, National University of Singapore; Sumit Agarwal, Jussi Keppo and Wang Zhiwen (2019), "The Causal Effect of Alcohol Consumption on Health, Crime and Socioeconomic Behaviours," Working Paper, National University of Singapore.

En Bloc

Property is always a hot topic in Singapore, even when the market is sleepy. During its heyday, when en bloc sales reached their peak, owners and non-owners were engaged in heated arguments as to which direction property prices were heading. Some owners, especially those with multiple properties, wanted prices to continue north; while those who had not bought or not bought sufficiently wanted a softening so they wouldn't have missed the boat.

In a land-scarce country with a density of almost 7,800 per square kilometre,[1] one would be hard-pressed not to be interested in property prices. A survey showed that two in five millennials in Singapore aspire to have multiple properties. More than half aged 21 to 36 years old are homeowners. Of these, almost a quarter (24 percent) already have multiple properties. This is higher than 17 percent of baby boomers

---

[1] Joanna Seow, "Dip in population density, but not in crowded feeling," *The Straits Times*, (16 January 2018), https://www.straitstimes.com/singapore/dip-in-population-density-but-not-in-crowded-feeling

aged 54 to 72 years and 19 percent of Generation X aged 37 to 53 years owning multiple residences.[2]

But can these millennials satisfy their housing aspiration? Can they afford to buy multiple properties, let alone one?

A major component of how much a property costs is land cost. In Singapore, more than 80 percent of the land parcels are controlled and supplied by the government. Two agencies oversee the land supply – HDB and URA – in which land parcels are sold through a tender process in which bids are made. Land sale schedules, released every half a year, include detailed information of each parcel which are made available to developers to make bidding decisions. As such, how much developers bid for a land parcel affects property costs when the property is developed and sold to individuals.

En Bloc Sales

"How about an en bloc sale? Does it influence property prices?" asked Teng.

He was thinking of SERS (Selective En bloc Redevelopment Scheme) in which the government renews older HDB flats. When a block of flats is selected to come under SERS, residents of that block get an opportunity to move to a new flat with a new 99-year lease within the vicinity of the old flat. Additionally, SERS flat owners receive compensation and re-housing benefits.

Teng was hoping that perhaps his block would be selected to participate in SERS. Then, it would be a windfall for him.

But Peter was thinking about en bloc transactions involving private properties. Much like the government releasing land parcels for developers to bid for, en bloc sales involve private owners coming

---

[2] "2 in 5 millennials want to buy multiple homes," *Singapore Business Review*, (22 June 2018), https://sbr.com.sg/residential-property/news/2-in-5-millennials-want-buy-multiple-homes

together to auction their collective plot of residential land to the highest bidder. Such private en bloc sales first start with the formation of a Collective Sale Committee (CSC) where at least 25 percent of the total number of property owners vote to decide to sell. After setting the reserve price in consultation with appointed lawyers, property consultants and independent valuer, the CSC proceeds to collect signatures from owners agreeing to the en bloc sale. When the majority consent is obtained, the CSC will launch the property for public tender exercise where interested developers will submit their bids.

"Mr Ong didn't say anything about en bloc sales but I can tell you what I think based on my experience," said Peter.

"OK. Here's a quiz for you. Guess what makes an estate more likely to go through an en bloc sale?"

"Age! The older it is, the higher the chance of an en bloc," jumped in Teng quickly. He is quite a bit of a *kiasu*. He enjoys competing with Siew Ling and do better.

"You are right. That's an easy one. Older properties are more likely to successfully go through en bloc sales. It's not just due to the inferior condition and lower property value of old dwellings, but it's also because there is less restrictive regulation legislating such old properties," explained Peter. "Next?"

> **Older properties are more likely to successfully go through en bloc sales.**

"Size of estate! The more units there are, the harder it is to get all residents to agree to the en bloc," was Siew Ling's turn to respond. She enjoys that little bit of *kiasu* spirit with Teng to see who can outdo the other.

"Siew Ling, you are spot on," as Peter smiled at the couple's endeavour to beat each other. "Estates with a large number of units are less likely to enter into en bloc sales. I read somewhere that one additional apartment unit decreases the probability by 0.02 percent.

"So it's tied 1-1 for Teng and Siew Ling. What else?"

"How about being near an MRT station?" Teng hazarded a guess. He wasn't sure whether that made sense but he badly wanted to outsmart his wife.

"Huh? How does that affect en bloc?" said Siew Ling as she rolled her eyes in disbelief. She was thinking of how her husband would say all kinds of stuff just so he could get more answers than she did.

"Well," said Peter as he paused for a while. "It actually does."

"There you go!" jumped in Teng with a little smirk on his face. He was elated that he got it right. Or so he thought.

"Wait, hold on. I haven't finished yet," Peter quickly interrupted before Teng got too swell-headed. "Proximity to MRT affects en bloc sales but in the opposite direction."

"Haha!" laughed out Siew Ling, not in a cynical manner but that her husband can be such a buffoon at times. Teng laughed too, but in bewilderment that he was right smack wrong.

"Let me explain. Properties located near MRT are prized properties because of the convenience afforded. So their land values are high. And precisely because of that, they are less likely to be en bloc targets as such en bloc redevelopments would be costlier, and hence, riskier. Moreover, I think existing residents are less willing to let go of this MRT convenience. They will have to relocate and it may not be near an MRT."

"So I guess it's minus 1 for Teng because he answered wrongly," teased a giggling Siew Ling.

"You're so mean," as Teng gently elbowed his wife.

"OK. What other factors?" said Peter as he brought the couple back to the quiz.

"I think freehold properties are more likely to be en bloc-ed than those with 99 years old," said Siew Ling.

Teng gave a sigh. He knew his wife was correct on this one.

"Yup. Freehold properties are 0.4 percent more likely to become en bloc properties than leasehold properties. The limited number of years left on a leasehold property makes it less tenable for a developer to buy the property en bloc," explained Peter.

"Any other factors?" prodded Peter.

"How about permissible plot ratio?"

Both Teng and Siew Ling gave him a blank look. They have no idea what a permissible plot ratio is.

"Permissible plot ratio is the development intensity allowed for a particular plot of land. It affects the maximum gross floor area of the development. Generally, if two developments have roughly the same land area but vastly different plot ratios, this means that one will be a lot denser or taller than the other. For example, The Pinnacle@Duxton has a plot ratio of 8.4, whereas the neighbouring Tanjong Pagar Plaza has a plot ratio of only 3.5. Then, The Pinnacle@Duxton would have a far denser development than Tanjong Pagar Plaza.

"So for a plot that has not reached its permissible limit, meaning there could have been more units built than it currently has, its en bloc potential is higher.

"Or if a plot has been granted a higher permissible limit, then en bloc probabilities are higher for these properties than those with a lower limit. I read somewhere that for every one unit increase in permissible plot ratio, the probability of an en bloc goes up by slightly more than 2 percent.

"One last factor," Peter concluded. "En bloc probability is higher for properties located nearer to the city centre."

"So, I win this quiz, right?" declared Siew Ling.

"Hmmph . . . hmmph," sniffled Teng, pretending to be a sore loser.

"But seriously, Peter, don't you think en bloc sales are getting a way bit out of hand? Some properties are still fairly new and yet they are en bloc-ed. And others are so rundown and deserve to be en bloc-ed but some residents are too greedy or emotionally attached that they block the deal," asked Teng. He had given rides to several passengers who complained of how their en bloc attempts were scuttled by greedy neighbours who just wanted more money.

> **[E]n bloc deals help in urban redevelopment and renewal especially in deserving old estates.**

"Say what you like but en bloc deals help in urban redevelopment and renewal especially in deserving old estates," responded Peter. "When the old dilapidated buildings are torn down to make way for new condos, it attracts younger families with higher incomes, stimulates commercial interests in surrounding areas and rejuvenates the vibrancy of the local community.

"And on top of that, I think we benefit too. When there's an en bloc, the government collects land development taxes that are used to improve local amenities and public transportation networks."

En Bloc Buyers

"Peter, do you remember once when my neighbour Professor Sing kept bugging you on whether you buy properties at a good price because you have insider information?" asked Teng.

"Hey, hello bro. It's not insider information. You cannot anyhow say that. It can get me into trouble," protested Peter.

"It's called better information. I'm a more informed person about the property market.

"But it is true that real estate agents could use their knowledge to suss out great deals for themselves. Many of my agent friends hang around with developers and other such contacts. And so before the market knows of it, these agents already know which are the potential en bloc sites and their chances of seeing the en bloc become successful. So they are more likely than the man on the street to have bought these properties before they went en bloc."

"Ahh . . . So again, knowledge is power," Siew Ling reminded herself as she recalled this same thought she had when Professor Sing was talking about real estate agents and how they have an advantage when buying properties.

"Peter, I had this passenger and he told me that he had gone through two successful en bloc deals! He said that after the first en bloc which he considered as a windfall, he wanted to stay in his second residence for the rest of his life. But an en bloc came for the second property and so he lucked out again," recounted Teng of this lucky passenger.

"Yeah, I noticed that tendency too," agreed Peter. "I noticed that existing en bloc residents have a higher chance to purchase another en bloc property. Perhaps they have an eye for spotting en bloc opportunties. And they are more familiar with the en bloc process and are aware of the potential capital gains an en bloc sale can bring. Or they are just very lucky."

> [E]xisting en bloc residents have a higher chance to purchase another en bloc property.

"But I also noticed that some people would just sell their condo at the secondary market even though they knew that the property would be undergoing an en bloc exercise soon. Why do they do that? Don't they want to wait and collect the en bloc windfall?" asked Teng.

"Yes, some people are like this," acknowledged Peter. "They would rather sell first and have the profit in hand. If they wait for the en bloc, it may or may not go through. There's uncertainty. So, if you are *kiasu*, you say 'No, I'd rather sell now and take a lesser but certain profit than to wait for an uncertain possibility.'

"And there are people who are willing to buy from them because they are risk takers who are banking on the en bloc to be successful. And I won't be surprised if some of these buyers are real estate agents. Remember what Professor Sing said? As agents, we are better informed. We know which estate is more likely to be successful in the en bloc exercise. And we know who are the residents who are more risk averse and do not mind selling it off for a definite profit. So real estate agents take advantage of this information."

Winner's Curse

"Peter, I've heard this term called 'winner's curse'. I'm not entirely sure what that means. Does it apply here?"

"Ahh . . . The winner's curse is a phenomenon that occurs in auctions such as land auctions or en bloc bidding, where the winning bidder overpays due to emotional reasons or incomplete information," explained Peter.

"It is the difference between the winning bid and the second highest losing bid weighted by the winning bid. So, if the difference is drastic, it means the winning bidder overpaid by a lot and the winner's curse is high. On the other hand, if the difference is small, it means the winning bidder did not overpay that much and the winner's curse is less.

"So developers bidding on an en bloc property should do their homework and not overbid aggressively. It may benefit the en bloc sellers a lot but it will be a winner's curse to the winning developer."

"OK, guys. Enough of this winner's curse and en bloc talk. Since I won the quiz, the treat is on me. Let's go to Nex and have some dessert," said a cheerful Siew Ling as she got the family ready for the outing.

WANT TO KNOW MORE?

This chapter is based on the following research: Sing Tien Foo and Chia Liu Ee (2018), "Speculators and Certainty Effect: Evidence from the Redevelopment Market," Working Paper, National University of Singapore. This research was also published as a commentary; see Sing Tien Foo and Chia Liu Ee, "What happens when the en bloc musical chairs stop?" *Channel News Asia*, (21 January 2018), https://www. channelnewsasia.com/news/singapore/commentary-what-happens-when-the-en-bloc-musical-chairs-stop-9864526

14

A Nudge, A Budge

S iew Ling quickly got Ethan and Ervin dressed up to go for dessert at Nex with Teng and Peter. Ah Kong and Ah Mah didn't want to go along because they were tired from having to look after the two rumbustious boys for the whole week. They wanted quiet time to themselves.

After cutting through the void deck of the next two blocks, they had to walk past a food court of another block before reaching Nex. This was the same route that Siew Ling had to take when she goes to work, and the same one too, that Ah Kong and Ah Mah use when they bring Ethan to his kindergarten. It was a route all too familiar to the family.

Siew Ling thought she could walk blindfolded to Nex. As she blanked out the chatterings from her two sons arguing who would make a better Captain America, and Teng and Peter still talking about en bloc properties, Siew Ling could recall not all but most of the landmarks along the way.

"There's the banner on the left about the Member of Parliament visiting the neighbourhood. Next to it is a banner on recycling. Then there's another banner about energy conservation," recalled Siew Ling as she recounted her walking route.

As they were approaching the food court, Siew Ling exercised her grey matter again. She tried recalling how each of the stall look like.

"The drinks stall is at the corner with a large sign that shows the various drinks from Coca-Cola. Then next to it is the stall selling steamed dumplings and some *kueh kueh*. The chicken rice stall is next. The uncle will hang the roasted chickens on the left and the steamed ones on the right. The Malay stall has a green signage with the crescent moon on it. And then there's the Chinese noodle stall with a shelf holding the various types of noodles. Below the shelf are metal bowls containing sliced mushrooms and fish balls," as the images came slowly to Siew Ling.

"Ahh . . . I got these right," smiled Siew Ling to herself as they walked past the food court. She was pleased. "Oh, yes! There's the notice board at the lift of the HDB block with a poster about switching off at the power socket."

Soon, they reached Nex. They went to the Icing Room so that the boys could have a place to sit and eat their dessert, while the adults could continue talking.

"Boys, did you notice the poster that tells you to switch off electrical appliances at the power points?" asked Siew Ling. She wondered whether her sons were observant. Children seemed to notice things that adults often take for granted.

The boys weren't listening to her. Their dessert – ice cream cake with the M&Ms sprinkled on them – was giving the boys a sugar rush. It was like having a little party in their mouths.

"Boys," said Siew Ling again, this time with a raised voice in a sterner tone. "Did you see any poster telling you how to save electricity?"

Ervin, at two years old, was too young to understand what his mother was talking about. But Ethan was more forthcoming.

"Mummy, do you mean the one with a girl pointing to a switch?"

"Yes, that's the one. Can you remember what she said?" asked Siew Ling.

Ethan was not sure of all the words on the poster but the illustration was sufficient for him to understand what the message was about.

"Ah Mah explained the poster to me. She told me that we should turn off the switch at the power point. And that would help us save money," replied Ethan somewhat nonchalantly as he continued eating his cake.

After a short while, feeling bored as his brother wasn't quite a fluent talker yet and his father and Uncle Peter were talking about some adult stuff, Ethan turned to his mother for companionship.

"Mummy, there's also a banner at the hawker centre, you know," he said. "And that one says 'Save energy. Save money'. Ah Mah told me we must switch off all appliances after use. Do not leave the switch on when we are not using the TV, computer or fan."

"Very good, Ethan," smiled Siew Ling. She was pleased that Ethan was learning the importance of conserving energy.

"And what else did the banner say?" tested Siew Ling to see if Ethan noticed.

"I know that one, Mummy. It says to switch off the air-con after a short while and use the fan instead. It could save us $400," said a delighted Ethan who knew he got it right.

And to test his mummy, he asked "And Mummy, do you know how many plates of chicken rice we can buy with $400?"

"I don't know, sweetie. How many?" asked Siew Ling, testing Ethan further.

"100!" said the young boy with both palms spread out and banging in the air. "If we use the air-con for a little while and then use the fan for the rest of the time, the money we saved in a year can buy us 100 plates of chicken rice! My favourite food," said Ethan as he grinned from ear to ear, excited that he could educate his mother on how to save on energy and spend on his favourite dish.

"And I think there was another poster, right?" asked Siew Ling.

"Yeah, there's a poster that mentioned using the thermos flask instead of the electric hot-pot," volunteered Ethan.

"But Mummy, if we use the thermos flask, it's quite troublesome for Ah Mah. She may run out of water when she needs it and it will take some time to boil," said Ethan who has a soft spot for his grandma.

Siew Ling nodded. "This is where we have to learn to adapt. It may be a little inconvenient but we can save money. Do you remember what the poster said about how much we can save if we used a thermos flask instead?"

"Mummy, you mean you can't remember?" asked the innocent boy, a little surprised that his mother has a short memory.

Siew Ling pretended that she couldn't recall.

"Mummy, it said that we can save $300 a year!" came Ethan's reply.

Siew Ling was beaming inside that Ethan had such a fantastic memory. Hopefully that would be put to good use, like in his studies. Not quite a Tiger Mum but still *kiasu*, Siew Ling wants her son to do well in school.

"Wow! $300 is a lot of money. And if we save all that money, what do you think we can use the money for?"

"Captain America toys!" shouted Ethan. Ervin joined in too, even though he didn't know what was going on. All he could recognise from the conversation was Captain America.

On their way back home, they chanced upon another banner that said there would be a talk on energy conservation. This would be held at the community centre the following Saturday morning.

"Oh great! I should be able to attend before I start work," thought Siew Ling. She was keen on keeping the household utilities bill down given that Teng's taxi-driving career seemed limited with the entry of Grab and the forthcoming distance-based toll charges.

The Energy Conservation Talk

As Teng was on the road driving, Siew Ling brought Ah Mah along for the talk on energy conservation. Ah Mah is quite an effective 'policewoman' at home in making sure that the lights and electrical appliances are switched off when not in use. But perhaps more can be done. Ah Kong had to stay at home to keep an eye on the two boys.

"Ma, this talk may be good for us. It's about a campaign to encourage families to save on their electricity bills," said Siew Ling.

"Oh . . . You mean like the campaign on saving water?" recalled Ah Mah on the campaign where households were given a smart meter attached to their shower hose that informed them how much water they were using when showering. She remembered that their neighbours, Josie and Sarah, participated in the study and actually cut down on water usage.[1]

"I'll ask Sarah to come along as well."

As it was a Saturday morning, the room was quite packed with working adults and young people as well, possibly students who were doing some energy projects for their school and might find the talk relevant.

In came a tall gangly man. He was introduced as Mr Leong, a consultant on energy conservation. He walked steadily to the front of the room where he was hooked up to a microphone and given a clicker for his slides.

"This man looks familiar," thought Sarah. "Where have I seen him before?"

The moment Mr Leong started speaking in his slow assured no-nonsense voice, Sarah remembered that he was the man who came to her secondary school a few years ago. He had spoken about the policy experiment involving a competition to promote energy conservation."Ah Mah. I know this man. He came to my school before to talk about saving electricity," whispered Sarah to Ah Mah.

"Shh . . . Listen, don't talk," said a somewhat annoyed Siew Ling.

---

[1] For more on this research on the effects of a smart meter on Singaporeans' water consumption, see Sumit Agarwal, Ang Swee Hoon and Sing Tien Foo (2018), *Kiasunomics: Stories of Singaporean Economic Behaviours*, Chapter 17 "Girl, Shower Faster, Save Water," (Singapore: World Scientific Publishers). To read the academic article, see Sumit Agarwal, Fang Ximeng, Lorenz Goette, Sing Tien Foo, Samuel Schoeb, Verena Tiefenbeck, Thorsten Staake and David Wang (2017), "The Role of Goals and Real-Time Feedback in Resource Conservation: Evidence from a Large-Scale Field Experiment," Working Paper, National University of Singapore, https://www.iame.uni-bonn.de/people/lorenz-goette/goals-and-real-time-feedback. This research was also published as commentaries, see Sumit Agarwal and Sing Tien Foo, "Targets, real-time feedback can cut water use in the shower," *The Straits Times*, (11 February 2017), https://www.straitstimes.com/opinion/targets-real-time-feedback-can-cut-water-use-in-the-shower; Sumit Agarwal and Sing Tien Foo, "Beyond price hikes and conservation campaigns, saving water through smart showers," *Channel News Asia*, (27 March 2018), https://www.channelnewsasia.com/news/singapore/nudging-conserving-water-beyond-price-hikes-10040642

"Good morning, everyone," greeted Mr Leong. "Thank you for coming to hear about this campaign on energy conservation.

"Let me start by asking how many of you have heard of the Paris Agreement?"

Almost all the younger generation raised their hands. Ah Mah didn't. She couldn't imagine what agreements could have taken place in Paris. Why not London? Or New York?

Mr Leong continued. "That's good to see. Now, how many of you know that Singapore is committed to the cause set out in the Paris Agreement?"

This time a smaller number, almost one-third of the audience raised their hand.

Mr Leong nodded to acknowledge that he recognised the profile of the audience.

"The Paris Agreement brings countries into a common cause to pursue efforts to combat climate change. Its aim is to strengthen global response to the threat of climate change. It has set out certain objectives, one of which is to undertake efforts to limit the temperature increase even further to 1.5 degrees Celsius.

"Singapore is committed to the Paris Agreement. Over here, our housing sector makes up about 15 percent of the country's total electricity consumption. So how can households foster an attitude and behaviour towards energy conservation so that we are responsible not only to ourselves but also to the society and the environment?"

Mr Leong paused to make sure that the audience was still with him.

"The National Environment Agency (NEA) previously ran a campaign involving school children. They worked with a few schools in which children were encouraged to nudge their parents to adopt a more conservative behaviour in terms of electricity consumption. They found that electricity consumption declined just by mere reminders from children to their parents and neighbours.[2]

"Encouraged by this outcome, NEA thought what if they could extend this beyond school children. After all, not all households have a school-going kid. And school children can only talk to a limited number of people. So, what if NEA were to use mass media tools like banners and posters? Wouldn't that reach out to a much wider audience?

"So NEA ran another campaign. In this campaign, they had educational banners put up in 62 hawker centres and posters on HDB notice boards for six months. Why hawker centres, you might ask.

"Well, we know Singaporeans love to eat and many go to hawker centres on a daily basis for dinners and suppers. So while they're eating and chatting with each other, NEA hoped they would also notice the banners.

"Compared to school children nudging their parents, this poster-banner campaign was a more subtle and non-personal way to let people know about energy conservation.

"So good so far?" asked Mr Leong to make sure that everyone followed him. It seemed all was good.

"Great! These posters contained information on energy conservation practices that will help households save on their electricity bills. Let me show you some of the posters."

Mr Leong showed the first poster on the projector screen.

"As you can see, the poster gives very practical advice on how to conserve electricity – common household chores that anyone can do to reduce electricity consumption. And to make it more salient and

---

[2] For more on this research on the effects of nearby construction on utilities bills, see Sumit Agarwal, Ang Swee Hoon and Sing Tien Foo (2018), *Kiasunomics: Stories of Singaporean Economic Behaviours*, Chapter 13 "Papa, Don't Forget to Switch off the Lights," (Singapore: World Scientific Publishers).

SAVE ENERGY SAVE MONEY

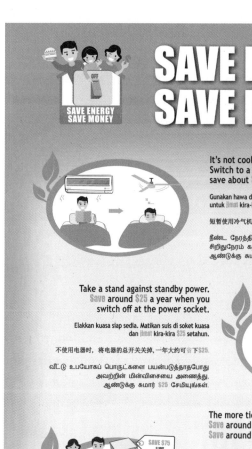

It's not cool to let the air-con run for a long time. Switch to a fan after a short while and save about $400 a year.

Gunakan hawa dingin bagi masa yang singkat dan beralih kepada kipas untuk jimat kira-kira $400 setahun.

短暂使用冷气机后，改用电风扇保持凉爽，一年大约可省下$400。

நீண்ட நேரத்திற்கு குளிர்சாதனத்தை இயக்குவது நல்லதல்ல. சிறிதுநேரம் கழித்து மின்விசிறியை பயன்படுத்தி ஆண்டுக்கு சுமார் $400 சேமியுங்கள்.

Take a stand against standby power. Save around $25 a year when you switch off at the power socket.

Elakkan kuasa siap sedia. Matikan suis di soket kuasa dan jimat kira-kira $25 setahun.

不使用电器时，将电器的总开关关掉，一年大约可省下$25。

வீட்டு உபயோகப் பொருட்களை பயன்படுத்தாதபோது அவற்றின் மின்விசையை அணைத்து, ஆண்டுக்கு சுமார் $25 சேமியுங்கள்.

More than **75% of households** practise this tip

The more ticks, the better!
Save around $260 a year if you buy a 3-tick air-con.
Save around $75 a year for a 3-tick refrigerator.

Lebih banyak✓, lebih baik!
Jimat kira-kira $260 setahun jika anda membeli hawa dingin 3✓.
Jimat kira-kira $75 setahun bagi peti sejuk 3✓.

购买较多✓的电器，节省更多。
使用三个✓的冷气机一年大约可省下$260。
使用三个✓的电冰箱一年大约可省下$75。

அதிக புட்குறிகள், மேலும் சிறந்தது!
3-புட்குறிகள் உள்ள குளிர்சாதனத்தை வாங்கினால், ஆண்டுக்கு சுமார் $260 சேமிப்பீர்கள்.
3-புட்குறிகள் உள்ள குளிர்பதனப் பெட்டியை வாங்கினால், ஆண்டுக்கு சுமார் $75 சேமிப்பீர்கள்.

SAVE $75 a year

SAVE $260 a year

National Environment Agency

* All calculations are based on electricity cost of $0.27 per kWh of electricity

real, monetary benefits are shown to demonstrate how such simple acts go towards financial savings.

"Let's take for instance the bottom picture on the left," instructed Mr Leong as he enlarged that part of the illustration. "The poster tells people how to be a smart shopper – buy appliances with three energy efficiency ticks. Can you imagine that a three-tick air-conditioning unit can save you $260 annually?"

Mr Leong could tell that some in the audience didn't realise the extent of monetary gains they could have benefitted from being a smart shopper.

But the response wasn't quite the 'Aha' moment that he wanted. At least, not yet.

"Now, let's see the top picture in the poster about air-conditioning and fans. We get that Singapore is very hot and humid, and using air-conditioning is almost a necessity. While we can't do much about our geographical location and hence, the associated humidity and heat, we can do something about how to make the weather more tolerable without hurting Mother Nature."

Mr Leong knew that especially among the millennials, issues concerning environmental sustainability is almost a sure-win to tug at their heartstrings.

"If you use the air-con because the weather is too muggy, by all means, do so. But please remember, you do not have to use the air-con the whole time. Set the timer to switch off after one or two hours when the room has been sufficiently cooled down. Then, switch on the fan to circulate and maintain the cool air. As the poster shows, you can save $400 by doing so!"

And that's when Mr Leong received the response he was orchestrating for.

SAVE ENERGY
SAVE MONEY

Beat the heat with a fan instead of an air-con. Save around $460 a year!

Hilangkan rasa panas dengan menggunakan kipas angin, bukan hawa dingin. Jimat kira-kira $460 setahun.

使用电风扇代替冷气机保持凉爽，一年大约可省下$460。

குளிரூட்டிக்குப் பதிலாக ஒரு மின்விசிறியைப் பயன்படுத்தி வெப்பத்தை தணித்திடுங்கள். ஆண்டுக்கு சுமார் $460 சேமித்திடுங்கள்

Don't let your electricity bills boil over. Use a thermos flask instead of an electric air-pot and save around $300 a year.

Elakkan penggunaan cerek elektrik. Gunakan termos air dan jimat kira-kira $300 setahun.

弃用保温电水壶，转用热水瓶盛热水，一年大约可省下$300。

உங்கள் மின்சாரக் கட்டணங்களை வரம்பு மீற விடாதீர்கள். மின்சார ஏர்-பாட்டுக்கு பதிலாக தெர்மோஸ் ஃபிளாஸ்க்கை உபயோகித்து ஆண்டுக்கு சுமார் $300 சேமியுங்கள்.

Leaving the storage water heater on can land you in hot water. Save an additional $110 a year by switching off the storage water heater after use.

Jimat tambahan $110 setahun dengan mematikan alat pemanas air simpanan selepas digunakan.

使用储水式热水器后，将电源关掉，一年大约可省下额外$110。

குளித்த பின்னர், வெண்ணீர் தொட்டியின் மின்விசையை அணைத்து, ஆண்டுக்கு கூடுதலாக $110 யை சேமித்திடுங்கள்.

*All calculations are based on electricity cost of $0.27 per kWh of electricity

National Environment Agency

And now, to hammer in the final nail, Mr Leong showed the second poster.

"Do you know that the energy consumed by using an air-con is similar to that of using 13 fans? And look at the money saved – a whopping $460 annually!"

There was an audible gasp. Mr Leong had indeed gotten their undivided attention now.

The Findings

"I want to share with you the findings from this NEA campaign," continued Mr Leong.

"They studied energy consumption from four groups of households depending on how far away they lived from the hawker centre: (1) those living within 0.5 kilometre of the hawker centre, (2) those living beyond 0.5 kilometre to one kilometre away, (3) those living beyond one kilometre to 1.5 kilometres away, and (4) those living beyond 1.5 kilometres to three kilometres away.

"The idea is that those living near to the hawker centre are more likely to have seen the posters and therefore, more likely to change their behaviour compared to those living farther away who are less likely to have seen these posters.

"So, energy consumption of these households was measured over time. Their usage was tracked for six months before the campaign started, six months when the campaign was ongoing and six months after the campaign ended. Six-six-six."

Again, Mr Leong scanned the audience to ensure that all could follow what he had said. It seemed so.

"Any guesses what was found?" asked Mr Leong.

As usual, the audience was somewhat hesitant to voice out their opinions in public.

"OK. The findings showed that there is about 0.5 percent reduction in the average electricity consumption among households living within one kilometre from the hawker centre. Those who lived closer to the hawker centre had more electricity savings. And as you live farther away, the effect dissipates."

> [T]here is … reduction in the average electricity consumption among households living within one kilometre from the hawker centre.

Ah Mah turned towards Siew Ling, winked her eye and whispered, "I'm one of those who contributed to the 0.5 percent reduction. I've been reminding Pa and Ethan not to waste energy."

Mr Leong continued. "Importantly, after the six-month campaign was over, the savings persisted. This means that people were still adopting good habits of saving energy despite no posters or banners reminding them to do so. That's very good news, isn't it?"

Mr Leong paused momentarily, then smiled.

"I'm sure you are tired of hearing my voice by now. So, let me ask you – what's so special about the findings? Any comments?"

Sarah, who is used to class participation in school, raised her hand. "Hi, Mr Leong. Thank you for your talk. You actually gave a talk at my school a couple of years ago about school children nudging their parents to save energy."

Mr Leong was somewhat surprised to hear that he has a 'repeat' member of the audience and hoped that he had converted her to be an energy saver.

Sarah continued. "I think the findings are fantastic especially given that these posters are non-personal. People do not feel the pressure to conform as may have been the case when children persuade their parents. I study psychology and I learn about the communication process. What do you think then was the key that got people to heed advice from a non-personal source?"

"Thank you for your question. It's good to know I have a 'repeat' listener here. It means I wasn't too boring in my talks," Mr Leong laughed.

"Seriously," said Mr Leong with no smile on his face, "I believe there are at least two factors that contributed to the campaign's success. First, in these messages, people were given objective dollar values as to how much they could save. It wasn't 'you can save some money' but rather 'you can save $300 if you do this'. By giving specificity to the monetary savings, the intention of the NEA campaign was to put money where their mouth is. They dare to and very publicly so, declare the savings that could have been achieved. This gives credibility to the message. People believe in the message. There's buy-in and so they are more willing to change their behaviour.

"Second, although banners and posters were used, and these I agree are non-personal sources of communication, the message wasn't. People were told '*You* can save . . .' or instances were shown where people can relate to such as using the air-con when sleeping. These are personal instances to them. They identify with these situations. They can relate to them. And they were told *they* can save from such energy-saving habits. It's not the society can save but individually, *their* household can save. Such personalisation of the message is also a key.

"Of course, not all social campaigns benefit from personal messages. In some cases such as anti-smoking campaigns, too strong a personal message can turn off people from even looking at the poster. This is what psychologists call defensive reaction. Fortunately, in this case, the personal messages worked because they concerned monetary savings. I do not know anyone who doesn't want to save money whenever they can."

Another hand was raised. A middle-aged man who came across as one who has seen the world asked, "The reduction in electricity usage is so miniscule at only 0.5 percent. That's not even a 1 percent reduction. Why would you say that the campaign is a success?"

"That's a good question," replied Mr Leong.

"Human behaviours are difficult to change. We do not expect people to change overnight in how they save energy especially since they are so accustomed to a certain level of comfort. Take for example, my teenage daughter. She's on her smartphone most of the time – WhatsApping, Googling or watching YouTube. Short of confiscating her smartphone, I cannot expect her to stop overnight.

"Likewise for energy consumption. It takes time to change. So, why is a 0.5 percent reduction a success?

"There are several yardsticks. One, this campaign compared to other campaigns is very cost efficient. The cost is essentially printing the posters and banners, and hanging them strategically at hawker centres. There is no incurrence of celebrity endorsements nor expensive glamourous commercials whether on TV or social media. It's a simple campaign that tells the facts with no bells and whistles. It also can be executed quickly. Yet, despite the lack of expensive attention-grabbing tactics, this campaign managed to get a reduction in energy usage.

"Moreover, as I've already said, the reduction in energy use was sustained even after the campaign ended. As such, the savings are even more substantial when we consider the post-campaign period.

> [T]he reduction in energy use was sustained even after the campaign ended.

"We should also recognise that the 0.5 percent reduction is only the start of a possibly permanent change in behaviour. This campaign should not be a standalone one. It should be part of a long-term programmatic exercise. Continuing with such reminders will fortify the initial reduction in energy use as well as encourage other residents who have yet to embark on energy conservation to start a more sustainable lifestyle.

"I believe you may have seen some of these posters and the banner again in your neighbourhood. This is part of the reinforcement exercise to sustain the good habit of saving energy."

Mr Leong hoped that his reply had won over the sceptical lot among the audience.

He said something else which seemed to gain the audience appreciation towards the campaign. "You know, there are several ways to get people to change their habits. One way is by using the stick – penalise people who overuse electricity by charging them a higher unit cost so that they will curb their consumption. The other is by their own volition because there's a carrot in the form of cost savings. This campaign seeks to get Singaporeans to change their habit voluntarily and enjoy the cost savings that come along with the good habit."

A final question was asked.

"I like the idea of using the air-conditioning for a short while and then switching to a fan thereafter. But I'll be sleeping when the air-con is still on. I get it that I can put it on timer, but I can't do that for my fan. I don't think fans have an auto switch-on mode. It has an auto switch-off mode. To wake up in the middle of the night to switch on the fan may disrupt my sleep. And even worse is I may not be able to go back to sleep again. Are there devices that will auto turn on the fan?"

Everyone laughed at this question, not because it was stupid or trivial but because it is so real. It's easy to say that one should switch from the air-con to the fan, but in reality, this may not be practical especially when one has already fallen fast asleep.

Mr Leong sighed. It's a tough question to reply because of the reality of what it is.

"I see your point. I'm in that same situation too. I hate to wake up in the middle of the night and not be able to sleep again," Mr Leong said. He wanted to show that he also faced the same issue and empathised with them.

"There are smart home technology available in Singapore. For new homes, such technology can be installed. For older homes, it may take a longer time to smart-proof. I believe there are some apps on smartphones that can help us auto-control our appliances. For those who do not have access to these devices that can programme our appliances to auto switch on and off, we will need to make adaptations of our own.

"As with most changes for improvements, some adjustments are needed which are not necessarily painless. There's the saying 'No pain, no gain'. So we need to think of how to go about making such adjustments.

"For parents with young kids who sleep earlier than them, parents can switch on the fan for them. The same for elderly parents who tend to sleep early, their adult children can switch on the fan for them.

"As for us the working adults and parents, some adaptation is necessary. Perhaps when you get up in the middle of the night to go to the bathroom, remember to switch off the air-con and turn on the fan. Use the fan's remote control so that it is less effortful and hence, less disruptive to going back to sleep. Or husband and wife can take turns doing this. I just hope no marital quarrels arise from this!"

Everyone laughed at the last point as the talk was brought to a close.

Siew Ling reminded Ah Mah to keep a closer watch on Ethan to ensure that he does not waste electricity. Ah Mah also thought of switching to using the thermos flask. And she'll have to keep a closer eye on Ah Kong too, as he's getting quite forgetful in not switching off the water heater.

WANT TO KNOW MORE?

This chapter is based on Sumit Agarwal, Mahanaaz Sultana and Sing Tien Foo (2019), "Public Media Campaign and Energy Conservation: A Natural Experiment in Singapore," Working Paper, National University of Singapore.

Calling Once, Calling Twice, Sold!

After the conversation with Peter about en bloc sales, Teng was excited to share that information with Professor Sing.

"Really?" remarked Professor Sing. "How interesting. Currently, I'm doing a study on land auctions and how property developers bid for them.

"In my current research, I studied how developers ensure that the prices of land pieces that they already have remain competitive."

"Aiyoh! These business dealings and strategies are too much for a simple guy like me," thought Teng. After all, he always had the impression that as a mere taxi driver, he's not up to wheeling and dealing. But nonetheless, he has always marveled at how property developers are savvy in their business decisions.

Sometimes he would hear from fellow drivers but more often from passengers of how ridiculous a price some property developers had bid for a piece of land, and how they thought that these developers were sure to lose money on them. But would developers be so silly as to overbid?

"Teng, developers engage in strategic bidding behaviour not only to generate a rising price pattern but also to participate without necessarily winning the subsequently launched sites," elaborated Professor Sing.

"Aiyoh! Sing, can you explain in easier English?" asked Teng as he scratched his head. "This is getting a bit too complicated for me."

"Can, can. Sorry, ah. Sometimes I get carried away because I forget I'm not presenting a research paper at a conference," laughed Professor Sing.

"Well, we studied all the tender prices submitted by all the land developers for all private residential land sales auctioned through the Government Land Sales. And we tracked each individual developer's bidding behaviour over time. By doing so, we could link one land plot to the next launched neighbouring plot."

"Why would that be important?" asked Teng.

"Ahh...," smiled Professor Sing. "When we know how much developers bid for Plot A and later Plot B and later Plot C that are geographically close to one another but launched at different times, we can compare the bids placed by the same developer and see whether prices tend to rise for subsequent land plots that are essentially close substitutes to one another. And on top of that, we can also observe how the developer bids for these similar lots and see if there is a pattern in the bids."

"So what did you find?" asked an eager Teng.

Although Teng is not selling his flat any time soon to buy a condominium, he still remembered well the public talk he had attended at NUS on inter-generational housing wealth mobility. If land prices were sold at a higher price over time, that would affect affordability. His thoughts were immediately on whether his sons could afford to buy their own properties in the future when they reached adulthood.

Price Increases

"Well, we found three things. The first is that developers' bids are higher when there was a previous land parcel sold within the last two years and located within four kilometres from the new site. Let me give you an example:

> [D]evelopers' bids are higher when there was a previous land parcel sold within the last two years and located within four kilometres from the new site.

Rank	Site 1 Launch: January 2011 Bedok Reservoir Road		Site 2 Launch: December 2011 Bedok South Avenue 3		Site 3 Launch: June 2012 Tanah Merah Kechil Road	
	Tenderer	Price per GFA**	Tenderer	Price per GFA**	Tenderer	Price per GFA**
1	United Venture Development (UVD)	$5010	FE Lakeside FCL Topaz Sekisue House (FSS)	$5750 (18%)*	Fragrance Group World Class Land	$7276
2	FE Lakeside FCL Topaz Sekisui House (FSS)	$4885	United Venture Development (UVD)	$5665 (13%)	Areca Investment	$7146
3	Best Desire	$4579	Kingsford Development	$5007	United Venture Development (UVD)	$6692 (18%)
4	First Changi Development	$4431	MCL Land	$4771	Verwood Holdings TID Residential Intrepid Investments	$6674
5	Allgreen Properties	$4008	Intrepid Investments Hong Realty Sunmaster Holdings	$4470	Sherwood Development	$6572
6	Sunmaster Holdings	$3875	Mezzo Development	$4123	Sing Holdings Maxdin	$6172
7	Leng Hoe Development	$3366	Soilbuild Group	$3910	Qingjian Realty	$6141
8	Mezzo Development	$3147			Hock Lian Seng Holdings Meadows Bright Development	$6128
9					FE Lakeside FCL Topaz Sekisui House (FFS)	$5996 (4%)
10					Sunway Developments	$5996

Tenderer names in italics are bidding entities that participated in all three auction sales.

* Numbers in parentheses indicate the percent increase in Gross Floor Area-adjusted bidding prices submitted by the same tenderer in the auction sequence.

** GFA stands for Gross Floor Area.

"In early 2011, the government launched a land parcel along Bedok Reservoir Road. Let's call this Site 1. This plot of land attracted eight bids. The highest bid was placed by United Venture Development (UVD) for $5,010 per gross floor area (GFA). The second highest bid of $4,885 per GFA was submitted by a consortium consisting of FE Lakeside, FCL Topaz and Sekisui House (FFS).

"After that there was another land auction at the end of the year for a nearby plot of land parcel along Bedok South Avenue 3. Let's call this Site 2. The distance between the two sites is about 3.2 kilometres. So they are pretty close to each other. This time, there were seven bids. Guess who bid?"

"I don't know. City Dev?" Teng hazarded a guess with the first name that popped in his mind.

"No lah. Remember, I said the findings were interesting and we could see a pattern in whether developers bid one plot after another plot in the same vicinity?" reminded Professor Sing. "The winner and the second highest bidder of Site 1 – UVD and FFS – also participated in the bidding for Site 2.

"But more interestingly is the prices they bid. UVD who won Site 1 increased its tendering price by 13 percent after adjusting for GFA. FSS who had the second highest bid for Site 1 also increased its bid. With an increase of 18 percent, FSS won Site 2 with a bid of $5,750 per GFA.

"Now comes Site 3 which was launched in June 2012. So, Teng, who do you think bid for this third site?" asked Professor Sing.

"UVD and FSS," came Teng's prompt response as he has learned the 'pattern'.

"You are right!" laughed Prof Sing. "Among the 13 tenderers were UVD and FSS. In the end, neither of them won this new site although UVD and FSS increased their bids by 18 percent and 4 percent respectively compared to their earlier bids for Site 2. The joint submission by Fragrance Group and World Class Land won for Site 3 with a bid of $7,277 per GFA."

"So, Teng. I'm a professor and I like to test people," smiled Professor Sing as he pulled his friend's leg. "What can you tell from these findings?"

"Aiyoh! Sing, how can you be like this?" said Teng as he feigned feeling the pressure of being a student.

"But OK, lah. I'll be a good student. Let me see . . .," paused Teng as he studied the numbers.

"First, the bidding prices have increased significantly. UVD and FSS have increased their bids over the 1.5 years."

"That's right," added Professor Sing. "UVD increased their tendering prices by 34 percent while FSS increased theirs by 28 percent in the course of the 18-month period. In fact, each subsequent parcel launch is associated with a notable jump in tendering prices. Anything else?"

Teng didn't seem to have an answer.

"The second thing is that the winner of a previous land parcel tends to participate in subsequent launches of new sites in the same area but does not necessarily win the new sites," explained Professor Sing.

"For instance, UVD continued to participate in the auctions for Site 2 and Site 3 after successfully winning Site 1. However, despite substantially raising its tendering prices, UVD did not win both subsequent auctions. Why do you think this is the case?"

"I think they wanted the whole area to belong to them so that when the condos are up, each estate is designed differently and yet have the same look and feel because they are from the same developer," responded Teng.

Property developers strategise their bids during land auctions. After winning a bid for a piece of land, they will bid again for a nearby land parcel at a higher price.

That way, by the time they sell the units from the 1st piece of land, the land price has gone up and they can make a higher profit.

But how do they know that the price they bid will influence the winning price?

Property developers do market intelligence to suss each other out.

But you said they bid again at a higher price?

That's right. By letting other developers think they are interested in the 2nd land parcel, other developers who are really keen in the 2nd land will submit an even higher price.

The higher winning bid raises the average property price. That way, the 1st developer wins on both sides – a lower cost on his 1st land parcel and a higher selling price when the property is developed.

"Then the whole area would look co-ordinated for a seamless landscape. Also, the developer would be familiar with the surrounding already after having worked on the first site. This makes it easier and less costly to work on the subsequent sites. I guess they tried but were unlucky not to win the other two bids.

"Well, that could be possible reasons," responded Professor Sing.

"Another possible reason is that after winning the first site, it is in the interest of the developer to ensure that the second and subsequent sites are higher priced than the first site. If the cost of the second land parcel is higher, it gives a price advantage to the first land parcel when the property units are developed and up for sale."

"Wow! These developers are so strategic," said an amazed Teng. "Luckily I'm just a taxi driver. If I were in business competing against them, I think I won't be able to survive."

WANT TO KNOW MORE?

This chapter is based on the following research: Sumit Agarwal, Jing Li, Ernie Teo, and Alan Cheong (2018), "Strategic Sequential Bidding for Government Land Auction Sales – Evidence from Singapore," *Journal of Real Estate Finance and Economics*, Vol. 57 (4), pp. 535-565, https://www.springerprofessional.de/en/strategic-sequential-bidding-for-government-land-auction-sales-e/13340368

Golden Spending in the Silver Years

An ageing population is a worldwide phenomenon. Singapore is no exception. Based on projections from the United Nations, some 47 percent of Singapore's total population will be aged 65 years and older by 2050.

The current retirement age in Singapore is 62. Employers must offer re-employment to eligible workers up to the age of 67, so that they have opportunities to continue working as long as they remain healthy.

However, our senior citizens are keeping themselves active and have longer life expectancy. According to the Ministry of Manpower, employed workers aged 65 and above made up 26.8 percent of the working population, up from 13.8 percent in 2006.[1] The government has introduced schemes such as the Special Employment Credit to

---

[1] Maegan Liew, "Seniors at work: The new norm for ageing in Singapore," *ASEAN Today*, (19 February 2019), https://www.aseantoday.com/2019/02/seniors-at-work-the-new-norm-for-ageing-in-singapore/

support employers and to raise the employability of older Singaporeans. It provides a wage-offset to employers hiring older Singaporean workers.

From the nation's perspective, other than the challenge of a shrinking workforce to support an ageing population, there are issues of reduced economic growth and increased healthcare and social services costs to consider. Hence, the healthcare packages – Pioneer Generation Package as well as the Merdeka Generation Package – help to defray medical costs and enhance social welfare. There is also the Silver Support Scheme (SSS) which provides additional support for elderly Singaporeans who had low incomes through life and who now have little or no family support.

From the individual's perspective, senior citizens continue working for various reasons – financial independence to cope with rising living costs; sense of purpose by contributing to their workplace and society; and develop stronger social bonds to be happy, avoid depression and keep dementia at bay. Research has shown that retirees are more likely to die sooner than expected due to idleness. The National Bureau of Economic Research in America found a robust 2 percent increase in male mortality after age 62 when they retire from the workforce and experience the associated changes in lifestyle.[2]

The Vowels

One Saturday, Ah Mah and her group of senior citizen neighbours, mainly women, were hanging out at the void deck after their *tai chi* lesson. Some of the neighbours, like Ah Kong and Ah Mah, were in gainful employment until they retired at 62. Some decided to work part-time to ease themselves into retirement lifestyle. Others continued working despite being past 62 years old.

---

[2] Maria D. Fitzpatrick and Timothy J. Moore (2018), "The Mortality Effects of Retirement: Evidence from Social Security Eligibility at Age 62," *Journal of Public Economics*, Vol. 157, pp. 121-137, https://www.nber.org/papers/w24127

They were discussing why some chose to retire and some didn't.

"My children wanted me to retire. They say 'Ma, you've worked hard for so long already to see us through to university. Now that we are working, it's time for you to rest and enjoy your silver years'," said the first woman neighbour.

"Wow! You have such filial children. You're very blessed," came the response from a second woman neighbour.

"Yes, I have wonderful children. They brought me to Taipei and Bangkok after I retired. And they continue to give me money every month to cover my daily expenses," recounted the neighbour.

"But then, one by one started having babies. So that part about me resting did not last very long. I'm now looking after two grandchildren – a two-year-old grandson and a six-month-old granddaughter. If my children were to hire a maid, it would be expensive. So I help them out."

"But you are enjoying your silver years, right?" asked another neighbour.

"Definitely. So I'm not resting but enjoying myself. My grandchildren are a handful but a joy," she replied.

"Sometimes I wonder whether my children encouraged me not to continue working because they anticipated I'll be helping them look after their children," she laughed half jokingly.

"For me, the reason why I continue working can be summed up in A, E, I, O, U," claimed the second woman neighbour.

Everyone was curious what she meant. The vowels?

"I want to be Active. I want to Enjoy. I want to be Independent. I want to remain Outgoing and I want to be Useful."

"Wah! I didn't know your English is so good, ah. You are the champion! We shall call you Mrs AEIOU," cheered Ah Mah.

"Hey! 60 is the new 40. Why should I shuffle quietly into retirement? I want to live a full life. I want to continue working as long as I can. And when I retire, I want to live comfortably, travel the world and indulge in my favourite hobbies," said the second neighbour while giving a little swing to her hips to show she's still a vivacious vibrant senior citizen.

"But what about your CPF? Did you withdraw CPF when you retired?" asked the second neighbour to the retired first neighbour.

"Well, I actually withdrew my CPF money even before I retired. Initially I thought I would just leave my money in CPF since it earns a higher interest than if I left it in the bank. But my other friends who are older than me kept urging me to withdraw the money. They had withdrawn theirs shortly after turning 55," said the first neighbour.

"Even before they retired?" asked Ah Mah.

"Yup," came the reply.

Planning for the Silver Years

"And they weren't shy about telling me how much they withdrew," the neighbour continued. "I think on average they withdrew about $15,000. That's 2.5 times their average monthly income. So their bank balance became fatter soon after turning 55."

"So you also withdrew your CPF when you turned 55?" asked Ah Mah.

"Yah, lor. I did because it's like peer pressure. When someone does it, you also do it," replied the neighbour.

"Was it easy to withdraw? Did CPF ask you a lot of questions?" asked the second neighbour.

"No. It was very fast. I thought it would take weeks but no, I got my money almost immediately," replied the first neighbour.

"So is $15,000 the magic number to withdraw?" asked the second neighbour who was still working. She was curious because she's eligible to withdraw her CPF savings.

"No, no, no," the first neighbour shook her head. "Upon reaching 55, you can withdraw at least $5,000 as well as CPF balances in excess of the minimum sum which currently is $171,000.

"I noticed that my friends who, how shall I say it," she hesitated for a while, "were more on the low-income and cash-strapped side tended to withdraw less than those who earned more and had more cash. Let me try to remember how much the amounts were.

"I think it was something like $10,000 for the lower income low-cash group, and twice that amount for the high income high-cash group."

"Ahh . . . That's because the higher-income group has more CPF funds to withdraw," said the second neighbour.

"But they are more cash rich. Why should they need to withdraw more? Or even withdraw at all?" said Ah Mah.

"And once you withdraw the cash, you could squander it all away and possibly become like our bankrupt neighbour," reminded the second neighbour of the recent misfortune of one of their neighbours.

"I also don't know why," agreed the first neighbour. "But I understand what you mean about squandering because I remember my lower-income friends telling me that within a year, they had used half of the withdrawn cash already. That's quite dangerous isn't it?"

"Definitely. I don't understand why either. By withdrawing the cash from CPF, they are foregoing interest rates of about 4 percent, while the bank interest rate is almost nothing. That's not wise, is it?" asked Ah Mah.

> By withdrawing the cash from CPF, they are foregoing interest rates of about 4 percent ...

"Unless of course they can channel the money into other assets that can bring in more returns," said the second neighbour.

"You mean like stocks?" asked Ah Mah.

"Not just stocks, but also bonds. Or maybe they want to invest in another property or in start-ups. There are more and more of these alternative investments these days," said the working second neighbour.

"Hmm . . . True, they could have started their own business. That's possible," said Ah Mah as she thought about Fatimah, her neighbour's sister, who started her own business under HOS.

"I remember reading in the newspapers about a study done by a local bank on how people in different age groups fared in terms of financial savviness,"[3] said the second neighbour, who because her motto is to be independent and useful, was constantly reading the newspapers to keep herself in the know.

"For us, 55 and older, we want to retire by 67 with $500,000. But unfortunately, we don't do well in keeping track of our retirement plans or have the ability to sustain the kind of lifestyle that we are used to after retirement."

"Oh dear! That's not good," said Ah Mah.

"But you know what," continued the second neighbour. "The young ones, those in their 20s – they want to retire by 56 with $1 million in their pocket!"

"Hah! Then they had better start planning now for their retirement. They'll have to invest early and wisely, and know the right way to grow wealth. If they don't or take excessive risks in their investment,

---

[3] Lee Qing Ping, "One in 3 adults doesn't invest: OCBC survey," *The Straits Times*, (16 July 2019), p. C2.

they might end up being disappointed and frustrated," said the first neighbour.

"What about your friends who are of the higher income bracket? Did they also spend their CPF withdrawal money just as fast?" asked the second neighbour.

"It didn't seem so. They seemed to be more careful," replied the first neighbour. "But you know what, there are always these retirement talks organised by banks, CPF, or even some financial experts. Why don't we arrange to go down to one of these talks one day. Maybe we can learn something from there?"

"But I'm working," said the second neighbour. "I can't go but can you please update me?"

The Seminar

Ah Mah and the first neighbour attended the seminar and took down notes for their group of senior citizen neighbours. With the second-hand Samsung smartphone that Teng had given her, she managed quite harrowingly to take some pictures of the slides that were shown on the screen.

The neighbours met up again on another Saturday.

"So how was the talk? Was it useful?" asked the working second neighbour.

"Quite good," said the first neighbour. "But although we tried to listen carefully and even took pictures of some of the slides, you know that at our age, we can only remember some of what was said."

"I took some pictures," said Ah Mah, quite proud of her achievement in being able to handle the smartphone. "Here they are."

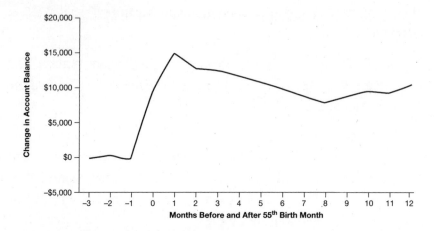

"This one shows how your bank account balance has changed when you reach 55. On the horizontal line at the bottom, '0' means the month a person turns 55.

"See? The moment you turn 55, your bank account balance goes up because you withdrew your CPF money and deposited it in the bank. But the balance dipped thereafter."

"Wow! I hope they didn't anyhow spend the CPF money," said the neighbour who didn't attend the talk.

"It seems that they spent more on their cards. Here's the screenshot I took on total card spending," said Ah Mah.

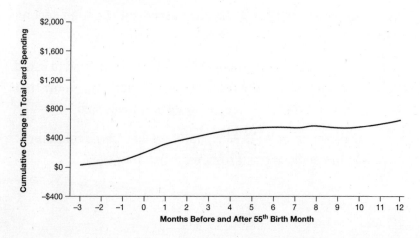

"Well, I think that's to be expected. They've worked hard and now that they can get their hands on the savings they'd stashed away all these years, I don't blame them splurging a little bit to reward themselves upon retirement," empathised the first neighbour who had withdrawn her CPF funds.

"Do you remember that we thought perhaps people would be putting their cash in other assets that would yield more returns?"

The second neighbour nodded.

"Not all did! The lower-income individuals spent their money on clothes and holidays. But thankfully, they also used the money to pay off debts that they might have," said the first neighbour as Ah Mah showed her another screenshot.

> **[L]ower-income individuals spent their money on clothes and holidays.**

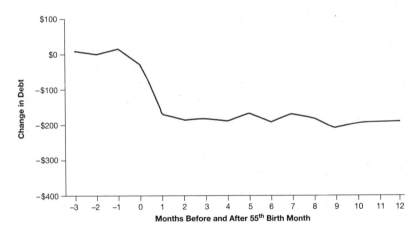

"But it's still worrisome isn't it that the moment you have your hands on what is supposed to be your retirement funds, you spend, especially among the lower-income group who have less savings," said the more savvy second neighbour.

"The smart ones are those with high income and are cash rich. They pursued investment opportunities such as property," said the first neighbour.

"But then again, we must be careful. At our age when there's less money coming in, we should not be undertaking excessive risk in our investments. We need to be extra *kiasu*. Otherwise, if we lose the money, we can't easily recoup it because we're no longer working," cautioned the second neighbour.

Both Ah Mah and the first neighbour agreed. As senior citizens, this isn't the season to take unnecessary investment risks.

"Look at this screenshot here – it shows an increase in the number of ATM withdrawals and use of cheques for purchases. This reiterates that people are buying more after they get their CPF funds."

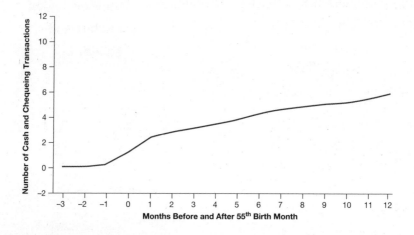

"You know, this exuberance among low-income Singaporeans when they get hold of their CPF funds can be a double-edged sword. What if they were ill-disciplined and started to overspend at the expense of their future retirement security? At 55, they have easily another 20-30 more years to live.

> [T]his exuberance among low-income Singaporeans when they get hold of their CPF funds can be a double-edged sword.

Medical bills can mount. Even with Medishield to cover part of hospitalisation costs, it's still prudent to save. They could become

NUS professors found that within 2 months of turning 55, Singaporeans' bank account increased by $15000.

They must have withdrawn their CPF money and deposited it into their bank account. But why? CPF money earns higher interest.

They use the money to pay off some debt. They also spend more on themselves. By the end of the 1st year after turning 55, the increase in the bank balance dwindles to a $10000 increase.

Did the NUS profs say anything whether there are differences in how the rich and the poor spend their CPF?

High-income people withdrew more. Their bank account balance rose by about $20000.
For low-income Singaporeans, they withdrew $10000 from their CPF, which is about 35% of their pre-55 bank balance.

Even though Singaporeans have flexibility on their CPF withdrawal timing and the withdrawal process is fast, it seems they withdraw their retirement savings almost immediately upon turning 55.

bankrupt in their silver years when they don't have earning power," said the concerned second neighbour.

"What are you saying? That the government should tighten the policy on withdrawal of a sizeable amount?" asked Ah Mah. "That would not go down well with the people. It's their money you know. That would be a political disaster."

"No lah. Not that drastic. But somehow, people will have to think smartly. Perhaps they should seek financial advice to work out a definitive plan to grow their wealth. First, they should moderate their spending when they withdraw their CPF money. Second, unless they have valid reasons for a sizeable withdrawal, leaving it in CPF yielding a much higher interest rate than in banks makes more sense. Otherwise, leaving the cash in banks earning a pittance seems financially unwise," explained the second neighbour.

"That makes sense," said Ah Mah. "But maybe these Singaporeans are *kiasu* and think that the government may suddenly change the regulations concerning CPF withdrawal. As the saying goes, a bird in hand is worth two in the bush. They'd rather have their money in their bank than in CPF."

Silver Support Scheme

"The talk also covered the Silver Support Scheme (SSS)," said the first neighbour. "You know, the one where the government gives cash payouts to the less privileged elderly to help them with their daily expenses?"

"Ahh . . . I think so although I can only vaguely remember," said the second neighbour. Her memory has been getting short as she ages even though she has been keeping herself active by playing mahjong and rummi-o.

"Under SSS, the government gives $300 to $750 every quarter to needy elderly to defray expenses. The money is automatically credited into their bank account," explained the first neighbour.

"At the talk, they said that for every $1 that an elderly receives from SSS, 65 to 75 cents of it is spent. And this was the same amount spent even among elderly who were not in the scheme and did not receive such support."

"So do you mean that the elderly's spending behaviour is the same regardless of whether they are under SSS or not?" asked the second neighbour.

"That's what the speaker said during the talk. I guess it makes sense because what else would you spend on during this season of your life? Necessities, right? And that kind of expenditure on food and medication should be about the same regardless of whether you are cash rich or poor. It's the young who spend on clothes, bags and eating out whenever a new restaurant opens," rationalised the first neighbour.

"Whatever it is, we must plan well for our silver years. It is not only being responsible to ourselves but also to our family," said Ah Mah.

Little did Ah Mah realise what lies ahead.

WANT TO KNOW MORE?

This chapter is based on the following research: Sumit Agarwal, Jessica Pan and Qian Wenlan (2018), "Age of Decision: Pension Savings Withdrawal and Consumption and Debt Response," Working Paper, National University of Singapore, https://papers.ssrn.com/sol3/papers.cfm?abstract_id=2487658; Sumit Agarwal, Qian Wenlan, Ruan Tianyue and Bernard Yeung (2019), "Supporting Seniors: Policy Evaluation of the Silver Support Scheme," Working Paper, National University of Singapore.

17

Pandemic Pandemonium

The Lunar New Year was just around the corner. Everyone was excited as here was another reason for neighbourly get-togethers. On that occasion, it would be the Sing family's turn to invite the neighbours for lunch.

But just a few weeks before the celebration, as Teng was watching the evening news with his parents and Siew Ling, they learnt about a strange virus that had hit the city of Wuhan in the Hubei province of China. Somewhat nonchalant then at the breaking news, they remarked that the timing could not have come worse as it was so near the festive period when people would be travelling back to their families for the annual celebration.

A couple of weeks later, just days before the Lunar New Year, they read about the lockdown in the city and the number of infections and deaths. Siew Ling, the ever *kiasu* one, decided to buy masks even though she did not know much about the virus. It was just an inkling.

She was fortunate. As the Chinese population in Singapore was caught up in preparation for the festive occasion, Siew Ling went to the nearest pharmacy when it just opened and was surprised to see a new stock of surgical masks wheeled in on a trolley by the supplier. She promptly snapped up two boxes containing 100 masks, spending a total of $19.80.

"That should suffice for now," she thought. "I hope things don't get worse."

At the Sings' Lunar New Year gathering, amidst harmless social gambling and feasting, nobody mentioned about the new virus in China. Siew Ling thought perhaps it was just her paranoia.

But as days went by and the number of reported infections and deaths skyrocketed, Singaporeans and people around the world panicked. This virus, named COVID-19, is highly transmittable. And because it is a new virus, little is known about it. No vaccine has been found yet.

Hand sanitisers flew off the shelves. People formed long queues to buy surgical masks, and that had to be rationed to only 10 masks per person.

On 12 March 2020, the World Health Organization (WHO) called the situation a pandemic. On 27 March 2020, the Director of the International Monetary Fund (IMF) said that the economic setback would be more serious than the Global Financial Crisis the world experienced in 2008-2009.

"Ma, you'd better not go out so frequently," cautioned Teng. "I heard this virus spreads very easily. It doesn't matter whether you are young or old, you can also be infected. And old people like you and Ah Pa are likely not to make it should you contract the virus."

"Yah, Ma," added Siew Ling. "This is no time to think you are strong and nothing can happen to you. We have to protect ourselves and everyone around us."

"Hey. We've gone through the Severe Acute Respiratory Syndrome (SARS) epidemic before. Don't worry," laughed Ah Mah, not having quite understood the severity of the health crisis.

"Ma, no. This is not like SARS," reinforced Siew Ling. "This virus is very contagious. We need to be more socially responsible. And because it is new, we do not know much about it. So we need to be even more careful. It's not like your normal flu."

Siew Ling began to teach the two boys how to wash their hands properly.

"Remember to sing the Happy Birthday song twice when you wash your hands with soap. Always with soap," reminded Siew Ling. "And wear your mask whenever you go out, especially when there are many people around. And practise physical distancing. Stay at least two metres away from other people."

"We know, Mummy," said Ethan as he started singing "Stay at home, I see you later. Stray from home, ICU later!"

Although the Singapore government gave out masks and each household also received a free bottle of hand sanitiser, Siew Ling wanted more as standby measures. She began scouting for even more masks both online and offline.

"What? It now costs $39 for a box of surgical masks! I can't believe it. I'd bought them for only $9.90 a box over Chinese New Year. These people are price gouging!" exclaimed an angry Siew Ling.

"Eh, why are you so *kiasu*?" sighed an irritated Teng as Siew Ling was hogging the computer searching for masks on Lazada.

"This is not about being *kiasu*, OK? It's about survival," came the retort.

Teng, on the other hand, was more concerned about how much he was bringing home each month. As more Singaporeans were infected with COVID-19 and more stringent governmental measures were put in place, Teng found his fare takings dwindling. Singaporeans were beginning to go out less although he did observe young ones still revelling and going out in groups. Although they added to his earnings, he did not think that such close socialising was wise.

He was not sure how truly severe the pandemic was but he knew his earnings had been adversely affected. Even Peter, his happy-go-lucky friend, was not so sanguine anymore as property sales came to an abrupt halt.

Mitigating Measures

To dampen the spread of COVID-19, many countries practised lockdown measures to minimise face-to-face human interactions. Factories were shut down. International travel was all but cancelled. But many economic activities depend on human-to-human interactions. So while these vigilant measures saved lives, they also generated a huge shock on the economy.

Demand for non-essentials fell off the cliff as people stayed home, while demand for essentials such as food, masks, hand sanitisers, and even toilet rolls skyrocketed. The lockdown also meant international travel and trade were crippled. Many planes were grounded as people ceased their travel.

Factory and flight closures greatly disrupted global production value chain and trade. The consequence is a significant decline in output, surge in unemployment, bankruptcy, and worries over financial stability.

The dilemma is the trade-off. The more stringent the measures were in flattening the infection curve to save lives, the faster and deeper would be the ensuing recession. The question then is "Can lives be saved without taking an excessive toll on the economy?"

The Singapore government embarked on nominal medical fees for testing and treating people who may have been infected with COVID-19. The rationale: They do not want people to delay seeing a doctor just to save on medical bill, essentially flushing out all the infected cases and minimising the spread.

Those who were infected were quarantined or hospitalised as their cases became more severe. Contact tracing was also relentlessly pursued to contain the infection. People who were entering the country also had to comply to a 14-day Stay-Home Notice before they could socialise.

But as the number of cases spiked, more draconian measures were instituted to stem the spread. This included having the whole population to stay at home for a month with no social activities with others not living in the same household, and closing all non-essential businesses.

Coronacoma

During the circuit-breaker period, Teng and the neighbours were Whatsapping each other on their group chat as they practised physical distancing.

"Hey guys! Hope you are staying safe. This is what my friend in China told me about the economic fallout from the China lockdown," wrote Professor Sing to Teng in his Whatsapp message.

"China's industrial value-add output fell by 4.3 percent and 25.9 percent in January and February of 2020, on a year-on-year basis. The slump is dramatic as the expected growth was about 5.5 percent. The economic impact of the lockdown is severe. The economic recovery appears sluggish. Moreover, the deteriorating pandemic situation across the globe is bringing an almost complete halt to the export sector in China and Chinese firms have difficulty accessing critical inputs provided by firms outside of the country."

"This is so bad," wrote Josie. "Can we go on Zoom? It's easier to talk than to type on Whatsapp."

So the neighbours started Zooming each other. They quite like that although they were practising physical distancing, they were not social distancing.

Josie continued on Zoom.

"As I was saying, all countries should co-operate. China was recovering and they were going back to opening their factories. Then other economies shut down and there's no demand. Then the China factories have to shut down because there's no business. This start-stop, start-stop is no good. They should be in lock-step motion. Otherwise, the economic engine can't get started to pull the global economy up. We may end up in an economic coma."

Johan, the banker neighbour, unmuted himself from Zoom and heaved a huge sigh.

"And there may be a flight to safety as the pandemic weakens the global economy. This may press down asset prices and stress the global financial system. Demand for the US dollar has soared. Asian banks may have vulnerable dollar exposure."

"Yeah! I heard some stock markets took a beating," added Teng.

"Yes, and who do you think are most affected by that?" asked Professor Sing. "Those who retired or about to retire. They are ones who have invested part of their assets in the market and have lost a hefty sum of their retirement funds. And among those who are working, a significant number will be laid off. With that, we've lost an economic generation.

"And the young ones, the Millennials ... They have not saved enough yet and now we will be depending on them to support the older folks who have suffered economically from this virus outbreak. So, essentially, we've two lost generations."

"So much gloom and doom," remarked Siew Ling.

"Some more gloom here," added Fadhilah. "With poorer consumer confidence, this will drive down purchases including property.

"And I won't be surprised if governments become more protectionistic. Already, there have been reported cases of confiscated imports of surgical supplies meant for other countries. When it comes to trade, I think we may see more protectionistic measures to help their own economy rather than the global economy."

"But why should people not spend more? This pandemic will be over one day, when the vaccine is found. It won't last forever," said Siew Ling.

"The health effects of the virus may be over, but the economic impact may be long drawn. And mind you, the vaccine will take one to 1.5 years to develop," reminded Fadhilah.

"Hey guys! Shall I ask my friend Sumit from NUS to join in this Zoom chat? I think he's doing some work on the economic impact of the pandemic," interrupted Professor Sing.

Everyone agreed. While waiting for Professor Sumit to join in, Johan added, "My bank did some preliminary analysis. There's a high probability that the recovery may be L-shape than V- or U-shape. Of course, that depends on how fast we can stem the spread. The faster, the better. Which means everyone must co-operate."

"What does 'L-shape' mean?" asked Teng.

"It means the economy will have a sharp drop and stays flat for quite some time. Like the letter 'L'," explained Johan. "During SARS, the recovery was fast, V-shape, because the pandemic was short and not drawn out."

"Why?" asked Teng.

"You see," continued Johan, "businesses have to incorporate

> **Businesses have to incorporate the risk of doing business arising from the virus as well as the economic impact thereafter. But in the case of COVID-19, it's difficult to accurately compute what the risk factor is.**

the risk of doing business arising from the virus as well as the economic impact thereafter. But in the case of COVID-19, it's difficult to accurately compute what the risk factor is.

"It is a new virus, that's why it's called novel coronavirus. And so we do not know with accuracy as to what the infection rate is or death rate is. Some people died at home without being tested for the virus. These were written off as flu or old age.

"There are reported cases of asymptomatic people, but we don't know how many there are. And how infectious they are and when people become more infectious. And there are also people who recovered and yet were later tested to still have the virus. There are so many unknowns about the virus that doctors and scientists are uncovering each day. As we learn more about the virus, these rates will be revised.

"All these are uncertainties. And uncertainties make it difficult for businesses to understand the risk involved as an outcome of the virus – risk such as another wave of infection or whether the virus will mutate. And so without understanding what risks you are facing when doing business, people shun away from economic activities. And that gives you the long plateau where economic activities take time to pick up."

"So what can be done to alleviate such fears and get out of this rut?" asked Josie.

Just then, Professor Sumit joined in the Zoom chat.

"Hi everyone! Thanks for inviting me to join in. Are you guys staying well?" asked a cheerful Professor Sumit. He was in his T-shirt and loose gym shorts, looking very cheerful.

"Sorry that I'm a bit sweaty. I'd just finished my online yoga class," said a smiling Professor Sumit. He moved his laptop around so everyone could see his surrounding area.

"Here's Sid, my baby boy. Say 'Hi'," beamed the very proud daddy. "Sid was watching me as I did my yoga. Times have changed, you know. This virus has accelerated many businesses to go online, even my yoga class! Businesses have to retool themselves.

"Are you guys talking about the pandemic and its economic repercussions?"

"Hi Professor. I'm Johan, one of the neighbours," introduced Johan to the NUS professor. "Yes, I was just telling my friends about the possible L-shape recovery."

"Hi Prof! I'm Josie, another neighbour. Thanks for coming in at last minute's notice. I was just wondering about how to get out of the downturn and recover as soon as possible," asked Josie.

"Aahh ... Well, this is where government stimulus packages come in," responded Professor Sumit.

"Governments at a time of crisis can step in and use strategic reserves or borrow from the future to cushion the downturns arising from such a crisis. Do you remember the Global Financial Crisis in 2008?"

Everyone nodded. The professor continued.

"House prices had fallen and people were over-leveraged. They had borrowed too much and had difficulty paying off their mortgage. This caused them to cut back consumption.

"So the United States government came up with several flavours of stimulus packages. There was a whole alphabet soup of them – HAMP, HARP, QE1 to QE4, The Dodd-Frank Act to name a few.

"These stimulus packages were meant to stimulate demand by reducing mortgage payments so that people can have more disposable income to spend. Some packages also had better terms and conditions on their mortgages to lower the default rate. These help to stabilise house prices.

"But when it comes to COVID-19, it's a different story altogether. The COVID-19 crisis is a supply shock to the economy. What do I mean by this?

"Due to social distancing and lockdown measures, people cannot go out to restaurants, shops, bars, and movies. This prohibits them from spending. Now, this would be transient if the pandemic was well under control, and people go back to their old ways of shopping, eating, and spending once the crisis is over.

> **[I]f the pandemic were long and there is wave after wave of widespread infections, over time, the supply shock causes unemployment and layoffs. This leads demand to drop on a more permanent basis.**

"But if the pandemic were long and there is wave after wave of widespread infections, over time, the supply shock causes unemployment and layoffs. This leads demand to drop on a more permanent basis."

"Isn't that already happening in some countries where businesses have gone bankrupt and people lose their jobs?" asked Siew Ling.

Professor Sumit nodded. "Well, that's why governments around the world have stepped up to announce various stimulus packages ranging from 5 to 30 percent of their annual GDP. Singapore, for instance, have packages that give relief to both the individual and small businesses. These packages try to protect jobs by telling employees that a portion of their monthly wages will be provided for by the government for an extended period of time.

"They also provide employers relief towards their rent payment, interest payment on their debt, and other costs that they incur. This will allow them to not fire their employees but just furlough them till the situation returns to normal and they can be hired back.

"Compare this to the U.S. In the U.S., employees are laid off by businesses. The unemployed can claim unemployment benefits from the U.S. government. This will have long-term implications as it is very possible that employers will take this opportunity to substitute capital for labour. For instance, they can permanently replace mortgage brokers, real estate agents, investment advisors, tax accountants, and even cashiers in restaurants with technology. This can have long-term effects."

Across the rooms, even though this was on an online platform, one could sense an "Aiyoh" moment.

"Luckily, the Singapore government handled this much better. At least that's what I think," continued Professor Sumit. "They are aggressive and bold, and have multiple supplementary budgets to reassure households, businesses, and financial markets that they are going to do whatever they can to save the economy and its people."

"How about health versus economics? Which is more critical – saving lives or building the economy?" asked Johan.

"That's so tricky," replied Professor Sumit. "Both packages must work hand in hand. If the population isn't protected from the virus, the economy cannot get going. So the medical programme has to ensure that there is massive testing, isolation, and contact tracing so that our hospitals are not overwhelmed. At the same time, the economic packages must ensure that when the society is fairly well protected from the virus, people are confident that they can go back as close as possible to pre-pandemic days of spending to generate the economy.

"Until we have the vaccine, it might well be that we'll have several circuit breakers every now and then to balance between health and economic considerations. The circuit breakers serve to curb the infection so that we are safe and our hospitals are not overwhelmed, but between circuit breakers, businesses may be opened with some safety measures put in place so that people can go out with confidence, take a breather, spend and help these businesses to survive so that more people are employed.

"Government packages cannot last forever. There comes a time when businesses have to fend for themselves. And so having circuit breakers and contact tracing to dampen the infection rate and build consumer confidence to support the economy is a longer term solution."

"So we want isolation and testing to contain the spread and possibly multiple but staggered circuit breakers so that we can experience some sense of normalcy every now and then to support businesses?" asked Siew Ling.

"Exactly. That's one possible scenario to consider," said Professor Sumit. "There are in fact two types of 'risks' that we need to overcome. First, is the risk of infection that stops people from going out. The second is the risk of losing a job if the economy goes bad. If people coop up at home and don't go out, they are healthy but the economy will experience a downturn. If they go out, they risk contracting the virus but businesses have some revenue at least for a while. It's tricky to keep a fine balance between the two."

Everyone nodded as they digested the information.

"And remember I said about the vaccine? Even when a vaccine is found, it will take time to manufacture and deliver to the masses. And from what I've read so far, these vaccines may offer limited protection. There's just a lot of unknowns right now," said Professor Sumit.

Teng chimed in.

"But these medical and economic programmes will come to nought if the people don't co-operate. I think Singaporeans have to play our part too. While there's testing and isolation, we must do our bit and not leave everything to the government.

"See what happened in some countries where people started partying and having a good time in bars? These places became hotspots and the infection rate climbed.

"We must be disciplined and adhere to physical distancing. And wear masks whenever we go out, especially to crowded places like the wet markets and supermarkets. Masking helps because if everyone masks up, there's mutual protection for everybody.

"I think some Singaporeans still don't play their part. They need to be socially responsible. The other day, I saw three old uncles getting together at the void deck chatting to each other, standing less than one meter apart, and not wearing masks. We are only as good as our weakest link, but if we work together, we can beat the virus."

"Absolutely," said Professor Sing. "We must not be complacent, even when the infection rate comes down. We must stay vigilant because there could be another wave. I remember reading that the Spanish Flu lasted three years because there were waves of infection. So we must never let our guard down."

"Yah! Several countries are experiencing another surge in cases after having the virus under control for a while. It's like having a war with an invisible enemy," added Teng.

Retooling

"So how can businesses survive? I've read on social media that many food places are closing down because there's not enough business," asked Siew Ling.

"E-commerce has definitely benefitted," Johan responded. "Businesses should have an online platform for sales to offset the slowdown in offline revenue. Look at Sephora – its online sales went up. But of course, not enough to compensate for the lost sales when the stores were closed during the lockdown."

"Delivery services also benefitted," added Teng. "I became Grab delivery man because no one was taking rides. And I see a lot of Ninja Vans around delivering purchases."

"Yes, businesses must adapt with the times," said Professor Sumit. "This pandemic has accelerated e-commerce. Of course, the writing was already on the wall that e-commerce is the future. But this virus has quickened the adoption of e-commerce.

> **[T]his pandemic has converted quite a number of Baby Boomers, those in their 50s and 60s, to buy more online. Their behaviour as consumers has changed. They have adapted to the new normal of buying products without touching or seeing them.**

"In fact, research shows that while Millennials and Gen Zers are the ones who clearly are comfortable with online purchases, this pandemic has converted quite a number of Baby Boomers, those in their 50s and 60s, to buy more online. Their behaviour as consumers has changed. They have adapted to the new normal of buying products without touching or seeing them, even though they are not very comfortable with this way of purchasing. So not only has online businesses boomed, they have also found a new set of customers – the Baby Boomers."

Siew Ling, with shopping on her mind, added, "And for physical shops, I think they have to demonstrate that it is safe to shop there. Merchandise displayed are purely for display purposes. So if its clothes, people who want to try on clothes will get new ones from the storeroom. And stores have to 'quarantine' these clothes after a customer has tried them on."

"And I also noticed more ads on social media as people stay at home. Even I work from home and have more breaks in between to look at Instagram posts," said Johan.

"Haha! Even my teaching has changed," injected Professor Sing.

"I have to retool my lessons for online teaching. I find I can only teach at most 80 percent of in-class content when I do online teaching. Time is spent in ensuring the microphones are switched on when speaking so that all can hear, I have to have more breakout sessions to break the monotony of just me talking, and it's definitely more difficult to assess the emotional aspect of the class online. I also don't know whether a student is really there all the time. I bet some go to the kitchen to get some food while the lesson is going on.

"Hey! Our 40 minutes of Zoom time is almost up. Wow! Time flies. I didn't realise we've talked for so long. You guys stay safe. Keep your distance from others."

"Take care. Keep well. Bye!" chimed everyone.

After the neighbours and Professor Sumit Zoomed out, Teng and Siew Ling gathered Ah Kong, Ah Mah, and the two young boys to the living room.

"Remember this," said Teng as he looked straight into their eyes. "We must do our part in keeping each other safe. Wash your hands frequently and with soap. Keep a good distance away from each other. And wear a mask whenever you go out. Together, we can overcome this crisis."

WANT TO KNOW MORE?

A large part of this chapter is based on a Zoom Chat Room Conversation titled *2020 Pandemic – The View from Asia*, organised by NUS Business School and Asian Bureau of Finance and Economic Research (ABFER) on 2 April 2020. Ongoing research is being conducted by the authors.

About the Authors

Sumit Agarwal, yoga fanatic and economics wiz, can untangle complex economics problems as adeptly as he can do most mindboggling yoga poses including head stands. Who would have thought that this Professor of Finance from the National University of Singapore (NUS) Business School is as enthusiastic about financial economics as he is about fitness.

As the Low Tuck Kwong Professor at NUS Business School and the Head of the Finance Department, Sumit had to take frequent taxi trips for his various meetings but he could never find a taxi when he needed one. That piqued his interest and the genesis of his research on Singapore.

Well known for his research relating to financial institutions, household finance, behavioural finance, and real estate and capital markets, Sumit brings a wealth of experience beyond intellectual rigour. He was a senior financial economist at the Federal Reserve Bank of Chicago and a senior vice president at the Bank of America.

With the ability to speak to the man on the street, Sumit is often quoted or featured in BBC, CNA, CNBC and Fox on issues relating to finance, banking, and real estate markets. His research is widely cited in leading newspapers and magazines like *The Wall Street Journal*, *The New York Times*, *The Economist* and *The Straits Times*.

Ang Swee Hoon lives and breathes marketing. As an Associate Professor of Marketing at NUS Business School and the Deputy Head of the Marketing Department, her students are often enthused by her passion in marketing. It comes as no surprise that Swee Hoon has been recognised on three consecutive occasions as an outstanding educator with the university's Teaching Excellence Award, putting her on the honour roll.

Her marketing mojo is evident in the leading textbooks *Marketing Management: An Asian Perspective* and *Principles of Marketing: An Asian Perspective* now in their 7th and 4th edition, respectively, that she co-authors with Philip Kotler, as well as in commentaries and media interviews. Swee Hoon also lends her expertise as advisor to several government boards.

Since obtaining her Ph.D. in Marketing from the University of British Columbia, Swee Hoon enjoys eclectic research including consumer happiness, counterfeiting, superstitions and advertising creativity. Her diverse research interests got her into reading on research outside marketing. This passion for acquiring new knowledge connected her with Sumit and Tien Foo, resulting in the earlier book, *Kiasunomics©*, followed by this sequel.

Sing Tien Foo is a Professor and the Head of the NUS Department of Real Estate, and the Director of the Institute of Real Estate and Urban Studies at NUS. Tien Foo is invited regularly to give views and comments on Singapore's property markets and housing policies. He serves in various capacities at government agencies including the

Land Appeal Board, Ministry of Law, Valuation Review Board, Ministry of Finance, and the Council for Estate Agencies (CEA), Ministry of National Development.

His keen interest in real estate has seen him work on topics relating to options, real estate finance and securitisation, REITs, and housing price dynamics. Tien Foo is the Founding Principal Investigator of the Singapore's NUS–REDAS Real Estate Sentiment Index, which receives wide media coverage. He is a co-author of *Singapore's Real Estate: 50 Years of Transformation*, which has a Chinese version "新加坡房地厂市场的变革与创新".

An outstanding scholar with a Ph.D. from the University of Cambridge, Tien Foo's expertise in real estate goes beyond Singapore's shores. He lends his knowledge and expertise by serving as the President of the Asian Real Estate Society and the Executive Board Member of the Global Chinese Real Estate Congress.